To Craig,

best wishes

Battle Exhaustion

Battle Exhaustion

Soldiers and Psychiatrists in the Canadian Army, 1939–1945

TERRY COPP

BILL McANDREW

McGill-Queen's University Press
Montreal & Kingston • London • Buffalo

©McGill-Queen's University Press 1990
ISBN 0-7735-0774-4

Legal deposit third quarter 1990
Bibliothèque nationale du Québec

Printed in Canada on acid-free paper

This book has been published with the help of a grant
from the Social Science Federation of Canada, using
funds provided by the Social Sciences and Humanities
Research Council of Canada.

Canadian Cataloguing in Publication Data

Copp, Terry, 1938–
    Battle exhaustion
    Includes bibliographical references.
    ISBN 0-7735-0774-4
    1. Canada. Canadian Army – History – Medical care.
    2. World War, 1939–1945 – Psychological aspects.
    3. Psychology, Military. 4. Canada. Canadian
    Army – History – World War, 1939–1945. 5. World War,
    1939–1945 – Canada. I. McAndrew, Bill, 1934–
    II. Title.
    UH629.5.C3C66 1990   940.54'7571   C90-090177-2

This book was set in 10 1/2 pt. Janson by
Nancy Poirier Typesetting Limited

To
Carolyn, Robin, and Ian
Linda, Monica, Reuel, and Robin

Contents

Acknowledgments

This work began as two separate monographs. The authors began to collaborate after each had established his own approach to the subject and, while much discussion and revision has taken place, the book before you remains the work of two authors. They jointly wrote the introduction. Terry Copp wrote chapters 1 and 2, the section on North Africa in chapter 3, and chapters 6 and 7. Bill McAndrew is the author of chapters 3, 4, 5, and the conclusion.

Terry Copp gratefully acknowledges financial support from the Hannah Foundation and Wilfrid Laurier University, which awarded a research grant out of funds partly provided by the Social Sciences and Humanities Research Council.

Terry Copp benefitted from discussions with the following neuropsychiatrists who served with the Royal Canadian Army Medical Corps during World War II: Dr John Burch, Dr Glen Burton, Dr Travis Dancey, Dr Jack Griffin, Dr Burdett McNeel, Dr Clifford Richardson and Dr Allan Walters. Doctors Dancey, Griffin and McNeel cheerfully responded to further questions over a five-year period. Dr Kingsley Ferguson, who as a young psychology student participated in a follow-up study of battle exhaustion cases, provided assistance in evaluating that work and offered helpful comments on an early draft of the manuscript. Dr Harry Botterell read and commented on chapter 2 on the basis of his experience at Number One Neurological Hospital. Dr Peter Van Nostrand provided information about his father and arranged a meeting with two of F.H. Van Nostrand's war-time colleagues. All of these men went out of their way to provide help with this project. Long-time friends and colleagues have been unfailingly helpful in commenting on parts of the manuscript, especially Craig Brown, Ken Dewar, Art Silver, Bob Vogel, and Suzanne Zeller. The advice of Brigadier (ret) Bryan Watkins and Brigadier Peter Abraham, director of British Army psychiatry, is gratefully acknowledged.

At various stages of the project research assistance has been provided by Stephen Flemming, Christine Hamelin, and Kathleen Hynes. Ms Hynes's research in the Public Record Office, London, England has been of particular value.

Evelyn Jones has typed and helped to edit successive drafts of the manuscript with good humour and great efficiency.

Bill McAndrew acknowledges the encouragement given him by Alec Douglas, Norman Hillmer, and colleagues at the Directorate of History. He is most grateful to the many veterans who, during stimulating battlefield studies, offered their hard-won insights into the reality of battle. They include: Lieutenant-Generals Henri Tellier and James Quinn; Major-Generals Bert Hoffmeister, George Kitching, and Pat Bogert; Brigadiers Bill Ziegler, Ian Johnson, and Sydney Radley-Walters; Colonels Strome Galloway, Clement Dick, Harvey Theobald, Jim McAvity, Brick Brown, Syd Thomson, Lockie Fulton, Tony Poulin, Jamie Stewart, and Bud Taylor; Major John Dougan; Captains Hunter Dunn, Egan Chambers, Bud Peto, and Doug Graham; Group-Captains Bert Houle and Dave Goldberg; Obersts Gerhard Muhm, Hubert Meyer, and Hans Von Luck. Many officers currently or recently serving in the Canadian Forces have arranged and participated in battlefield studies and workshops concerned with battlefield behaviour. They include: Lieutenant-Generals Charles Belzile, Richard Evraire, and Kent Foster; Major-Generals Bob Stewart, Clive Milner, and Jack Dangerfield; Brigadier-Generals Ian Douglas, Tom DeFaye, and D.R. Williams; Colonels Jim Allen, Rick Neugebauer, Thane Wheeler, Bill Sutherland, Doug Moreside, and Herm Hirschfeld; Colonels Brian McGrath, Ernie Beno, and Ray Crabbe, along with the directing staff and students of successive courses at the Canadian Land Forces Command and Staff College, the Canadian staffs at Central Army Group and No. 4 Allied Tactical Air Force Headquarters at Heidelberg, and the officers of the 1st Regiment Royal Canadian Horse Artillery at Lahr. They have all taught him a great deal. Dr. A.E. Moll also offered much helpful advice.

Abbreviations

ADMS   Assistant Director of Medical Services
BEF   British Expeditionary Forces
CEU   Canadian Exhaustion Unit
CMHQ   Canadian Military Headquarters (UK)
CO   Commanding Officer
CPA   Canadian Psychological Association
DDMS   Deputy Director of Medical Services
DGMS   Director General of Medical Services
DMS   Director of Medical Services
EMS   Emergency Medical Services
FDS   Field Dressing Station
MNI   Montreal Neurological Institute
MO   Medical Officer
NCO   Non-Commissioned Officer
NYD(N) Not Yet Diagnosed (Nervous)
PPCLI   Princess Patricia's Canadian Light Infantry
R22eR   Royal 22e Régiment
RAF   Royal Air Force
RAMC   Royal Army Medical Corps
RCAMC   Royal Canadian Army Medical Corps
RCR   Royal Canadian Regiment
RHLI   Royal Hamilton Light Infantry
RMO   Regimental Medical Officer
SEC   Special Employment Company
SPO   Selection of Personnel Officer

Colonel Colin K. Russell, one of the early promoters of the Canadian Army's Second War psychiatric service, was largely responsible for establishing No. 1 Neurological Hospital at Basingstoke. (Department of National Defense [DND])

Brigadier E.A. McCusker was the senior medical officer of I Canadian Corps in Italy in 1944. His views on proper battlefield behaviour were shaped by his experience in World War I. (DND)

Brigadier K.A. Hunter, a permanent force medical officer, was Assistant Director of Medical Services with the 5th Canadian Armoured Division in Italy. He was the army's senior doctor during the Korean War. (DND)

Dr H.H. Hyland was a neurologist who acquired considerable psychiatric experience at Toronto General Hospital before the war. He was senior neuropsychiatrist at Basingstoke until his return to Canada in 1942. (Courtesy Dr Robert H. Hyland)

The officers of No. 1 Field Ambulance, Barriefield Camp, 1939. Dr Arthur Doyle, second from the right, accompanied the 1st Canadian Infantry Division to Sicily and Italy in 1943. He established the army's first psychiatric practice in battle. The picture to the right shows Dr Doyle in 1965. (Courtesy Susan Doyle)

Dr Burdett McNeel at Debert Camp in 1942. He later commanded No. 1 Canadian Exhaustion Unit in Normandy. He encountered much resistance from commanders who looked upon psychiatrists as unwelcome intruders. (Courtesy Dr McNeel)

Dr Burdett McNeel, centre, with Personnel Selection Officers at Headley Detention Barracks, where they conducted a pre-invasion screening of 1,400 prisoners in 1943-44 to identify potentially effective soldiers and incorrigibles. (Courtesy Dr McNeel)

A Personnel Selection Officer conducting an interview to assess the suitability of a recruit. A brief interview proved to be an imperfect means of assessing personality and psychological stability. (DND)

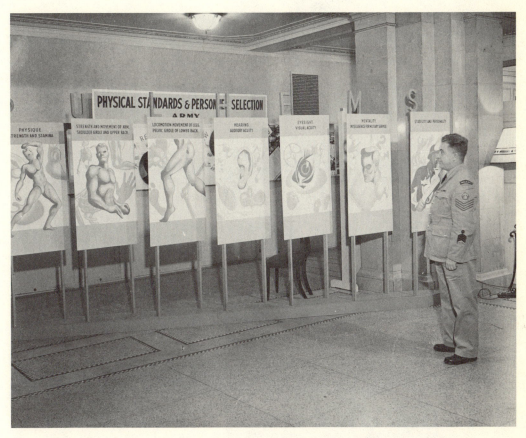

A wartime recruiting centre displaying the PULHEMS medical classification system that was introduced in 1943-44 to try to place round pegs in round holes. Variations of the system were adopted by the British and United States Armies. A description of its functional categories is given in appendix 1. (DND)

Colonel William Line taught psychology at the University of Toronto before succeeding Brock Chisholm as the army's Director of Personnel Services. He was responsible for implementing the program of mass psychological screening of recruits. (Archives in the History of Canadian Psychiatry)

The Chief Psychiatrist in the Directorate of Personnel Services, Dr John Griffin, was its principal link with the army's medical service. He was one of the first workers with the National Committee for Mental Hygiene (Canada). (Archives in the History of Canadian Psychiatry)

Dr Brock Chisholm, a decorated infantryman in World War I, became Canada's first private psychiatric practitioner in 1934. He founded the army's Directorate of Personnel Services and became its senior medical officer as a Major-General in 1942. After the war he headed the World Health Organization. (Archives in the History of Canadian Psychiatry)

Dr Robert Gregory in 1946. He was the psychiatrist of the 3rd Canadian Infantry Division when it landed in Normandy in 1944. His caseload grew quickly as the battle of attrition in the bridgehead worsened. (Archives in the History of Canadian Psychiatry)

A World War I veteran of the Royal Flying Corps, Dr. F.H. Van Nostrand was the Chief Psychiatric Consultant with the Canadian Army Overseas. He was universally respected by his professional colleagues, and his common-sense approach to psychiatry helped to break down the considerable resistance of military commanders to its practice in the army. (Courtesy Dr A.E. Moll)

Dr A.E. Moll during training in England. Military psychiatrists had to be self-sufficient and familiar with military ways. While an Area Psychiatrist in England, Moll had to devise a system for screening volunteers for parachute training. (Courtesy Dr. A.E. Moll)

The staff of No. 2 Canadian Exhaustion Unit in the Gothic Line near Rimini, Italy, 1944. Dr A.E. Moll is seated on the left. A Corps unit, the CEU received cases from forward medical installations, applied basic psychotherapy, and either returned men to their units or evacuated them. (Courtesy Dr A.E. Moll)

Dr J.C. Richardson was senior neuropsychiatrist at Basingstoke until 1944, when he moved with the 1st Canadian Army to the Continent, where he coordinated the clinical work of the field psychiatrists. (Courtesy Mrs Ruth Gould)

Dr Charles Gould conducted a psychiatric out-patients' clinic in England until 1943, when he went to the Mediterranean to take charge of a general hospital psychiatric ward. His detailed observations are given in appendix 2. (Courtesy Mrs Ruth Gould)

Physically and emotionally scarred casualties in an improvised medical unit in Italy. (DND)

A psychiatric conference at Basingstoke in 1943. Dr F.H. Van Nostrand is seated fifth from the left. In the second row J.C. Richardson is third from the left and Dr A.E. Moll third from the right. Dr Burdett McNeel is third from the left in the top row. (Courtesy Dr A.E. Moll)

Battle Exhaustion

Introduction

"Sergeant! ... W.A.T. for Private Turvey ... And send the others away, can't see them this morning.

Turvey went along, baring his arm for another inoc, but he found that W.A.T. was only a very amusing game called the Word Association Test ...

When it was over there was a wait ... The sergeant filled in the time with sedate chatter about the captain ...

"He's really going to enjoy talking with you, Turvey. Isn't often he takes time to lay on a W.A.T., poor fellow. Generally he interviews twenty in a morning and has to write out a diagnosis and recommendations on all of them by 1500 hours so I can type them in time for the Medical Board."

"Gosh, are there that many nuts around here every day?"

"Well, of course" – the sergeant coughed good-humoredly – "we don't use the word 'nut'. Not in psychiatry. We have all sorts of *cases* though, you'd be surprised. Psychopaths, aggressive or inadequate," the sergeant rolled the words fondly, "suspected epileptics, schizoid personalities, manics. And scads of neurotics – compulsives, depressives. But battle fatigues mainly. Anxiety states, you know."

"What're they all in a state about?"

"O, about getting killed, mostly ..."

"Course, it's all very hard on the captain. He's very young, you know ... Had a sheltered home life, then went direct from interning into the army. Hasn't had much of a chance to develop himself as a clinician. Sent straight over here a month ago. Now he gets enough material in one day to last him a year on Civvy Street, and no time to analyze it. Some of it really shocks him, too. He's kinds of a shy type really. Has personality problems himself. All these psychiatrists have."

Earle Birney[1]

Earle Birney's description of Turvey's encounter with a Canadian Army psychiatrist is based on his own observations as a personnel selection officer in North-West Europe. The humour, as in all Turvey episodes, has particular appeal to those who served in the army, for Turvey's adventures are firmly grounded in reality. This study is in many ways a long, involved, academic footnote to Birney's description of army psychiatry and the "anxiety states," scared "about getting killed," that psychiatrists dealt with.

Copp's interest in the field was sparked by studying the experience of Canadian infantry battalions in the North-West European theatre of operations during World War II for his series of books, *Maple Leaf Route*. Military historians, he found, have made little effort to understand the role that battle exhaustion played in the conflict and his work began as a limited attempt to explain the nature, extent, and varying incidence of psychiatric casualties in battle.

McAndrew was pursuing similar research on the Italian campaign. Coincidentally he participated in several workshops on battlefield stress held by Canadian Forces units and began a series of on-site battle studies with Canadian and German serving officers and veterans. Trying to reconstruct old battles with former duelling participants raised a great many questions about what soldiers actually do on a battlefield, and the discussions on stress offered a clue. Like Copp he realized that in their preoccupation with weapons, tactics, technology, and grand strategy most historians have ignored the vast human dimension of battle. Taking battlefield behaviour for granted seems odd because soldiers' behaviour presumably dictated military results. Did soldiers routinely follow orders? Sacrifice themselves more or less willingly? Run away? Become ill? Hide? Behave courageously? Being human, unsurprisingly they did all these things, and behaved in varied other ways as well. While most soldiers performed their unpleasant chores doggedly, sometimes with exceptional valour, others were unable to withstand the stress of battle. How many there were, whether they were treated as medical casualties or otherwise, and what happened to them were open questions.

No historian begins a major research project without a fairly clear idea of what questions he is going to ask and what answers he expects to find. The historian also understands that research will force the modification of both questions and answers. When we set out to study the problem of battle exhaustion the questions framed and the answers sought concerned the *situation* in which soldiers found themselves. This standpoint was reinforced by our reading of recent American, Israeli, and British research on what is now called combat stress reaction or battleshock. Modern armies assume that anxiety states are inseparable from battle and will rise and fall in relation to such factors as morale and intensity of combat. The current wisdom is that such casualties can be quickly returned to duty if frontline treatment based on the principles of proximity (to the battlefield), immediacy (to the trauma), and expectancy (of rapid return to unit) is available.[2]

The existing literature on the Canadian Army in World War II provides little indication that psychiatric casualties were a significant problem for

Canadian soliders. One chapter of the official medical history[3] does, however, offer a general summary of "Neurology and Psychiatry." It was co-authored by a number of army psychiatrists and we were able to contact seven of these men, who agreed to discuss their wartime experiences.

Oral history requires careful preparation; fortunately the military records held at the National Archives contain a good deal of information about psychiatric work in the army in Canada and Britain, as well as material on battle exhaustion. At first reading it seemed that a lot of energy had gone into psychological testing and psychiatric screening of soldiers and recruits. Apparently very large members of young Canadians had proved incapable of meeting army standards of mental stability or of surviving the stress of routine army life and had been rejected or discharged on psychiatric grounds. Others did not reveal their "inadequacies" until exposed to combat, where they quickly broke down because of their "predisposition" to neuroses. This view did not attract our immediate sympathy. Our enquiries into the battlefield made it seem more likely that breakdowns were the result of the collapse of unit morale and/or of individual morale in specific battle situations rather than a matter of "inadequate personalities." Nevertheless we quickly realized that our research would have to range far beyond the battlefield. It would be necessary to examine the concept of battle exhaustion and to understand the system that had recognized and legitimated it. This required a basic understanding of the state of the profession of psychiatry in the pre-war period. A brief outline is offered here so that the particular history of Canadian army psychiatry may be understood.

IN THE LATE 1930s the term psychiatrist was applied to three reasonably distinct types of physicians. First, in terms of status, were the neuropsychiatrists. For example in Toronto, where Duncan Graham was professor of medicine, University of Toronto and physician in chief, Toronto General Hospital,[4] only academically qualified neurologists were allowed to practice neuropsychiatry. Graham, like so many of his counterparts in the interwar years, was determined to bring scientific method to the practice of medicine. Beginning in 1920 he "built a staff grounded in clinical medicine, testing them as seniors and residents in medicine, then sending them away for post-graduate clinical study and usually to qualify for the MRCP (England). Extra training in physiology, biochemistry or pathology as a preparation for research was demanded."[5]

GRAHAM BELIEVED THAT PSYCHIATRY did not lend itself to the application of scientific method. The men he entrusted with neuropsychiatry took an interest in neuroses and would offer patients some explanation of what might lie behind neurotic behaviour but they knew of no scientifically based treatment for such transient mental states, and relied on occupational therapy. Indeed Dr Goldwin Howland, the head of the neurology division, was the principal architect of occupational therapy in Canada.[6] Psychotic patients were transferred from the hospital to an asylum as soon as the diagnosis of "nil organic findings" was confirmed.

The professor of psychiatry at the University of Toronto, Clarence B. Farrar, was quite content with this situation. Farrar's appointment was not at Toronto General but at the provincially controlled Toronto Psychiatric Hospital, the centrepiece of the Ontario mental illness treatment system. Farrar was a leading figure in the mental hospital psychiatry of the era. As editor of the *American Journal of Psychiatry* and a specialist in the treatment of schizophrenia, Farrar was able to attract a number of promising physicians to the one-year university diploma course in psychiatry. There was good communication between the mental hospital psychiatrists and the neuropsychiatrists but most accepted a division of responsibility that left chronic mental illness to the asylum and neuroses to the neuropsychiatrists.

Mental hospital psychiatry was experiencing a period of rapid innovation in the late thirties. Insulin-coma therapy for the treatment of schizophrenia[7] was accidentally discovered in 1933. Knowledge quickly spread from Vienna to North America and by 1937 many Canadian asylums had established insulin-coma wards.[8] No one really understood the mechanisms of the treatment, but putting patients into repeated comatose states seemed to improve their condition. By the following year Metrazol, a chemical which induced violent convulsions, was in use[9] with catatonics, manic depressives, and schizophrenics. Metrazol quickly fell into disfavour because the convulsions were found to produce compressed fractures of the vertebrae. It was soon replaced by electric shock, which could be more easily controlled. Mental hospital psychiatrists might not have had the status of neuropsychiatrists, but in 1939 many believed that innovative physical treatment methods were opening up important new horizons.

The third group of psychiatric practitioners were usually referred to as "mental hygienists." The mental hygiene movement had been created by the crusading zeal of Clifford Beers, a sometime mental asylum patient who wrote *A Mind That Found Itself*, the story of the treatment (or ill-treatment) of his own illness and of his recovery. Beers founded the American National Committee For Mental Hygiene during World War I. The Canadian Committee was established in 1918 under the energetic leadership of Clarence Hincks and C.K. Clarke. By 1939 the movement was encountering public indifference in reaction to its exaggerated claims.[10] In Canada the focus had narrowed to mental health education in schools and psychological testing.[11]

Where were Freud and the other adherents of psychoanalysis in this picture? No one interested in mental illness could have been ignorant of Freud's ideas, but few of those who worked as psychiatrists in Canada seem to have incorporated more than the most general Freudian concepts into their thinking. Freud's death in September 1939 occasioned a number of tributes in the academic journals.[12] The general tone was laudatory but the image conveyed was of a brilliant thinker who had helped to shape the twentieth century rather than an architect of modern psychiatry. Karl Menninger, for example, wrote: "Perhaps no other one individual in the field of science lived to see the thinking of the entire world so profoundly modified by his discoveries within his lifetime as Freud. Galileo, Dalton, Lavoisier, Darwin, these and others contributed discoveries which greatly modified our thinking and our ways of living, but the effect was more gradual in its permeation. For not only medical science and psychological science and sociological science, but literature, and anthropology, pedagogy and even popular speech show the influence of Freud's discoveries."[13]

Farrar, who certainly rejected most of Freud's ideas, took a more sceptical approach in the obituary he wrote, though he did concede that "it is good that the phenomena [sic] Freud occurred."[14] But neither the *Bulletin of the Menninger Clinic*, the *American Journal of Psychiatry*, nor other specialized journals turned away from their preoccupation with the new physical methods. These seemed to promise successful treatment of the large numbers of patients that psychoanalysis, even if it worked, could never touch. Volume 96 (1939–40) of the *American Journal of Psychiatry* contains eighty-seven articles – the majority deal with either insulin-coma or Metrazol. Only one article deals directly with Freud and that is a study of attitudes towards psychoanalysis among neurologists, psychiatrists, and psychologists. The author, who admitted he regarded "psychoanalysis as reactionary," sent a questionnaire with a four-point scale to a "haphazardly selected" group of practitioners. The neurologists were overwhelmingly sceptical of the claims of psychoanalysis. Members of the American Psychiatric Association were less negative, but only 25 out of 179 wished to indicate their "wholehearted" acceptance of psychoanalysis.[15]

The physicians interviewed for this book rarely mentioned Freud or psychoanalysis until asked and then tended to see them as irrelevant to military psychiatry. No one ever referred to Freud's own work on war neuroses. Dr Travis Dancey, who was a young mental hospital psychiatrist running an insulin-coma ward in 1939, described McGill University and the pre-war Montreal medical community as resolutely anti-Freudian even before Dr Ewan Cameron arrived in 1942 to head the new Allan Memorial Institute.[16] Cameron rejected Freud and all other psychoanalysts. Now notorious for his use of various physical treatment methods with reckless disregard for their effects on patients, Cameron in the early years was a mainstream psychiatrist heading to the top of his profession.[17]

The academic medical community in Toronto was similarly free of Freudian influences. Farrar ensured that psychoanalysis was not part of the teaching at Toronto Psychiatric Hospital, while Graham and Howland were equally determined to keep Freud out of the general hospitals and the medical school curriculum. When Canada's first private psychiatrist, Dr Brock Chisholm, began a Freudian-influenced psychiatric practice in Toronto he was resolutely ignored. Graham did talk to Chisholm, but was not impressed and firmly rejected suggestions that his expertise be used at Toronto General.[18]

THIS WORK BEGINS with an account of the establishment and development of the psychiatric branch of the Royal Canadian Army Medical Corps (RCAMC) in England. The men who created this service were all drawn from the academic medical world of McGill and the University of Toronto. They saw themselves as neuropsychiatrists working within the framework of general medicine and neurology. Their task was to diagnose and treat individuals who suffered from mental illness. Psychotics, roughly defined as those suffering from major disabling diseases, such as schizophrenia and manic depression, were held at the neurological hospital until they could be returned to Canada, discharged from the army, and committed to an asylum. Psychopathic personalities, a term then applied to chronic social deviants who usually had long criminal records, were also discharged as soon as their sentences were served. This category included those who did not conform to the norm. Homosexuals, or at least those accused of homosexual acts, were given this label and returned to Canada for immediate discharge. Other soldiers whose behaviour repeatedly challenged army discipline were also diagnosed as psychopathic.[19]

The largest group of patients sent to the neuropsychiatric hospital in Basingstoke, Hampshire, were neurotics. The terms neurosis or psychoneurosis were used, without much precision, for a variety of mental states that made it difficult or impossible for the individual to function adequately in a given environment. Most neuropsychiatrists differentiated between chronic neuroses, which pre-dated military enlistment and were thought to be deeply embedded in the personality, and acute neuroses, which had developed in previously normal personalities. It was generally accepted that some individuals were predisposed towards neurosis because of childhood experience, but since many case histories did not elicit signs of predisposition and did provide evidence of successful long-term social adaptation the neuropsychiatrists accepted the reality of acute neuroses brought on by the circumstances of military life.[20]

The research of William Sargant strongly reinforced the view that a disabling anxiety neurosis could develop in a stable personality. Studies of British soldiers evacuated from Dunkirk indicated that many men who broke down during the withdrawal of the British Expeditionary Force (BEF) had no predisposing characteristics and were psychiatric casualties because of their specific experiences in a disastrous retreat.[21] Sargant's views on diagnosis and treatment were very influential at Basingstoke.

The neuropsychiatric model of dealing with mental illness *as it arose* was seriously challenged by psychologists and some psychiatrists who believed that personnel selection could screen out potential problem cases. In Canada, as in Britain and the United States, social scientists of all kinds yearned to bring their expertise to bear on the war effort. The Canadian Psychological Association (CPA) had been lobbying the military to introduce personnel selection through psychological testing since the outbreak of the war.[22] After 1941 army psychiatry in Canada was strongly influenced by men who saw themselves as social engineers. Brock Chisholm, Jack Griffin, and Bill Line, the men who created army psychiatry in Canada, believed that they could scientifically screen, categorize, and utilize the nation's manpower.

The neuropsychiatrists resisted, but to no avail. Increasingly army psychiatry overseas was also drawn into the work of personnel selection. Interest in acute anxiety neuroses, the "shell shock" of World War I, lapsed and when the Canadians entered battle on a large scale in 1943 the army was ill-prepared for "battle exhaustion," the psychiatric problem brought on by combat. The British and Americans had been equally committed to a personnel selection model and were also forced to improvise their own approaches to the psychiatric crisis on the battlefield.

Second War battlefields provided psychiatrists with an unlimited practice. Those in Italy were particularly lucrative. As Allied soldiers advanced spasmodically against the topographical grain of the country they met skilled and well led German troops fighting in easily defensible mountains. Despite overwhelming air, artillery and tank superiority, it was left to infantrymen to climb the mountains and throw the enemy off. This was not the war which planners had envisaged. Organizations and manning policies were based on the assumption that the war would be fought by mobile, mechanized forces. Accordingly, personnel selection officers channelled the most qualified men to armoured, gunner and other specialist corps, leaving the infantry too often as the depository of the less educated, the less motivated and sometimes even the less physically fit.[23] No one was quite sure just what type of individual made the best infantryman. Compounding the irony, Allied planners grossly underestimated the kind of reinforcements that they would need. When actual casualty lists replaced projected estimates a monumental problem became evident. There were too few trained infantrymen to replace losses. Combat infantrymen, perhaps ten percent of total Allied manpower, produced at least seventy-five percent of casualties including psychiatric ones. A retraining programme had rapidly to be devised to convert, for example, redundant anti-aircraft gunners into riflemen. It was at best a partial and ineffective response.

As the Italian campaign wore on the world of the combat soldier and the world of the supporting troops grew further and further apart. In the rear areas the hundreds of thousands of men in the Allied lines of communications created a rich, diverse, corrupting sub-culture. The black market flourished, venereal disease reached epidemic proportions, and the battlefield was a safe distance away. Less than 10 per cent of the allied soldiers in Italy ran the risk of meeting death in combat. Injuries due to enemy action accounted for less than 20 per cent of all hospital admissions. And yet a small number of men were repeatedly asked to leave the safety of the rear areas and return to battle. Inevitably the incidence of desertion, absence without leave, self-inflicted wounds, accidental injuries, and psychiatric breakdown reached levels previously unheard of. Psychiatrists in the Allied armies were called upon to explain the causes of this behaviour crisis as well as to diagnose and treat the men caught up in it. The Canadian story described here differs only in detail from the experience of the other Allied troops in Italy.

The invasion of North-West Europe on 6 June 1944 launched a campaign that culminated in the surrender of the enemy's forces after just eleven months. During the initial stalemate in Normandy and in other periods of heavy fighting the battlefield produced large numbers of psychiatric casualties. Shortages of trained reinforcements were a major problem, for once again it was an infantry-man's war. But the malaise that almost overwhelmed the Allies in Italy never developed in North-West Europe. Army psychiatry in this campaign focused on attempts to prevent, limit, or cure breakdown in battle. Desertion, absence without leave, and other crimes against the military code occurred, but the numbers were not alarming.

The topic of psychiatric casualties in battle has attracted a good deal of attention in the aftermath of the war in Vietnam and the more recent Arab-Israeli conflicts. It should be stressed that this study is a purely historical work analysing some aspects of the relationship between psychiatrists and the Canadian military from 1939 to 1945. It is presented as a chapter in both the history of war and the history of psychiatry.

CHAPTER ONE

No. 1 Nuts

The Development of Army Neuropsychiatry, 1939–1942

The Canadian Army mobilized for war in the late summer of 1939 with a national call to arms. Just after noon on 1 September Army Headquarters alerted military districts, which in turn spread the word to local militia units. Commanding officers paraded their soldiers, called for active service volunteers, then filled vacancies with other recruits from nearby communities. Enthusiasm varied regionally and from unit to unit. The Chief of the General Staff noted that the "infantry was not coming along as well as might be desired."[1] Infantry soldiering was not the most appealing life, particularly for those who considered it somewhat redundant in an age of modern mechanized warfare. Nonetheless, more than 58,000 joined up in the first weeks. Most formed the cores of the 1st and 2nd Canadian Infantry Divisions. The 1st shipped to the United Kingdom in December 1939 and the 2nd several months later. In due course the 3rd Infantry, 4th and 5th Armoured Divisions, and 1 and 2 Armoured Brigades followed to compose the First Canadian Army. These fighting elements of the overseas army numbered about 100,000. A like number were employed in bases and support facilities.

The RCAMC, like all other branches of the Canadian Armed Forces, was magnificently unprepared for rapid mobilization. As late as November 1939 there were only 42 medical officers and 11 nursing sisters in the permanent army.[2] But unlike other branches of the armed services, which would have to train most of their recruits in the elementary arts of war, the RCAMC could draw upon its militia units and upon the medical community at large with the certain knowledge that its key volunteers had been professionally trained.

Initially there was little evidence that the medical corps was capable of organizing these recruits to serve effectively. The system of medical examination for recruits had changed little since World War I and, despite representations from the medical community, no provisions were made for routine chest x-rays, urinalyses, or Wassermann tests. It was also decided that it would not be necessary to employ specialists on medical boards because "In any instance where a specialist's report is considered necessary to establish a candidate's fitness, the individual should be rejected by the board."³

Criticism of the army's methods of examining volunteers came from all directions and before the end of 1939 re-examination of all recruits was ordered. It was to include a chest x-ray, chemical urinalysis, and a more detailed physical.⁴ Psychological testing for the selection and classification of army personnel was also considered. A conference on "The Use of Psychological Methods in Wartime" held in Ottawa on 2 October 1939 concluded that "it would be advisable to introduce into the recruiting examinations, intelligence and aptitude tests"⁵ and urged that the Director General of Medical Services (DGMS) be asked to cooperate with the CPA, which had offered to devise and implement the tests.

The chairman of the conference was Canada's most distinguished scientist, Sir Frederick Banting, the co-discoverer of insulin. Prominent among the advocates of testing at the meeting was Major-General A.L.G. McNaughton, President of the National Research Council. McNaughton had been Chief of the General Staff from 1929 until 1935 and in early October he was anxiously awaiting the call to return to the colours. When the call came it was to the post of Inspector-General of the units of the 1st Canadian Division with a view to commanding the Red Patch Division when it was sent overseas, not to the post of Chief of the General Staff, the senior position in the military.

Without McNaughton's direct involvement psychological testing stood little chance of being accepted. The Chief of the General Staff, Major-General T.V. Anderson and the Adjutant-General, Major-General H.H. Matthews showed no interest in the idea. Neither the senior medical officer Colonel J.L. Potter nor his successor as DGMS, Brigadier B.M. Gorssline, would voluntarily have anything to do with "psychological methods." Indeed a meeting of psychiatrists called to discuss approaches to psychiatric problems in the army was flatly told that "there would be no testing and no psychiatric screen at enlistment."⁶ The examining boards were to "reject obvious misfits, subsequently unit medical officers were to make their diagnosis and refer difficult cases to regional consultants for disposal."⁷ When new instructions to medical boards were issued in early 1940 doctors were told to establish "that the recruit is sufficiently intelligent" by questioning him. Obvious misfits were defined as those "with a history of nervous breakdown ... residence in an institution ... drug addiction ... or a family history indicating nervous instability such as migraine, eccentricity etc."⁸

The lack of concern for intelligence testing, not to mention any form of personality evaluation, reflected the attitude of the Canadian medical profession toward psychology and psychiatry. The overwhelming majority of doctors inside or outside the army sincerely believed that well-trained physicians, particularly those who had served as medical officers in World War I, could evaluate an individual's ability or stability as well as any psychiatrist and better than any psychologist. If the medical board had doubts about an individual's mental fitness its job was to reject him, not to diagnose him.

There is a good case to be made for this point of view, but during the early fall of 1939, when more than 50,000 Canadians enlisted in the army, some overworked medical boards did not take the time to evaluate carefully all of the volunteers. A number of recruits with a history of mental illness[9] and many more who were mentallly deficient were enrolled in the army as category A or B personnel, the two classifications that placed no limitations on military service.

The attitude of the RCAMC towards intelligence testing and psychiatric screening was clear enough, but what did it intend to do with psychiatric casualties produced by the stress of war? The Canadian Army had admitted to 15,500 "neuropsychiatric disabilities" in World War I – 9,000 of them diagnosed as "shell shock and neurosis."[10] It had to be assumed that similar casualties would occur again.

The Canadian government's chief adviser on this question was Dr J.B.S. Cathcart, Chief Neuropsychiatrist in the Department of Pensions and National Health. Cathcart was a veteran of World War I medical services and had extensive experience with shell shock cases. In the fall of 1939 he and his colleagues were primarily concerned about "the pension question." After World War I large numbers of veterans received pensions on the basis of neuro-psychiatric disability. There was a strong belief that such pensions, by formally recognizing the existence of a psychoneurosis, reinforced the condition instead of helping to cure it.

Cathcart was familiar with Dr Thomas W. Salmon's study of American psychiatric casualties in World War I[11] and with the similar ideas about forward treatment of such cases expressed in the British government's exhaustive post-war study of the problem.[12] He assumed forward treatment would be provided, but insisted that the number of psychiatric casualties and thus pension cases could be dramatically reduced if the term "shell shock" could be changed to reflect the view that the condition was a behaviour disorder. "As soon as the whole army learned that instead of being listed as shell shock these casualties were described Below Standard, the flood would stop."[13]

Cathcart's views on the efficiency of forward treatment and the desirability of finding a new name for shell shock represented the conventional medical ideas about World War I psychiatric casualties. Cathcart himself had little influence on the Canadian Army's approach to the question. Throughout the summer and fall of 1939 his department was engaged in a bitter jurisdictional dispute with the army. The Department of Pensions and National Health was attempting to establish a claim to treat all military casualties "after they had been cleared from the field of conflict."[14] The Department of National Defence had no intention of allowing this to happen and it was unwilling to follow Cathcart's advice on any subject. Thus, it welcomed Dr Colin Russel's proposal to establish a neurosurgical and neurological hospital that would deal with psychiatric cases as a specialized unit in the Canadian expeditionary force bound for France. Russel became the army's adviser on all neuropsychiatric questions.

A graduate of McGill (MD 1901), Russel studied neurology and psychiatry at Johns Hopkins, then under the direction of William Osler. He then spent several years in Zurich, Berlin, and Paris, working with leading continental neurologists. In 1905 he interned at The National Hospital for the Relief and Cure of the Paralysed and Epileptic. The National Hospital, or simply "Queen Square" after its location in London, was the mecca of twentieth century neurology and when Russel returned to Montreal he was able to establish himself as a leading figure in neurology – a relatively new clinical specialization in Canada.[15]

Russel volunteered for the medical corps in World War I and by 1917 he was in charge of neuropsychiatry at Granville Special Hospital for Nervous Cases, a Canadian army establishment at Ramsgate, England. He published a number of articles on his experiences with shell shock patients and was regarded as an expert on the subject. After the war he became clinical professor of neurology at the Montreal Neurological Institute (MNI).[16] In the late thirties Wilder Penfield's MNI was a world famous centre of neurosurgery and Russel's reputation was further enhanced by his association with it. In fact Penfield was no particular admirer of Russel and was deeply disappointed when Russel, not he, was authorized to organize a specialized unit for overseas service.[17]

Russel was brought back into the army as a Lieutenant-Colonel with the title of Consultant Neuropsychiatrist. He outlined his very definite views on the origin and proper treatment of neuroses in a paper published in the *Canadian Medical Association Journal*, December 1939. Although he had never been near the front lines Russel was confident that all fear reactions – "anxiety, trembling and jumpiness ... mental confusion or even almost a stupor" could be handled with "common sense treatment of rest, food and an understanding appreciation."[18] He believed that men suffering such symptoms could be returned to duty in a few days. The real problem, and the task of neuropsychiatrist, he continued, was the treatment of "a large class, which became larger, the further one got away from the front [who] exhibited all the evidences of conversion hysteria – the so-called shell shock." Russel believed he knew how to deal with these cases. Hysteria is the "great simulator," he wrote, and it can involve "blindness in one or both eyes, mutism, associated or not with deafness, convulsions of a major or minor type ... profuse sweating ... paralysed extremities ... or a host of other manifestations ... I have seen examples of all of these and cleared them up by purely psychic treatment and very quickly."[19]

According to Russel the cause of such hysteria was either an "extraordinary suggestibility" or the absence of "high moral standards." It could be cured by the use of faradism (the application of an electric current producing a severe, painful shock) until the hysteria was abandoned, isolation, or by the use of a "wire brush," a special feature of Russel's treatment program in World War II.[20] The wire brush, charged with an asymmetric alternating current, was applied to the paralysed limb. With these methods Russel claimed "to return over 71.4 percent back to full duty ... The cure of the psychoneuropath really consists of a mental contest resulting in the victory of the physician. This, in conclusion, is the secret of psychotherapy."[21]

Russel wanted the hospital staff to include two neurosurgical teams, which would use specially fitted vehicles that Mr McLaughlin of Oshawa"[22] was preparing. The link between Russel's special hospital for the treatment of war neuroses, "in the zone of the army where strict discipline is maintained,"[23] and a mobile neurosurgical unit may seem obscure, but it was clear to him. The army's neurological hospital was to be modelled on the MNI, which served to isolate neurology and neurosurgery from general surgery and medicine. Canadian academic medicine before the war the treatment of neuroses in hospitals was the exclusive province of neurologists who, because of their interest in neuroses, described themselves as neuropsychiatrists. If neurologists were to be grouped with neurosurgeons, then the neurological hospital must also be the noncustodial psychiatric hospital.

This approach was unique to McGill, where Wilder Penfield had created his institute with a great deal of publicity and Rockefeller money. At the Toronto General Hospital neurosurgery was very much part of general surgery, just as neurology and neuropsychiatry were firmly wedded to general medicine. Dr Kenneth McKenzie, who like Penfield had worked with the great neurosurgical pioneer Harvey Cushing, had begun his neurosurgical service at Toronto General in 1924. By 1939 McKenzie's unit at Tornto, not Penfield's highly publicized operation in Montreal, was the major Canadian centre for neurosurgery.[24]

McKenzie believed that it made no sense to separate surgical specializations, especially in wartime when multiple wounds could be expected. What, he asked "would be the procedure in cases where wounds of the abdomen or chest were associated with wounds of the spinal cord and consequent paralysis?"[25] McKenzie's arguments were difficult to refute, and his approach to neurosurgery fitted in with the plans of the British Army. Thus, McKenzie's model ultimately prevailed in the war zone, with neurosurgical and neuropsychiatric units being attached to base hospitals.[26]

But this was in the future. In 1939 Russel used the public prestige of Wilder Penfield to counter McKenzie's criticisms. At a meeting chaired by Brigadier Gorrsline, Penfield dismissed McKenzie's objections with the statement that general surgeons would be brought to the neurological hospital. Their scheme, Penfield insisted, allowed for "the cooperation and teamwork of neurologists and neurosurgeons which, in the Montreal Neurological Institute, we find of such mutual advantage."[27] The meeting concluded with an agreement that the special unit, to be called No. 1 Neurological and Neurosurgical Hospital would take the field with the Canadian troops scheduled for France.

The Montrealers had prevailed, but the hospital could not function without the assistance of Toronto doctors. William Cone, Penfield's assistant, was to be senior neurosurgeon, with Harry Botterell from Toronto as his second. Russel was the senior neuropsychiatrist, with H.H. Hyland from Toronto General Hospital next in rank. The junior neurologists were Fred Hanson, a young American who was working at the MNI when war broke out,[28] and Clifford Richardson, a Toronto neurologist who combined experience as a house physician at Queen Square with work at the Tavistock Clinic and the London Institute of Psychoanalysis. In 1939 neither Hanson nor Richardson knew very much about shell shock or the military. Enlistment, in Richardson's words, "was just the natural thing to do." He had gone on a walking tour of Germany in 1936 and had been amazed by the atmosphere of Hitler's Reich. He was clear on the "threat and danger of Nazi philosophy" and was certain such "a fanatic leader, such dangerous ideas had to be stopped."[29]

The winter of 1939-40 offered Richardson and the other volunteers the opportunity to practise that supreme military virtue – patience. The 1st Division with its medical units arrived in England just before Christmas. Quartered at Aldershot in ancient barrack buildings without central heating, the whole force seemed to catch influenza or colds. An outbreak of German measles added to their misery and Colonel R.M. Luton, the senior medical officer overseas, made arrangements for Canadian soldiers to be admitted to British army hospitals.[30] When the medical staff for the first two Canadian general hospitals arrived in February of 1940, there were no buildings for them to work in, and there was no particular need for their services. Discussions between Ottawa and London centred on the medical establishment required for the Canadian units going to France to join the BEF. National Defence headquarters seemed incapable of coming to a clear decision on this question but it was agreed that the group of neurologists and neurosurgeons, who had already been dubbed "No. 1 Nuts," were intended for the war zone in France and therefore could be sent overseas.[31]

Colin Russel, Bill Cone, and Harry Botterell left for London in May 1940 and arrived just as the evacuation from Dunkirk was taking place.[32] The 1st Canadian Division would not be going to France in the foreseeable future and sending the neurological hospital overseas was no longer a priority. Cone and Botterell kept busy with research at Queen Square while Russel worked to keep his hospital idea alive. Lord Camrose, the proprietor of the *Daily Telegraph*, offered his country home, Hackwood Park, a spacious mansion near Basingstoke in Hampshire. Russel somehow persuaded Canadian army authorities in London to authorize the agreement. No one in Canada had thought to cancel the move of the rest of the hospital staff and in September 1940 No. 1 Neurological Hospital, usually called simply Basingstoke, opened for business as a 200-bed hospital. The nurses, twelve from the MNI and eight from Toronto under Matron Myra MacDonald,[33] were housed in the Camrose family rooms while the doctors settled into the servants' quarters. Construction of Nissen huts for additional wards began and the hospital community settled into a familiar routine.

The Minister of National Defence, J.L. Ralston, eventually noticed the hospital's existence when the costs of establishing the unit were brought to his attention. Why, he asked, was a unit designed for service in France developing into a new and expensive stationary hospital in England?[34] Colonel Luton's reply argued that "the hospital will accompany our expeditionary force to the field when the time comes" and "it would be an error to dissolve a unit upon which a great deal of money ($50,000) had been expended."[35] The idea of sending the hospital overseas was not formally abandoned until 1942, when it was agreed that new methods of evacuation and treatment made the original role of the hospital "undesirable."[36] By that time Basingstoke had acquired a vital role as both an army hospital and an Emergency Medical Services (EMS) hospital for the country of Hampshire. No. 1 Neurological was in place for the duration.

Basingstoke was well placed to receive patients from Southampton and other English port cities devastated by the blitz of 1940-41. The neurosurgeons had steady work because the army had allowed large numbers of young Canadians to ride high-powered motorcycles on the wrong side of narrow roads even under blackout conditions. The resulting mayhem was such that German propaganda broadcasts suggested supplying a motorcycle for every Canadian soldier.[37]

Determining whether a physical basis existed for a number of the puzzling post-traumatic syndromes these motorcycle accidents produced taxed the staff's collective skill. Epilepsy was, however, "the most common 'organic' condition encountered" and required careful investigation. A diagnosis of epilepsy was automatic grounds for return to Canada and many epileptics had tried to conceal their condition by taking anti-convulsants or relying on the protection of friends. Neurosyphilis, sciatica, neuritis, migraine, and narcolepsy were also encountered, but it was obvious from the first weeks that the main work of the No. 1 Nuts would be with patients requiring the attention of the neuropsychiatrists.[38]

Diagnosis and treatment of neuropsychiatric cases were under the direction of Colin Russel until repeated bouts of illness, which he attributed to his age and the English winter, led him to request repatriation to Canada in early 1942.[39] Russel was most interested in the cases of conversion hysteria that closely resembled the kind of shell shock he had dealt with in England during World War I. Russel used the electric wire brush treatment with a few of these patients[40] but simple psychotherapy, reclassification, or reassignment was usually all that was required. Most of the patients admitted to Basingstoke were suffering from a psychoneurosis manifested by a wide variety of symptoms – strong fear reactions, chronic headaches, enuresis, gastric illness, uncontrollable restlessness, exaggerated physical weakness, muscle tics, obsessions, phobias – the list was almost endless.

H.H. Hyland, who had considerable experience with similar patients at Toronto General Hospital, established the basic routines in psychiatric treatment. Hyland had joined Howland's neurological service at Toronto General Hospital in 1930. Ward G, with twenty to thirty beds for organic neurological disease and twenty-five to forty beds for nervous and mental disease, was the largest neurological and psychiatric service in Canada and the model for most of the country.[41] Hyland had been trained in neurology at Queen Square but he had developed a strong interest in psychiatry. He approached the problem of mental illness with the neurologist's conviction that there was a "physiological basis of mental functions and dysfunctions." The differences between "normal," "neurotic," and "psychotic" disorders were, he wrote, "narrow and ill-defined." The symptoms of mental stress "also occur in varying degrees in normal persons. In others these same symptoms tend to be carried to such an extreme as to merit the term neurotic."[42]

Hyland's flexible, practical approach to psychiatry was generally shared by his junior colleagues, although Richardson and Hanson were less committed to the virtues of psychotherapy. Richardson had become disenchanted with psychoanalytically influenced psychiatry while working at the Tavistock Clinic and attending sessions at the London Institute of Psychoanalysis in the mid-thirties. He had little confidence that anything could be done with the hundreds of patients who arrived at Basingstoke with long records of neurotic reactions to the stress of civilian and army life and was quite certain that "return to Canada and discharge" was the correct procedure for chronic neurotics as well as for psychopaths and alcoholics.[43] This view sometimes led to difficulties. On one occasion Richardson told a chronic bedwetter that he would be "returned to Canada." By next morning word had spread and the ward stank of urine.[44]

The number of reboardings, which reclassified soldiers as unfit for military service, was causing the Canadian military authorities some concern by 1941. Between February 1940 and March 1941, 2,135 troops of all ranks were returned to Canada for discharge and 21 per cent of these were classified as mental cases – "chiefly anxiety neuroses, chronic alcoholism or mental deficiency."[45] In addition to these, hundreds of other Canadian soldiers were, or had been, neuropsychiatric patients at No. 1 Neurological Hospital or No. 15 General Hospital. The problem began to reach epidemic proportions in the winter of 1941 and Luton appointed a "committee on cases of anxiety neurosis"[46] to study the matter.

The committee met at Basingstoke on 13 January 1941 and the first order of business was to change the name of the committee and the scope of its investigation. Since the whole range of mental illness was to be examined, the title Functional Nervous Diseases was adopted and the Official Nomenclature of Diseases 1931 was used to enumerate the five diagnostic categories: 1. Mental deficiency; 2. Chronic alcoholism and drug addiction; 3. Functional psychoses; 4. Psychopathic personalities; 5. Psychoneuroses.

The Committee decided that the "higher grade of defectives ... would be able to perform routine tasks quite efficiently"[47] and should only be discharged if they had behaviour problems that did not respond to army discipline. Drug addicts, chronic alcoholics, and functional psychotics were to be returned to Canada forthwith.

The broad category of psychopathic personalities was also easily disposed of.[48] Generally neuropsychiatrists used this term to encompass a variety of chronic social misfits who had been arrested for burglary, larceny, petty theft, robbery with violence, homosexual activity, or absence without leave. These patients were referred to Basingstoke from various prisons and detention barracks. They were to be returned to Canada and discharged from the service unless there was clear evidence that they would respond to military discipline.

This left the largest category, the psychoneuroses. In 1940 psychoneurosis was a catch-all term for a variety of personality disorders that made it difficult, or impossible, for an individual to function adequately. Major Hyland, as the senior neuropsychiatrist (Colin Russel was absent due to illness), presented the case for the retention and treatment of all anxiety and hysteria cases. At Basingstoke a good deal of attention was paid to each patient[49] with treatment "initiated by a careful evaluation of physical, psychological and sociological components." A detailed case history with "questioning about childhood environmental influences, parental attitudes and relationships, phobias, school and work record, disposition towards sports and physical dangers, sexual habits, adaption to difficulties, mood changes, details of army experiences, etc." followed a thorough physical. Then came a systematic mental examination "surveying intellect as well as emotion" and a detailed discussion of the factors "causing the immediate mental conflict and tension." Hyland believed in repeated talks with patients so that "repressed fears and conflicts" could be aired again and again. The immediate problems that had caused or at least precipitated the neurosis were to be dealt with where possible, but when the problem was insoluble Hyland urged a "philosophical outlook" and the avoidance of continued "emotional thinking." In selected cases "hypnosis, sodium pentathol, suggestion by use of faradism and occasionally prolonged narcosis" were tried.[50]

Hyland's argument for intensive treatment of all psychoneurotics was challenged by Major F.H. Van Nostrand, the neuropsychiatrist from the Canadian Army's No. 15 General Hospital at Bramshott. Van Nostrand expressed the view that "the majority of these soldiers were of little use, even when they returned to their unit." In his opinion, slight strain would probably cause them to break down again. Hyland replied that those who "responded to psychotherapy should be given another opportunity to carry on with their unit." If they broke down a second time "they could be brought before a medical board for reclassification."[51] The committee agreed to postpone a policy decision until a follow-up study of patients returned to their units from both hospitals could be undertaken.

Van Nostrand's background was very different from Hyland's. He had served in World War I as a stretcher bearer and then joined the Royal Flying Corps. Between the wars he had devoted his energies to rebuilding the family farm north of Toronto and acquiring a medical degree. After graduation he joined the staff of Christie Street Hospital for Veterans and for the next ten years he dealt with a variety of psychoneurotic patients.[52] For him, psychiatry was applied common sense; one tried to get patients to face up to their problems and to function as well as possible.[53] The majority of patients at Bramshott, like those at Basingstoke, had long histories of pre-war problems and had been in and out of mental institutions. Van Nostrand was quite certain that intensive psychotherapy would have little lasting effect on such men. He also believed that a second group of soldiers, who had developed neurotic symptoms in England without exposure to combat, were failing to cope with the normal stress of army life. If they could not be dealt with effectively by Regimental Medical Officers (RMOs), chaplains or unit Commanding Officers (COs), it was unlikely that hospitalization and diagnosis as a neurotic would accomplish anything. Indeed it was probable that such treatment would reinforce the patient's sense of himself as a sick person.[54]

The follow-up studies took a very long time to complete. But a preliminary report based on sixty-five case histories of men who had no previous history of mental instability was made available by Hyland in October 1941. The Committee on Functional Nervous Diseases was told "that out of 65 cases which had been returned to their units for an average of three months, 70.2 per cent of the in-patients and 43.7 per cent of the out-patients were doing full duty efficiently and without complaint." Hyland also told the committee that he had studied fifty-four other patients who had not been returned to duty and he was struck by "the frequency of poor family and personal history as a background in these cases." The committee decided, after some discussion, that those cases showing a "bad personal and family history" should be recategorized and sent home, while those "who have a good background and respond well to treatment"[55] should be returned to duty.

In April 1942, Richardson produced a more detailed study of patients from Basingstoke. During an eighteen-month period the hospital had admitted 1,712 psychiatric cases of which 649 were diagnosed as psychoneurotics. Fifty-five per cent of these were returned to duty. The follow-up study was able to obtain adequate information on only seventy-five of these men. The data on this group gave a different impression from the earlier report, for just 25 per cent of the men "remained well and efficient during periods of three to fifteen months after discharge to duty." If these cases were in any way representative, the Canadian Army was not decreasing wastage very effectivey. Richardson was disturbed by these statistics but he attributed the high failure rate to the large number of patients who "should never have been taken into the army because of nervous instability"[56] and pointed out that British Army experience with psychoneurosis was very similar.

British experience with mental disorders among soldiers who had not been exposed to combat was indeed strikingly similar. More than 100,000 men had been medically invalided out of the army in the first year of the war with gastric, mental, and nervous problems,[57] and thousands more had been treated and returned to duty with an uncertain prognosis. The extent of the problem had led to an acrimonious public debate which took place in *The Lancet* and other leading medical journals. Calls for an end to civilian doctors treating soldiers were made on the grounds that "the Englishmen regard soldiering as terribly hard for the poor boys: and at the slightest opportunity pampering the soldier becomes a favourite pastime."[58] Complaints about malingering and "skrimshanking" were also common but the central focus of the professional debate was between those who doubted that the "neurotic could be freed of his neurotic tendencies"[59] and those who were confident that psychotherapy could return a significant proportion of soldiers to full duty.

The Lancet came down strongly on the side of those who favoured a rigorous policy. The army "would no doubt lose some valuable soldiers, the editor declared, but it would be rid of some thousands of men who are of no use to it at all."[60] The British Army, struggling to obtain its share of manpower in an unequal competition with the air force and the navy,[61] was unwilling to adopt this attitude. The consulting psychiatrist to British Army at home, Brigadier John R. Rees, had come into the Royal Army Medical Corps (RAMC) from his position as medical director of the Tavistock Clinic, an Institute of Human Relations committed to social psychiatry in the broadest sense. Rees and the psychiatrists he brought into the service with him were strongly committed to a treatment approach that emphasized various therapies – psychoanalytical and occupational. Ultimately the British Army even established a separate facility for the intensive retraining of psychoneurotics.[62]

The Canadian neuropsychiatrists at Basingstoke were divided on the question. Van Nostrand and Richardson were firmly on the side of *The Lancet* but Hyland remained committed to a treatment model. The Canadian Army was not interested in their views, however. It refused to accept the notion that large numbers of men should be returned to Canada when all signs pointed to a looming manpower shortage. No. 1 Neurological Hospital would continue to function as a treatment centre for the more severe neurotic cases and a custodial centre for psychotics awaiting shipment back to Canada. RMOs were urged to keep mild psychoneurotic cases with their units. If referral to a psychiatrist was necessary, they were to be seen as outpatients as Basingstoke before admission was considered. The treatment of psychoneuroses at the hospital continued throughout the war with little sign of any improvement in recovery rates.[63]

The time, energy, and scarce resources devoted to the treatment of neuroses in the Canadian Army may seem disproportionate in view of the poor results, but the army's concern for reducing wastage encouraged medical personnel to devote considerable attention to soldiers as individuals. Quite apart from the moral value of this approach, it did achieve some measure of success. One young officer spent four weeks at Basingstoke under treatment for anxiety neurosis with conversion symptoms. Released to his unit, he had to return to the hospital after a short stint of regimental duty. After a second, much shorter, treatment session the young man was able to cope with his duties. He ultimately developed into an outstanding senior combatant officer in the Canadian Army. It might be argued that No. 1 Neurological justified its existence by this case alone.

THE CANADIAN ARMY'S DEFENSIVE ROLE in England prevented its neuropsychiatrists from gaining direct experience of battle neuroses. But the Canadians kept in close touch with their British counterparts, who were attempting to understand casualties they described as NYD (N), Not Yet Diagnosed (Nervous).*

The BEF had gone to France in 1939 with a clear set of assumptions about this problem. The experience of the last phase of World War I led most medical officers to believe that in a well-trained unit there would be few breakdowns, except after prolonged combat. Soldiers who exhibited nervousness or more extreme symptoms in these circumstances would be treated with rest, reassurance, and firmness. This therapeutic regime would be carried out as far forward as possible, at a Field Ambulance or Casualty Clearing Station (CCS). No specialist would be needed at these advanced posts. Psychiatrists would be available to treat serious cases at a neuropsychiatric centre attached to a general hospital.

The events of May and June 1940 prevented the testing of these assumptions. As the BEF retreated to Dunkirk very large numbers of acute anxiety neuroses developed and all that could be done was to evacuate them to England. The British Army at home had made no provision for such casualties,[64] and it was decided to send them to the Emergency Medical Services (EMS) neurosis centres originally set up to deal with the civilian psychiatric casualties expected from air raids.

Sutton, a sub-unit of the Maudsley Hospital, was the main EMS centre receiving military patients from the BEF. Here, William Sargant and Elliot Slater

---

* British medical authorities preferred to avoid the World War I term "shell shock". The official preference was that forward medical officers use NYD (N), for Not Yet Diagnosed, (Nervous). In practice a wide variety of terms including psychoneurosis, anxiety neurosis, battle neurosis, shock, exhaustion, and battle stress, were used by doctors until the terms "battle exhaustion" or simply "exhaustion" took hold.

led a team of psychiatrists and neurologists who were firmly committed to a physiological approach to psychiatric research. Their first major report, published in *The Lancet* on 6 July 1940[65] began by distinguishing between the cases "of acute *shell shock*" seen after Dunkirk and the neurotic disorders treated during the "Phoney War." The latter group exhibited "personality deviations, constitutional instability and lack of stamina which could be readily established from their past history." The acute cases of war neurosis from France, on the other hand, demonstrated that "men of reasonably sound personality may break down if the strain is severe enough."

Sargant and Slater noted that "compared to the average population" there was probably a greater proportion of men who "had suffered from nervous troubles in earlier life" among the acute cases, but they were struck by the number of individual histories showing good adaptation to army life, with "normal intelligence, personality and work record." Such men had broken down under the stress of the withdrawal to, and evacuation from, Dunkirk.[66] "It was an accumulation of strains, both physical and mental, of great intensity – bodily danger, continuous physical exertion, loss of sleep, insufficiency and irregularity of meals, intermittent but perpetually recurrent bombardment and the sight of comrades and civilian refugees being killed around them ... the necessity of continued withdrawal from the enemy, the impossibility of striking back produced a sense of frustration that contributed to a disastrous effect on the mind." Their patients' symptoms were "remarkably uniform: thin, fallen-in faces, pallid or sallow complexions, the whole expression of the body was one either of tension and anxiety or of a listless apathy ... The patients complained of the usual symptoms of the acute anxiety state: sleepiness, terrifying bad dreams, a feeling of inner unrest and a tendency to be startled at the least noise."

If the manifestations of anxiety were intense, they were also of short duration "even with a minimum of treatment." Some who had difficulty in staying asleep were given sedatives while the more severe cases were given a course of continuous narcosis, inducing sleep for the greater part of every twenty-four hours over a period of several days to a week. The doctors believed that "the longer the symptoms are allowed to last, with knowledge of the patient, the more deeply they will be ingrained and the more likely they will be to recur as future behaviour patterns."

Sargant and Slater also believed that "both for the patient and the doctor it is necessary to know the proximate cause of the breakdown." If required, hypnosis was to be employed to accomplish this. Sodium amytal, the most common sedative, produced an "easily controlled hypnoid state," which could be used "for the recovery of amnesia, for the reinforcement of suggestion and for the relief of hysterical symptoms." The prognosis for the recovery of these men was uncertain but the severity of their experience had convinced many of them that they would not return to battle without breaking down. The authors were initially reluctant to accept this suggestion, arguing that "only a history of previous neurotic illness or symptoms in civil life should exclude the patient ... from front line ... service."

Six months later a report was published on 1,500 cases seen by Sargant's group at Sutton Emergency Hospital.[67] It began with a firm statement that "it is impossible, by psychotherapy to reconstitute the make-up of a personality ... the neurotic cannot be freed of his neurotic tendencies." In military life, where the curing of symptoms results not in return to full activity as a civilian but to renewed service in the army, "treatment encounters the same difficulties but does not offer the same reward." The correct policy, Sargant and Slater now argued, was to return the neurotic who had broken down to civilian life where the best chance of readjustment lay. Sargant recalled this period in his 1967 publication, *The Unquiet Mind*: "Our experiences of Dunkirk taught us the folly of trying to patch up soldiers and expect them to face again the stresses that caused their breakdown ... In World War I neurotics had as a result, been kept with the Colours until they broke down completely. Some were shot for cowardice; but the example did the others no good ... under strong or continuous stresses no threats of exemplary punishment can prevent breakdowns."[68]

THE SUTTON HOSPITAL team also came to believe that "the most important lesson" of Dunkirk and the Battle of Britain was the need to prevent "a neurotic pattern of thought or behaviour from remaining fixed in the patient's brain for a minute longer than necessary."[69] The nervous system was to be protected from further stress by immediate sedation with sodium amytal or other barbiturates. Sargant noted that success in relieving acute symptoms only worked well when the patient was treated early enough and this led him to advocate the use of sedatives as far forward as possible. This treatment or even rest alone would lead to the disappearance of acute symptoms, since there was "a considerable tendency to spontaneous recovery." Even so the patient must be forced to "re-experience the violent emotions that the battle scenes have aroused." According to Sargant "this process – abreaction – has a prophylactic, as well as an immediate therapeutic effect."[70]

Sargant also reported on a new form of physical treatment that became known as insulin subcoma or modified insulin treatment: "In addition to sleep therapy, a modified form of insulin treatment is useful in some cases for breaking down the vicious circle of anxiety and loss of weight. Increasing doses of insulin are given in the mornings up to a maximum insufficient to produce coma or hypoglycemic excitement, followed three hours later by 12 oz. of potatoes or 7 oz. of sugar. The treatment is without any of the risks associated with insulin coma and generally produces a rapid gain in weight and improvement in physical condition."[71]

The work of William Sargant, Elliot Slater, and the Sutton Emergency Hospital group had a profound effect on policy towards battle neuroses in the Canadian and United States Armies. Both Fred Hanson and Clifford Richardson visited Sutton Emergency Hospital and Sargant addressed Canadian neuropsychiatrists on a number of occasions in 1941 and 1942.[72] Sargant's physical methods of treatment were adopted at Basingstoke and, since all Canadian neuropsychiatrists had to spend time at the hospital, a standardized notion of forward treatment of battle neuroses was developed. This did not mean all Canadian psychiatrists accepted Sargant's other findings. There was particular reluctance to believe that men of normal personality would break down in large numbers and strong resistance to the notion that such men could not be returned to full duty.

DURING 1942 THE HOSPITAL at Basingstoke continued to expand, and huts occupied more and more space on the vast lawns of Hackwood Park. Van Nostrand was transferred to No. 1 Neurological as the new commanding officer and in June Colin Russel, now almost sixty-five years of age, returned to McGill. Herbert Hyland was the senior neuropsychiatrist overseas but Canadian Military Headquarters offered Russel's job as consulting neuropsychiatrist (and the promotion to full colonel) to Van Nostrand. Shortly afterwards Hyland returned to Canada and his work at Toronto General Hospital. Richardson became the senior neuropsychiatrist at Basingstoke.

Two other McGill men left Basingstoke along with Russel in 1942: Cone returned to the Montreal Neurological and Hanson joined the United States Army. Hanson had been restless at No. 1 Nuts and had sought out action in some bizarre ways, including taking part in motor-torpedo boat raids in the Channel.[73] In May 1942 he transferred to the United States Army at the request of the senior medical officer in the US European theatre of operations, and became the unofficial adviser on neuropsychiatric problems to an army that had not yet recognized their existence. He was able to gain permission to join the 2nd Canadian Division for the Dieppe raid "to observe the stress of actual combat" and then actively sought a role in the North African campaign. He reached the front in Tunisia in March 1943 and was able to initiate the development of frontline treatment for combat neuropsychiatric casualties. Hanson's brilliant record in organizing psychiatric facilities in Tunisia and developing immediate treatment procedures led to his appointment as consultant in neuropsychiatry, North African theatre. Later in 1943 he played a major role in establishing for the United States Army a complete system of psychiatric services based on the lessons learned at Basingstoke.[74]

The Canadian Army's neuropsychiatric tradition, which associated psychiatry with neurology and general medicine, was unique. In the British Army psychiatry was linked with personnel selection and psychology rather than with the medical services, and RAMC physicians frequently ignored the advice of the specialist in psychological medicine.[75] The Canadian system was also unusual in having a single central institution, the hospital at Basingstoke, to serve as a training centre for all psychiatrists in the overseas army. The neuropsychiatric hospital was much admired by British and American doctors because medical priorities seemed to outweigh military priorities. But this situation could not last. The Canadian Army in England was under growing pressure to emulate the British Army's personnel selection program. Van Nostrand and Richardson could do little to prevent the reorganization of Canadian army psychiatry to make room for psychological medicine.

CHAPTER TWO

Square Pegs and Round Holes

The Impact of Personnel Selection

Churchill and MacKenzie King have struggled on for years;
What good, without psychologists, are blood and sweat and tears?
But now the Bott Battalion's on its way, so give three cheers,
The War will soon be won!

What a dirty trick on Hitler!
Why not play the game with Hitler?
Who will break the news to Hitler
That Bott and all his brainy boys are hurrying off to war?
Quoted in C.R. Myers, "Edward Alexander Bott"

At the outbreak of war the Canadian and British Armies had rejected intelligence testing and psychiatric screening of recruits, but by the beginning of 1941 both armies believed they were facing a severe shortage of manpower, particularly of skilled tradesmen. The British had begun using a verbal intelligence test for new recruits in July 1940 but its main purpose was to isolate dull and backward men for referral to a psychiatrist. During 1941 a series of experimental studies led to the establishment of a British army directorate for the selection of personnel. By mid 1942 an army-wide program of intelligence and aptitude testing was underway.[1]

The British Army's personnel selection branch was created to implement the theories of those psychologists who believed that the occurrence of shell shock in World War I was dependent on "previous psychoneurotic history and inherited predisposition, on inadequate examination and selection of soldiers fitted for the front line."[2] The psychologists not only claimed to understand the origins of the problem, they also were confident that the various intelligence and personality tests devised since the last war could select those who were fit for combat.[3]

The Canadian Army at home had started intelligence testing in 1940 but the experiments were not followed up until early 1941 when personnel of the Canadian Armoured Corps training at Camp Borden were examined. (Those with lower intelligence scores were posted to the infantry.) The Minister of National Defence, J.L. Ralston, began to take an interest in the issue and in April 1941 the National Research Council gave the CPA a grant of $2,000 "to further its studies of intelligence and aptitude measurement."[4] E.A. Bott, professor of psychology at the University of Toronto, was sent to England to consult with the armed forces overseas and to find out what the British were doing. He was given the rank of group captain in the RCAF and most of his subsequent work was with the airforce.

Bott was a major figure in the Canadian university community. He was chairman of the psychology department at the University of Toronto and president of the new (1938) CPA.[5] When war broke out Bott, along with other psychologists, had volunteered his services to the country. Although it received little encouragement the CPA developed a standard test, the M test, intended to determine "learning ability."[6]

This test drew heavily on the United States Army's Alpha and Beta tests, which had been developed during World War I. The original tests had created a ferocious controversy in the United States when the *Army Report* on the wartime testing program was published. The editor, Robert M. Yerkes, claimed that the tests, which had been administered to 1.7 million American soldiers, successfully measured "inborn intelligence." This "native intellectual capacity" could, he argued, be expressed by assigning a mental age to each soldier. The testers had determined that the average white draftee had a mental age of 13 and from this they inferred that anyone with a mental age of between 7 and 12 years was a "moron" with very limited potential. This produced the information that 30.3 per cent of all whites and 79 per cent of all blacks were "morons."[7]

The methodology, assumptions, and values of the testers were sharply attacked by many commentators including Walter Lippman, who ridiculed the entire concept of mental age.[8] Psychologists did not remain on the defensive for long – too much depended on public acceptance of the validity of their tests. By 1938 they had developed a variety of more sophisticated IQ tests. Few psychometricians still claimed that 30 to 40 per cent of the population was ineducable,[9] but psychologists as a group continued to believe that a very large percentage of the population had limited abilities. Bott and his colleagues in Canada shared these assumptions.[10] When this bias was combined with the commonplace view that modern war would be fought with complex machines requiring users with above average intelligence the stage was set for large-scale rejections of suspect volunteers and draftees.

While in England Bott had a chance to administer the M test* to a number of groups and to consult with British and Canadian psychiatrists. British psychiatrists, or at least those in charge of army psychiatry in Britain, were very supportive of Bott's ideas. The Canadians were much less enthusiastic. Colin Russel was flatly opposed. He argued that well-trained medical officers, NCOs and officers could select men as "precisely" as psychological tests could. Moreover, he warned, "psychological group tests cannot be expected to pick out the recovered psychotic, the psychopath, the temperamentally unstable or the man who is going to lose his will to carry on."[11]

Brigadier J.A. Linton, the Director of Medical Services (DMS) for the newly established I Canadian Corps, strongly supported testing although he had no clear idea of what the available tests measured. He had chaired the committee examining the question in Canada and had become convinced that in a large organization like the army "we are bound to have square pegs and round holes. If we can prevent them from coming together ... we should save an enormous amount of time and effort." In addition, the number of functional diseases could be decreased, he believed, "if any simple procedure [for early diagnosis] can be adopted." The problem, according to Linton, was "how mental inertia can be overcome in those who for various reasons cannot or will not correlate military problems with the present century."[12]

Russel was not present at the meeting of June 1941, which decided to establish a personnel selection branch for the Canadian Army overseas, so there was little debate. The new branch was to report to the adjutant-general not to the DMS, but "medical officers with special neuropsychiatric training" were to be attached. The meeting also recognized that the RCAMC had very little confidence in psychological testing. It was agreed that intelligence tests might be of use in the initial selection of recruits and officer candidates, or in choosing personnel for technical employment, but only if used in conjunction with existing methods. Intelligence tests, the psychiatrists still insisted, were "of no use in the detection of mental disease."[13]

Neuropsychiatrists were not the only ones to express their reservations about the advent of personnel selection. The staff officers at Canadian Military Headquarters (CMHQ) were concerned that intelligence tests would be used to eliminate "mental defectives who are well-behaved and amenable to discipline." Both the British and Canadian Armies had long experience in utilizing men

---

* The M test, which could be administered to large groups, was made up of eight short sub-tests. The first three were non-language picture tests designed to be understood by illiterates, 4 and 5 dealt with knowledge of tools and basic mechanical aptitudes, 6, 7, and 8 were conventional arithmetic, vocabulary, and relationship tests.

· of below average intelligence and there was a strong belief that such men could "make useful soldiers providing their limitations are appreciated."[14] Those who could not find any niche in existing military units were surely so limited as to require discharge.

Brigadier Linton did not accept this view. In the fall of 1941 he began a campaign to establish "labour battalions." He argued that there were people in every unit "unfitted for the duties a soldier must perform in the modern army." Commanding officers were too often guilty of placing such people in jobs where their deficiencies were not readily apparent. This, according to Linton, was dangerous because they would break down under the pressure of battle. To illustrate his argument Linton described four privates finally brought forward for medical reclassification: "One man is a driver and is defeated by every roundabout. Under ordinary conditions he is a fairly good driver but he usually leaves the roundabout on the same road by which he entered ... [The others] have been tried in every position in the unit, even as batmen. In their desire to do a good job they polish the inside of Sam Browne belts with disastrous effect on clothing."[15]

The British Army had created an Auxiliary Military Pioneer Corps to employ "dull and backward" soldiers as unskilled labourers. During the retreat to Dunkirk several companies in the Corps had been given arms and had fought with determination.[16] After Dunkirk all companies in the renamed Pioneer Corps were either armed or at least trained to use arms, until it was decided that many men could not absorb the training. Unarmed labour battalions were reconstituted within the Pioneer Corps. Such units were at first differentiated from the armed companies by the designation "Q." When Jack Rees, the consulting psychiatrist, pointed out the obvious connotation of Q, the terminology was changed to "unarmed" for the remainder of the war.[17]

Linton was determined to develop a similar system in the Canadian Army. His efforts to promote psychological testing and labour battalions were strongly supported by General McNaughton and even by National Defence Headquarters in Ottawa. There had been a palace revolution in Ottawa – the new chief of staff, Harry Crerar, and his vice-chief, Kenneth Stuart, had informed the adjutant-general that a special directorate of personnel selection was to be established under Colonel G.B. Chisholm, who would be assisted by a civilian advisory commission.[18] The new directorate was to develop a systematic program of personnel selection, ultimately classifying all men in the army, and seeking to identify potential officers, men of high intelligence, men suitable for trade training, men showing neurotic reactions, and men of low intelligence.[19] This program was much more ambitious than the one developed for Canadian troops in Britain, its comprehensive aims clearly reflecting the attitudes and ambitions of Canadian psychologists.

The new director, Brock Chisholm, was to become one of the leading public figures in Canada after the war. Now best remembered for his attack on the myth of Santa Claus as damaging to children, his service as Deputy Minister of Health and President of the World Health Organization is largely forgotten. Chisholm was a remarkable man by any standard. He had fought as an infantry-man in World War I, winning a Military Cross. After earning his MD at the University of Toronto, he studied at the Tavistock and other hospitals in London. He later lectured at the Yale Institute of Human Relations before returning to England for further experience in psychiatry. In 1934 he set up practice in Toronto as a psychiatrist, becoming the first such private practitioner in Canada.[20]

Chisholm had never lost his interest in the military and by the outbreak of the war was a militia brigadier. Placed on active service with the rank of colonel, he commanded part of a military district in Northern Ontario for two years. During this period Chisholm produced a widely distributed pamphlet, *A Platoon Leader's Responsibility for the Morale of His Men*, which contained in six pages nearly all there is to say about management of men in the army. The pamphlet explained the role of good morale in preventing anxiety states and insisted that such morale could only be produced by build-ing a group, "a mutually protective entity which is more than the sum of its units."[21]

A man of enormous energy and charm, Chisholm had a wide circle of friends and admirers. One friend, Harry Letson, was Deputy Adjutant-General, and it was he who had persuaded Ken Stuart (then Deputy Chief of Staff) to bring Chisholm to Ottawa to advise on training. Letson and Stuart were rising powers at NDHQ, soon to become heads of the two key branches of army administra-tion.[22] On 4 August 1941 Stuart called a meeting to set forth the need for an organization to "classify officer and other rank personnel."[23] Both Chisholm and Bott were present to explain the details of an organization that would soon become the largest psychological testing enterprise in the country's history.

While Chisholm was getting things organized in Canada, Major J.W. Howard,[24] a professional psychologist, was sent to England to begin "sifting" the Canadians overseas. In December 1941 seventy-five officers were recruited from various units in Britain and, after a one-week course, they were offi-cially designated Selection of Personnel Officers (SPOs) and sent off to test and interview the army.[25] One week's training was deemed sufficient to equip an officer to administer the M test and to conduct a brief interview. It was the neuropsychiatric division of the RCAMC that was to provide qualified psychiatrists to examine the misfits and doubtfuls uncovered by the tests or by the psychological interview.[26]

Russel, in his last months as Consulting Neuropsychiatrist, was still fighting a rearguard action against the whole scheme. Early results indicated that as many as 6,000 soldiers would be referred for psychiatric examination. Russel noted that this "seems a great number." He thought the psychologists should stick to identifying and reassigning people who were being misused by the army, "for example, good mechanics working as kitchen help." The mentally backward could be sent to a labour battalion by the RMO if there was no place for "hewers of wood and drawers of water" in the battalion. "As for the prepsychotics," Russel wrote, "I do not believe special treatment beyond the understanding care of the RMO is indicated. If they get beyond his ability they should be sent to the Neurological Hospital." Russel was equally certain that the "prophylaxis of the anxiety neurosis also rests with the Regimental Medical Officer"[27] and that nothing would be gained and much lost by attempting to identify potential neurotics.

CMHQ was too strongly committed to psychological testing to accept this advice and in the summer of 1942, the new Consulting Neuropsychiatrist, Colonel F.H. Van Nostrand, was informed that additional staff would be made available and that full cooperation with the personnel selection branch was essential. Van Nostrand, who shared Russel's disdain for the psychologists, nevertheless asked for a rapid increase in the number of neuropsychiatrists. "It is estimated," he wrote, "that one per division will be required plus at least two for Canadian Reinforcement Units ... and one for each large body of troops which is geographically isolated."[28]

Van Nostrand did not want these positions filled by a group of civilians sent over from Canada. There were, he believed, enough neuropsychiatrists in the Canadian Army overseas who could be assigned to this duty. Additional psychiatrists, he wrote, "preferably but not necessarily neuropsychiatrists," should be requested from Canada and a minimum of two should be French Canadians. These would have to undergo "a period of training in army neurology at No. 1 Canadian Neurological Hospital"[29] before being sent to army units. Van Nostrand appointed neuropsychiatrists to each of the Canadian military regions in the United Kingdom, assigning them to CCSs or army general hospitals.[30] To prevent them from being absorbed into the hospital routine they were attached to, not on the strength of, the medical units. The regional neuropsychiatrists were to screen referrals and send only the more serious cases to No. 1 Neurological.

The DMS now hoped he had a system in place for the "diagnosis and disposal" of the army's personnel problems. In March 1942 No. 1 Canadian General Pioneer Company was created "to employ illiterates and men with low mental standard who were unable to absorb training."[31] This meant that "mental deficiency" could be swiftly dealt with by the personnel selection branch and neuropsychiatrists could concentrate on functional nervous disorders, which in 1942 were rising to a much higher level "than during the worst of the blitz period."[32] During the first eighteen months of its operation, September 1940 to April 1942, Basingstoke had admitted 1,171 psychiatric cases. Although Basingstoke was now receiving only the most serious cases, the next eighteen months saw a further 2,427 admissions.[33]

Some increase in functional nervous diseases because of "the prolonged sojourn of the Canadian Army in Britain" and the cumulative stress of "boredom, separation from families, inactivity and indefinite waiting"[34] was to be expected but the numbers seemed unaccountably high. The disastrous Dieppe raid of August 1942, another possible factor, made only a small contribution to the increase. Of the slightly more than 2,000 Canadians who returned to England (out of 5,577 who embarked for Dieppe) 586 were wounded and a large number were "exhaustion" cases, who were treated with rest and sedation. By mid-September just eight men from among the survivors had been admitted to Basingstoke.[35] The remainder had returned to full duty.

Since neither combat nor boredom is a sufficient explanation, it seems likely that the rise of psychiatric casualties in the Canadian Army may have been a by-product of the introduction of psychological testing. Van Nostrand had warned the DMS that "it is unwise to suggest to a borderline individual, who has not yet become a problem, that he is mentally different from his fellows, and, as such, requires special consideration."[36] The DMS was not influenced by this advice and instead urged "close cooperation of unit commanders, RMOs, neuropsychiatrists and the Personnel Selection Board.[37] Personnel selection officers were to conduct a psychological examination, including a psychiatric history covering family, school, and employment records, as well as a personal history covering religious problems, sexual adjustment, police record, and alcohol or drug addiction. "Psychopathic trends," the instructions stated, "are frequently indicated by difficulties or unusual attitudes towards religion or sex; or by chronic trouble with the law." The instructions did caution that "great care should be exercised ... to avoid suggesting symptoms or disabilities,"[38] but Van Nostrand had little confidence that this would happen.

THE EFFECTS OF PERSONNEL SELECTION on the army overseas were a pale reflection of what was developing in Canada. The instructions circulated in Britain were essentially a copy of those in May 1942 to medical officers examining volunteers and conscripts at home, except that there was no warning about the dangers of suggestibility.[39] In Canada, staff officers of the personnel selection directorate – young men given commissions on the basis of university degrees or some university attendance – were testing, interviewing, and diagnosing other young men with the kind of assurance that only profound ignorance can provide.

The personnel selection directorate was authorized in August of 1941 but Professor Bott and the CPA had been preparing for the great day for almost two years. Bott had lined up a group of CPA members to fill the officer psychologist positions. These men, to be called army examiners, were to undertake the training of the assistant army examiners, who would actually give the tests and the initial interviews.[40] Bott also brought to Ottawa one of his brightest young colleagues at the University of Toronto, Bill Line, who was to become Chisholm's deputy and eventual successor.[41] Line was joined in Ottawa by his close friend and collaborator, Jack Griffin, MD, who took on the job of psychiatrist at the directorate, a task involving liaison with the RCAMC.

Line and Griffin had worked together at the Toronto headquarters of the National Committee for Mental Hygiene (Canada). They both championed preventive mental hygiene and were strongly committed to the virtues of psychological testing.[42] Intelligent and well-informed, they knew that whatever claim to legitimacy such testing could make depended on the validity of the test, the skill of the examiner, and the cooperation of the person being examined. Line, in particular, must have known that the hastily created personnel selection system could not meet even minimal standards for such evaluations.

In January of 1942 when Line had the opportunity to review the results of the first month's work with soldiers already in the army, the extent of the problem could not be ignored. Line prepared a memorandum, classified secret, informing assistant army examiners to stop using "diagnostic terms (or phrases that smack of diagnosis)."[43] Medical officers and not the examiners were, he wrote, the proper authorities to use terms such as "psychopathic inferior, feeble minded mental defective, moron, imbecile, neurotic, hysterical, sexual pervert, psychotic, insane." The use of these words in a "casual way" was unacceptable. Equally unfortunate was the constant use of slang expressions in documents that a serving soldier had the right to see. Popular phrases like "ignorant hobo," "needs a good thrashing," "should be put through the mill," were, Line wrote, "expressive of the feelings of the examiner" but of no other value. "Even when the soldier's limitations are such that he is not likely to respond to training," he warned, "it is still desirable to state his case without diagnostic reference or recommendations for discharge."[44]

Line could complain about the excesses of the new "psychologists" but the system was in place and in the next three years examiners referred thousands of men for psychiatric assessment. The shortage of psychiatrists frequently meant long delays between referral and diagnosis, placing the soldier in a position where his symptoms were unlikely to diminish. One of Griffin's first tasks as the personnel selection psychiatrist was to visit training centres to determine the reasons for the large numbers waiting to see the psychiatrists.[45] In one military district 182 men had been discharged for psychiatric problems in the first four months of 1942 and a further 81 men had been downgraded to limited service in Category c. In 1941 only 16 per cent of discharges had been for wholly medical reasons, whereas the rate in 1942 was 36.9 per cent for psychoneurotic causes alone. The DMO was described by Griffin as "fairly cooperative" but "a bit worried over the extent of neuropsychiatric problems in his district."[46] Griffin was unable to suggest any solution to the problem other than the appointment of more psychiatrists to provide expert opinion and to limit the waiting period.

The expansion of the army's psychiatric branch was accomplished in the face of obstacles that might have overwhelmed a less energetic man than Jack Griffin. When he arrived in Ottawa in the fall of 1941 Griffin was met with open hostility by senior RCAMC officers. Brigadier Gorssline, DGMS, had rejected Griffin's offer of assistance in developing mental hygiene services in 1939 and he had not changed his mind in the interval. "He said to me," Griffin recalled, " 'Well, you got in eh? ... remember under no circumstances will you treat anybody in the army for a psychiatric condition'."[47]

Medical Corps opposition to personnel selection and psychiatry persisted until Chisholm became the army's senior medical officer in September 1942. In the meantime Griffin managed to have a number of psychiatrists who were already in the army transferred to training and recruiting centres. There were only a few academically qualified neuropsychiatrists around and Griffin relied on a number of younger mental hospital psychiatrists whom he had come to know through his work with the National Committee for Mental Hygiene.

During the 1930s some remarkably able doctors who could not afford post-graduate study or even the costs of setting up a medical practice applied to provincial ministries of health for employment in the mental asylum services. Positions were available, particularly in Ontario, where the provincial government had provided funds both to improve medical treatment and to establish community mental health clinics.[48] These clinics gave mental hospital psychiatrists the opportunity to work with adult neuroses patients, a type not normally seen in the mental hospitals.

The supply of neuropsychiatrists and mental hospital psychiatrists was quickly exhausted in 1942 and a large number of vacancies remained. Griffin moved to establish training courses for psychiatrists at McGill and the University of Toronto. The seven-month program was open to RMOs who had served at least six months in the army. Each month three such doctors, selected with "considerable care," started the course at each university's psychiatric teaching hospital, "acquiring the fundamentals of formal psychiatry." Two further months were "spent in the medical wards of a general hospital under the direction of a capable teacher of psychosomatic medicine and neurology." A month in a veteran's hospital and two months on the job in a military establishment completed the training.[49] These fledgling psychiatrists were to provide the manpower for the full development of an army psychiatric program between 1943 and the end of the war.

It is not clear whether Griffin thought that the presence of psychiatrists on medical boards would reduce the number of rejections and discharges, or simply improve the accuracy of such screening. The consequences appear to have been an increase in the number of psychiatric discharges and in the percentage of recruits, volunteer and conscript, rejected for psychiatric reasons.[50] Retrospectively, Griffin and other psychiatrists involved in screening developed doubts about their work, but during the war, even while complaining that the few minutes available for an interview were inadequate, psychiatrists relieved the army of thousands of "neurotic" recruits.

In 1945 Griffin published a follow-up study based on a sample of the 22,000

men who had been released from the army as psychoneurotics.[51] Griffin and
three junior psychiatrists identified 1,650 of those who had been discharged
from military districts in central Canada between January and October 1943.
Information was eventually obtained on 560 of the group through interviews
with the individual, and/or his wife, his mother, and his friends. In all but
about 20 per cent of the cases, two or more sources were used. The mother
was the most common single source, the wife and the ex-soldier himself
the next.

The researchers asked their informants about the individual's present health
as compared to his condition while in the army. Forty-five per cent of the
men were *perceived* to be in worse health – there was no medical exam –
52 per cent in the same health and just 3 per cent were considered to be better.
This extraordinary persistence of ill health was difficult to reconcile with the
employment record of the men, since 43 per cent had obtained a better job
after discharge than they had held before enlistment. Just 18 per cent reported
worse employment conditions. The investigators attributed the improvement
in job status to economic conditions and rationalized other problems in their
methodology and results. They concluded that one of the most disturbing
aspects of their study was the finding that two-thirds of those questioned
"believed themselves to be suffering entirely from some physical disability
and showed no insight into the relevance of nervous and emotional factors."
The psychiatrists urged that greater attention be paid to giving these men
"more insight into their condition."[52]

Canadian rates of discharge for psychiatric reasons were not unusual. In
the United States separations from the army for neuropsychiatric disorders
accounted for half of the 1.1 million men discharged during the war, and the
American rates increased dramatically in 1943 when the United States Army
embraced psychiatric consultation. During 1944, when the extraordinary manpower losses to the United States Army had forced changes, the rates declined
with equal rapidity.[53] In Canada, however, "nervous and mental discharges"
continued to increase in absolute numbers and as a proportion of all
discharges.[54]

The problem of wastage through psychiatric discharge was only one aspect
of the enormous impact of personnel selection on the manpower resources
of the Canadian military. The application of such procedures to the examination
of volunteers and conscripts at the recruiting depots was of much greater consequence. The laissez-faire policies of 1939-40 may have allowed large numbers
of unfit men to enter the army but the advent of the assistant army examiner
and the psychiatrist certainly kept very large numbers of perfectly fit men
out of the army.

Detailed statistics are available on the disposition of men called up under
the National Resources Mobilization Act of 1940, legislation that permitted
the government to conscript men for service within Canada only. Of the
1.8 million men called up 53 per cent were found to be fit for service anywhere,

13 per cent were placed in category B for restricted employment and 34 per cent (607,782 men) were found medically unfit.[55] Between 25 and 45 per cent of the medically unfit were rejected for psychiatric causes. Few statistics were kept on the number of volunteers rejected, whatever the reason, but it seems that there were proportionately fewer psychiatric rejections among volunteers.[56]

In early 1943 the chief of staff and many other senior officers became aware of the rising tide of rejections and their complaints forced Chisholm to modify the guidelines for medical boards. Circular Letter no. 210 introduced a new category to be used by army examiners and psychiatrists called "accept for recheck."[57] The idea was that doubtful cases were to be enlisted and then reexamined before the completion of basic training. There was some difficulty in getting the personnel selection staff to implement the program and in October 1943 Chisholm noted that while no reports were yet available from four military districts, some data were available from the other six. During the month of June 1943 10,100 recruits had been examined in these districts and 6 per cent had been accepted for recheck. Subsequent examination "reveals that 70 to 80 per cent of these men are adjusting satisfactorily and are absorbing full military training without difficulty." Chisholm suggested that the new policy "seems to be working out well" and he set out procedures that he stated would "insure the maximum number of recruits being accepted and ... also ensure a continuous check on psychiatric standards of acceptance in the various reception centres."[58]

This modification of the psychiatric screen enabled the army to recruit thousands of young men but it seems to have raised few questions in the minds of the psychologists and psychiatrists in personnel selection. One small program to provide special training for "unsuitable" recruits was started in March 1944 when the psychiatric rejection rate had risen to 37 per cent. A training base at North Bay, Ontario was selected for the experiment and Dr G. Scott, an experienced psychiatrist, was placed in charge.[59]

The 111 men in the first group were carefully studied and their subsequent military careers surveyed. Scott's most disturbing finding was that most of the 35 men labelled s4 (rejection for instability) had been incorrectly graded. The assistant army examiners had rejected men who were simply "immature, poorly motivated youths with profuse, inconsequential complaints or mature men who wished to avoid service." They were regraded s1 and sent on to advanced training. Most of the remainder, those accepted for recheck, were retained in the army. Scott concluded that the stability ratings "assigned on induction were too severe." He also reported that the North Bay conditioning program was "effective in salvaging and stabilizing mild psychiatric disabilities for further duty."[60] The results of the North Bay experiment challenged many of the assumptions of personnel selection but by late 1944 when Scott's report was available little could be done.

The neuropsychiatric branch of the Canadian Army overseas was directed by men who did not share this enthusiasm for personnel selection. In the spring of 1943 Van Nostrand prepared a lengthy report on "Neuropsychiatry in the Canadian Army (Overseas)," which was published in the *Canadian Medical Association Journal*. The tone of the article was restrained but Van Nostrand insisted that he was "not convinced that the incidence of functional nervous disease in the Canadian Army (Overseas) will be materially reduced by all the special measures which have been introduced." He went on to note that "the selective tests now in use do not accurately predict which soldiers will break down under the stress of service."[61]

Van Nostrand continued to believe that a regimental officer or competent NCO could identify disabling neuroses. Most of those suffering from psychoses would also be diagnosed quickly and routinely by medical officers; and the psychopathic personalities could be identified by their crime sheets. He believed that all of these should be discharged from the army. Richardson was somewhat less certain (or less experienced) than Van Nostrand but there was no fundamental difference of opinion between them.

The views of Van Nostrand and Richardson were to some extent academic. Canadian Military Headquarters in London was determined to place personnel selection on a scientific basis. A proper place must be found for everyone in the army overseas; if square holes did not exist, they would have to be created. The problem was that personnel selection was classifying growing numbers of men for whom special places would have to be found. The creation of No. 1 Pioneer Company in March 1942 had initially provided jobs for 100 men. By the fall, it held 320 men, 78 per cent of them having a diagnosis of "mental deficiency without psychosis."[62] A second pioneer company was created in June. These companies were used for heavy labour such as loading and unloading coal, road building, and evacuation. Morale was said to be high and their work was greatly valued.[63]

In November 1942 staff officers in London proposed the creation of a pioneer corps modelled on what they understood to be the British example. This new corps was to be composed of "the estimated 5,000 illiterates who were serving in the Canadian army overseas."[64] General Andrew McNaughton, the senior Canadian officer overseas, vetoed the proposal, not because he rejected the assumption that illiteracy was a product of mental deficiency, but because he believed that the army's illiterates had too low a mental capacity for inclusion in a British-style armed pioneer corps.[65] McNaughton was one of Canada's most distinguished scientists, the former head of the National Research Council. If he could accept the personnel selection argument that an illiterate was incapable of absorbing complex military training, then it was not surprising that other senior officers accepted this view as scientifically based.

The idea of a broadly based pioneer corps was abandoned but the army continued to create ad hoc pioneer companies for heavy labour. Three were established in November 1942 and by March 1943 the personnel selection system had identified enough additional illiterates and mental defectives to staff at least five more companies. No. 6 company was authorized in April 1943, but a shortage of suitable NCOs and officers delayed the creation of further units. By fall 1943, with Canadians in action in Italy and preparation for North-West Europe absorbing the staff in England, no one was prepared to authorize the formation of additional pioneer companies. Soldiers waiting for such assignment in reinforcement and holding units were reabsorbed into the army mainstream.

The pioneer companies performed useful tasks and relieved other army units of much routine work, but they also absorbed significant numbers of men who would have performed satisfactorily in regimental postings. Studies of the combat performance of men judged to be mentally deficient by United States Army psychiatrists indicate that limited intellectual ability is not necessarily an indicator of unsatisfactory military performance.[66]

Canadian pioneer companies were not limited to those who performed poorly on intelligence tests. An attempt was made to make use of men diagnosed as "potential habitual offenders" to create a special training company. This effort was a complete failure,[67] but Dr G.S. Burton, the neuropsychiatrist attached to No. 1 Pioneer Company, reported that the small group of psycho-neurotics in his unit were doing satisfactory work and it was decided to use a new pioneer company to try to "salvage" such men. There had been a good deal of criticism that the soldiers' neurotic symptoms "seemed to vanish as soon as they reached their objective (Canada)," and this might be a solution.[68] Van Nostrand had little confidence in salvaging anyone but he hoped that the experiment would reduce the incidence of neurotic reactions by eliminating the prospect of a return to Canada from the army's folklore about psychiatry.[69]

There was no shortage of candidates for No. 4 Company and by June 1943 155 men with average or better M test scores were working on a variety of landscaping and redecorating projects. It proved to be impossible to judge the value of the experiment. Most men adjusted well to the new environment, but very few improved sufficiently to return to their original units.[70] In spring 1944 nine new units, designated Special Employment Companies (SECs), were created to handle psychiatric casualties in operational theatres. By then such men were not expected to rejoin their original units and the new companies were simply labour companies made up of men with low stability ratings. It seems unlikely that placing men diagnosed as neurotic in labour companies instead of returning them to Canada or England discouraged breakdowns in the rest of the army. Many Canadian officers believed that "symptoms calling for recategorizing on the basis of stability" were part of the folklore of the army and were widely discussed in the reinforcement units.[71]

During 1943 personnel selection officers concentrated their efforts on a program to re-examine and reclassify the entire Canadian Army overseas, according to the criteria of the new PULHEMS* system. This ambitious scheme foundered when the 1st Division left for the Mediterranean and other combatant units were caught up in the intensified training for Overlord. A second scheme was proposed to develop job descriptions for each position in the army and then reassign those who had too much or too little intelligence for the particular job. The British Army had just completed a similar program and was in the midst of transferring surplus "high grade" personnel to units that were short of such types.

General McNaughton fully supported this proposal in a letter written to commanders of all formations and units in England: "I fully appreciate that this policy will to a degree cut across the lines of individual preference and will affect to some extent the control that an officer ... has over personnel of his Corps or unit. It is inevitable that it will result in the removal of men whose loss will be felt. Notwithstanding these disadvantages, however, I am convinced that the action is necessary for the well-being of the Army as a whole, and I therefore asked all Commanders loyally to accept my decision."[72]

The commanders of the 2nd, 3rd, and 4th Divisions objected strenuously. The Canadian Army was modelled on the British system of distinct regiments, raised in specific areas of the country. While functionally much the same, each Canadian infantry or tank battalion was the active component of a regiment with a treasured historical tradition and battle honours dating back to at least World War I. Each regiment treasured its distinctive dress and customs and its regimental lore. The army sports program, a vital part of training, began with competition among the companies or squadrons, but the best men competed for the regiment and became local heroes. Group identity and loyalty were based on these traditions.[73]

McNaughton's readiness to disturb the hard-won cohesion of combat units for "the well-being of the army as a whole" alarmed Lieutenant-General Harry Crerar, the Corps Commander. Crerar, who would succeed McNaughton as army commander in 1944, had surveyed his units to assess the effects of the scheme. He told McNaughton that reallocation was threatening the territorial identification of some units. CMHQ was, Crerar wrote, "making the fundamental error of judging efficiency ... required towards winning the war

---

* PULHEMS: P for physique; U for upper and L for lower and locomotion; H for hearing and ears; E for eyes; M for mental capacity; S for stability. Grade 1 represents fitness for service anywhere; 2 fitness for anywhere but front line combat; 3 fitness for line of communication duties; 4 fitness for Canadian service only; 5 unfit. It is important, if tautological, to point out that those battle exhaustion cases which had been graded were rated 1.

by the technical efficiency of an administrative system ... this is a fundamental error because, whether we like it or not the average man is not a 'scientific animal' and he reacts more importantly to emotion than to logic. An administrative system which fails to take this situation into full account will not produce successful military results.

"The same observation applies to a unit. If the officers and men which it comprises are imbued with mutual regard and confidence, and a desire to maintain ... the reputation of the regiment ... then that unit will most certainly do what is required towards winning the war, whether or not it produces desired answers to certain administrative questions."[74]

Despite Crerar's protest the personnel selection branch continued to classify and reallocate throughout the war. The unpublished history of the branch notes that the SPO was seen as a dangerous intruder by most units. The author writes:

The experience of one SPO is typical; he reports that the CO of the Holding Unit to which he was first posted was "definitely antagonistic" and men were made available for interview only when and if training was not obstructed. This CO was a veteran of the last war. The CO of the next Holding Unit in which this SPO worked was a younger man, was much more cooperative and indicated his "willingness to see a demonstration" of what this new personnel selection procedure could do. In understanding the coolness of the reception which SPOs were given it is more important to realise that COs had some justification in believing that they were agents of a superior body, CMHQ, that was trying to spy out and remove some of their best men. Added to this was a general attitude of scepticism towards the whole conception of psychological testing. It was not easy for the SPOs to overcome this opposition because they were themselves mostly inexperienced in the whole philosophy and untutored in the validity of testing and interviewing ... There is no need to disguise the fact that the method which had been chosen for applying selection procedures to the overseas Army was NOT one designed to create the mutual confidence of SPOs and unit COs.[75]

Regimental officers were not the only ones who challenged the selection and reallocation system. Burdett McNeel, then the psychiatrist attached to the Canadian detention barracks, was struck by the high percentage of the 1,600 detainees who were from holding units where the reallocated were sent while awaiting new postings. He wrote:

Whatever the practical advantages may be of having an army flexible to the degree that any man may be transferred anywhere at any time there is a decided disadvantage in its effect on morale as a great many of these men, particularly those of low intelligence level, become strongly attached to, and well incorporated in a unit only to be transferred to a strange unit where they have neither interest or security. It still appears true that no high degree of stability can be achieved in a unit without it being more or less a family group or a group of families. It is our opinion, that transfers, reinforcements, etc., would be better in units about section strength with their own NCOs, if not officers, attached. It is bad enough for a simple man to have to face the unknown fortunes of war without having to face the unknown in the organization which is supposed to give him support. It may also be stated that many a simple man has become confused by ruthless transplantation on the basis of a set of figures on his documents who could have given good service in a unit where his capacities were known and utilized.[76]

On the eve of the invasion of Sicily Canadian army psychiatry was in a state of transition – the neuropsychiatric branch of the RCAMC had been a reluctant and cautious participant in the various attempts to classify and reclassify Canadian soldiers, but like all organizations, it had embraced the opportunity to increase its own ranks. By the spring of 1943 there were more than a dozen psychiatrists at work in England. Inevitably they began to function more as a part of personnel selection than as a separate medical specialty.

One of the many consequences of the focus on testing and reclassifying was the development of a new diagnostic category for soldiers who presented behaviour problems, but could not be labelled as suffering from a psycho-neurosis. The term used, "psychopathic personality, inadequate," was most unfortunate and afterwards army psychiatrists were deeply embarrassed by it.[77] They had sought to find a term to describe the soldier who had failed to become an efficient and useful member of his unit. Inadequate, they insisted, meant inadequate for the army. Psychopathic personality simply indicated that the behaviour that was seen to cause the problem arose from the basic personality of the individual, not from a neurosis.

The invention of this category meant that large numbers of soldiers who may have simply required a new posting or a more sympathetic officer, who had read Chisholm's advice on man-management, were given a pseudo-scientific psychiatric label. This procedure was carried over into preparations for battle-field psychiatry, where terms like "grossly inadequate personality" were used to describe men who became unfit for fighting service without suffering from any significant acute neurosis. The categories "inadequate with added battle neurosis" and "adequate with battle neurosis" were also used.[78]

These three terms were thought to cover all types of breakdowns the psychiatrist or RMO would be likely to see in combat. There was no agreement about what proportion of psychiatric casualties would occur in each category, and no consensus about symptoms. The specific diagnostic decision, with its important implications for treatment, prognosis for return to duty, and future pension rights, was left up to the individual psychiatrist.

The Canadians also decided to accept the new British terminology for forward diagnosis of psychiatric casualties.[79] Originally the term Not Yet Diagnosed

(Nervous), had been used, but in late 1942 Brigadier G.W.B. James, the psychiatric specialist in the Mediterranean Theatre, began to insist on "Physical Exhaustion" or simply "Exhaustion." James hoped that this term would better express what he believed was the temporary nature of the soldier's breakdown.[80] The Canadians and British gradually developed the term "Battle Exhaustion." The Americans, also influenced by James, used "Combat Exhaustion."

CHAPTER THREE

Into Battle

Psychiatry in the Mediterranean
Theatre: North Africa, Sicily, Ortona

The smallest detail taken from an actual incident in war is more instructive to me, a soldier, than all the Thiers and Jominis in the world. They speak for the heads of states and armies, but they never show me what I wish to know – a battalion, company or platoon in action. The man is the first weapon of battle. Let us study the soldier for it is he who brings reality to it.

Ardant Du Picq

The expansion of Canadian army neuropsychiatry in response to the demands of personnel selection had drawn attention away from the original purpose of the branch – the treatment of stress-related neuroses. Since no Canadian army units were in continuous combat before July 1943, the priority attached to personnel selection seemed logical. The whole Canadian Army appeared to have settled in for a protracted stay in England and most psychiatrists came to share the general preoccupation with classification.

At Basingstoke Neurological and Plastic Surgery Hospital (plastic surgery was added in early 1943) Richardson was unhappy with the changed priorities, arguing that the chronic shortage of medical officers at the hospital severely handicapped the treatment program. "Psychiatric casualties," he wrote, "require special facilities ... psychotherapy, physical methods ... and rehabilitation must be carried out concurrently." Successful treatment meant changing the attitude of neurotic patients. It was necessary to "instill confidence and stimulate morale by every possible means." This could only be done if there were enough medical and general duty personnel to establish a routine in which "an atmosphere of recovery and enthusiasm predominated."[1]

Richardson's complaints were not really addressed until June 1943 when Dr Allan Walters arrived at Basingstoke. Walters was a colleague from Toronto General Hospital and a man of enormous energy. Like Richardson he was thoroughly trained in neurology, but he was also a psychiatrist experienced in various treatment procedures, from Freudian-influenced psychotherapy to the most advanced physical techniques, including Sargant's insulin sub-coma method. Walters took over the direction of the neurosis wards at Basingstoke and introduced his methods to younger psychiatrists doing their tour at the hospital.[2]

Richardson and Van Nostrand were also anxious to train psychiatrists, regimental medical officers, and infantry commanders in the prevention and treatment of psychiatric casualties on the battlefield.[3] When the 1st Canadian Division was selected to participate in the invasion of Sicily, Van Nostrand was able to persuade McNaughton to authorize the immediate appointment of a divisional psychiatrist. He selected Dr Arthur Manning Doyle.

Doyle had arrived in England in August 1942 as one of the first mental hospital psychiatrists to join the neuropsychiatric branch. He had good academic credentials as a neurologist but, in the circumstances of the mid-1930s, had not obtained a hospital appointment.[4] Instead he had joined the Ontario Provincial Hospital (asylum) Service where he had been a pioneer in the development of community mental health clinics.[5] Doyle, unlike most of his counterparts, had dealt with hundreds of cases of neurosis in the clinics of the Ontario Service. A militia medical officer recruited into army psychiatry in Canada by Jack Griffin, Doyle had been senior psychiatrist in Military District 6 (the Maritime provinces) before his posting to the United Kingdom.

Doyle was able to gain practical field experience before joining the 1st Division. Exercise Spartan, the First Canadian Army's massive field exercise in March 1943, was especially useful. During this exercise he treated 121 patients. By his estimate 12 per cent of these were "basically psychiatric problems."[6] As a result of the experience Doyle developed his ideas on handling neuropsychiatric cases in a paper for Colonel Van Nostrand: "Plan for the Efficient Triage and Treatment of Acute Neuropsychiatric Casualties."[7]

Doyle's paper codified many aspects of the continuing debate between those involved in personnel selection and those concerned with providing care for acute cases of psychiatric dysfunction on the battlefield. He identified both stages of the overall problem: the preparatory training period and actual combat. In the first, he thought, there was a steady stream of training casualties:

almost all of whom are soldiers with long histories of mental instability or defect. Many of these should never have been enlisted. They are for the most part chronic constitutional cases whose ineptitude comes to light as the troops become better known to their Officers and NCOs, as the stiffened program of training reveals their weaknesses and the pleasing novelty of military life merges into grim reality of daily routine. These cases are the psychologically inferior, the defective, the unstable exactly as found in civilian life. Proper methods of selection would weed out the totally unfit at the enlistment level. The others require placement in special branches of the army where their impaired abilities may be useful rather than harmful. The main psychiatric job here is one of identification and reallocation of persons suffering from chronic or constitutional neuropsychiatric disorder.[8]

Doyle had already experienced this phase and it left impressions that he retained throughout the remainder of the war. They were reinforced when he joined the 1st Division in Scotland for amphibious landing training before the division embarked for the Mediterranean. His chief concern was to weed out the weak, as he wrote later: "During the waiting and equipping period in May and June 1943, in the concentration areas in Scotland, there was ample opportunity to visit at least all medical and infantry units, and to assist the Medical Officers in culling out obvious psychiatric misfits. The units most conscious of the need for good personnel management made considerable use of this opportunity, but others unfortunately neglected an opportunity or did not see the need to weed out their ranks. Incidentally the Psychiatrist can beware of those units who do not have work for him in quiet times. They may be extremely good units; more likely they are the lesser prepared who are unaware or neglectful of their personnel problems and will provide him with much trouble when the test of action comes."[9]

This culling of obvious misfits was not the same thing as a general screening. Doyle dealt with men referred to him by unit officers, providing an on-the-spot mechanism for downgrading and reallocation to other duties. Doyle's enthusiasm for weeding the ranks of those who presented behaviour problems was in no way unique. Both the British and the Canadian psychiatric services were close to a consensus on this point, including those like Van Nostrand who were leery of mass psychiatric screening.

Doyle's projections for the second or combat stage of the problem reflected William Sargant's influence: "Immediately troops go into action the psychiatric picture undergoes a drastic change. The casualties are then mainly acute clinical syndromes occurring in ostensibly stable individuals. Exhaustion states, stuporous states, manic states, acute terror reactions occur, and they occur in appreciable, sometimes large numbers as we know from the experience of the last war and from campaigns of the present conflict."[10]

He suggested a medical handling system based on two premises: that combat psychiatric illness was short-lived and that rapid forward treatment offered the best prognosis. It would be a grave error, Doyle concluded, to evacuate cases to general hospitals, delaying their return to their fighting units and wasting manpower, to say nothing of the incalculable effect on morale of both the casualties and other troops. Forward treatment facilities should be planned to provide rest, food, sedation, reassurance, and reasonable security for patients for up to seven days. The ccs was likely the best unit to handle cases, and the forward neuropsychiatrist and the commander of the station must work closely as a team. "It should be emphasized that the neuropsychiatrist cannot accomplish his task alone. His work is essentially Medical and he and the officer in charge of medicine at the ccs will have to be partners, a team assuming mutual responsibility for each other's duties where practicable so that a 24 hour service may be maintained. Unless this joint endeavor exists the objectives of this plan will never be attained."[11]

The only physical requirements would be a few extra tents, stretchers, and nursing orderlies for the ccs. The patients themselves would do most of the regular work as part of their occupational therapy. "This project," Doyle concluded, "is reminiscent of the corps or divisional rest stations well known in the last war and indeed should static conditions develop it is anticipated that divisional and corps Medical Units will again open their own rest stations while the ccs psychiatric centre will close and the psychiatrist assume the duties of consultant to the Medical Units in the area."[12]

Doyle's proposals were developed without direct reference to, or knowledge of, attitudes towards psychiatric casualties in the British Eighth Army, which the 1st Canadian Division was preparing to join. British forces in the Mediterranean had done very little to organize forward psychiatry. The Eighth Army medical plan for the invasion of Sicily called for the evacuation of psychiatric casualties to Malta or North Africa and made no provisions for forward treatment behind the regimental aid post.[13] The psychiatric policy of the British Army in the Mediterranean arose out of the medical experience in that theatre of war, where battle casualties of any kind were a small proportion of total hospital admissions.[14]

The official medical history, relying on notes made by Brigadier G.W.B. James, the consultant psychiatrist, stresses that the campaign against the Italians (December 1940–March 1941) produced few acute cases – "less than 200 for all services."[15] Even the battles in Greece and Crete, with the difficult evacuations of troops under air attack, are described as having caused "a very small number of battle neuroses."[16] Since James's own figures indicate that in 1941 one in every six battle casualties was psychiatric,[17] it is clear that the British Army was ignoring a problem which would become important once large-scale fighting began.

The battles of the spring and summer of 1942 and especially the withdrawal to the El Alamein line forced acknowledgement of large numbers of cases that seemed to be associated with fatigue and nervous exhaustion. This led James to begin using the term "exhaustion" rather than anxiety neurosis for breakdowns occurring in combat. He also began using the term "campaign neurosis" to describe veteran soldiers who had broken down. "Men," he wrote, "can probably do two years after which there is an increasing risk of nervous breakdown."[18] For the second battle of El Alamein and the pursuit to Tunisia, a psychiatrist was attached to a mobile general hospital in the hope of saving a higher percentage of exhaustion cases, but the Eighth Army went into the difficult battles in Tunisia without a system of forward psychiatry and doctors evacuated most patients to Tripoli without attempting forward treatment.

The Australian and New Zealand units in the desert did not share the British

Army's reluctance to institutionalize forward psychiatry. In May 1941 the Australian division besieged in the tiny port of Tobruk established a war neurosis clinic that treated 207 men over a three-month period. The forward clinic was in a bomb-proof underground shelter under an anti-aircraft gun and close to a heavy anti-aircraft battery. Dr A.J. Sinclair reported that "treatment, in so far as it could be carried out, consisted primarily in the provision of adequate rest, if necessary, with the use of soporifics. Thereafter, there was a frank discussion of the nature of the patient's fear and of the distinction between fear and cowardice. If the personality of the patient was good enough attempts were made to teach the patient to discipline his fear and to prove to him he was still capable of first class work while still afraid."[19]

The psychiatrist diagnosed 62 of the men as suffering from "simple fear states," which he did not consider to be a neurosis. He was able to return 33 of these men to their unit and all but 5 were able to stick it out for some time. A further 70 men were classified as suffering from "anxiety neurosis." Rest and sedatives seemed to work equally well with this group and he returned half to their units. Sinclair concluded that "anxiety neurosis in soldiers has a relatively good prognosis if treated early." Case histories were not particularly revealing. Half the patients reported some family history of "neurosis," half did not. Sixty-one percent were judged to have a "poor personality" but Dr Sinclair did not elaborate.[20]

A second Australian psychiatrist, Dr H.R. Love, reported on a group of 174 men treated in a tented Field Ambulance. His methods and salvage rate were similar to Sinclair's. Love's report, published in *The Medical Journal of Australia* in August 1942,[21] showed a broad familiarity with the research literature on anxiety neuroses and a remarkable degree of certainty about their prevention and care. He concluded that "with proper handling the number of men who require to be sent out of the unit lines may be reduced to a negligible figure. It requires confidence in diagnosis, prompt action as to treatment and a certain hardness of heart."[22] Their experience in Tobruk convinced the Australians "that the acute nervous disorders of war are best treated near the front line"[23] and the Australian 9th Division, which remained in North Africa as part of the Eighth Army, assigned a psychiatrist to one of the division's clearing stations.[24]

The 9th Division's medical services continued to develop their own approach to forward treatment in 1942: "Soldiers arriving at the ccs were examined and asked almost at once to contribute a pint or so of their blood for the blood bank. Liberal fluid was then given and the patient was fed and put to bed with a generous sedative. As soon as he was rested and the symptoms relieved, the soldier was got up and took part forthwith in the work of the desert station ... The contribution of whole blood by psychiatric casualties was found to be a sound psychological aid to treatment. It gave the soldier the feeling that he was doing something for his comrades, that by voluntary sacrifice of blood he 'atoned' for his breakdown and was made to feel that he remained a useful member of the group by which he feared he might be regarded as an outcast."[25]

The New Zealand Expeditionary Force did not develop forward treatment until the summer of 1942, when it set aside a divisional Field Ambulance as a rest centre. This proved so successful that the New Zealanders never developed special exhaustion units. Either a man was fit to return to his unit after four or five days of sedatives and rest or he was evacuated to base. The force's adviser in psychiatry, Lieutenant-Colonel John Russell was quite matter of fact about exhaustion and "a considerable percentage, probably the majority" of cases were "referred to Base for grading and then placed in some suitable occupation."[26] The Maori battalion pioneered a system of "battle friends" who lived and fought with a new replacement or anxious veteran but this approach to limiting psychiatric casualties seems to have been unique. The early development of forward psychiatry in the Australian and New Zealand contingents provided a model for other Allied armies, but the British medical system for the evacuation and treatment of "battle exhaustion" remained unaffected by the Anzac example.

If forward psychiatry was relatively underdeveloped in the Eighth Army it was completely ignored in General Kenneth Anderson's First British Army, which took part in the Allied landings in North Africa. Both military commanders and medical administrators in the First Army were strongly opposed to the presence of psychiatrists and flatly refused to accept an adviser at army headquarters. Two psychiatrists did join the force in December 1942 and one of them was able to work in a forward area for a short time. At a base hospital in Algiers a second psychiatrist employed the full range of physical techniques in treating an "enormous number of neurosis cases." The First Army's failure to provide any form of forward treatment meant that virtually all acute cases were evacuated without sedation. By the time treatment was available the condition of many men had deteriorated and it was not possible to return more than a small number to their unit.[27]

The American forces had also arrived in North Africa unprepared for psychiatric battle casualties. Most of the United States Army Medical Corps had forgotten its work with shell shock in World War I. As one senior medical officer remarked: "I think that none of us had any appreciation of the magnitude of psychiatric problems that would occur in the combat zone. I must acknowledge that early in the war I was to a great extent influenced by our long time practice, in the peacetime army, of thinking in terms of schizophrenia and major depression ... None of us realized the great number of acute anxiety states and other acute conditions that would need immediate psychiatric help in the combat zone until after the invasion of North Africa."[28]

In both the United Kingdom and the United States some American medical officers were trying to establish a psychiatric service geared to combat. Fred Hanson, who had left Basingstoke and the Canadian Army in the spring of 1942, was serving as a consultant in neuropsychiatry to the American forces marshalling in Northern Ireland. Hanson had developed a coordinated program of psychiatric services that was producing good results in training, but the senior medical officer for the United States invasion forces decided to wait and see whether such a program was needed in a combat zone.[29] Meanwhile the Surgeon-General's office in Washington had decided to act on its own initiative and had sent Roy R. Grinker to Algeria. Grinker became one of the leading figures in American psychiatry, and his book *Men Under Stress*, based on his experience with Army Air Force pilots in North Africa, remains one of the classics of modern psychiatry.[30]

Grinker arrived in North Africa lacking any authority to establish a psychiatric service and at first he simply treated American psychiatric casualties at a British general hospital in Algiers. Here British doctors were experimenting with sodium pentothal as a method of inducing abreaction in patients evacuated from the fighting in Tunisia. For Grinker this experience was seminal in the development of his theory of narcosynthesis, which he later applied to the treatment of combat stress among pilots.[31] Grinker switched his work to the Army Air Force when Hanson took over army psychiatry.

Hanson first reached Tunisia as one of two psychiatrists attached to the US II Corps. He arrived in the aftermath of the disastrous battle of Kasserine Pass, which had humiliated the Americans and brought General George Patton to the temporary command of II Corps. Given Patton's subsequent notoriety for slapping neuropsychiatric casualties in Sicily, it is ironic that Hanson and his associate, Louis Turien, began to establish the prototype for American forward psychiatry while working under Patton's command.

Hanson's work in Tunisia was based directly on William Sargant's research. Establishing himself at a ccs, he used instant sedation, rest, and abreaction, returning 30 per cent of acute casualties to combat duty within thirty hours.[32] In April 1943 the new Corps Commander, Major-General Omar Bradley, approved the first directive on army psychiatry in a combat zone. It established the term "exhaustion" as "the initial diagnosis for all combat psychiatric cases"[33] and required the use of sedation at battalion aid stations and during the evacuation of psychiatric casualties. Hanson's success in organizing an effective treatment program led to his appointment as consultant in neuropsychiatry for the North African theatre. Shortly thereafter Circular Letter no. 17, Neuropsychiatric Treatment in the Combat Zone,[34] established many of the basic procedures to be used by the United States Army for the remainder of the war.

DOYLE, WITH THE REST of the Canadian forces, went to the battlefields of Sicily directly from the United Kingdom. After participating in two assault landing exercises over the beaches at Troon in Scotland, Wetshod and Stymie I, he boarded a Dutch merchantship, *Alcinous*, as ship's doctor for the voyage to the Mediterranean. He went ashore on D-Day, 10 July, and helped with the treatment of wounded and sick patients at a beach dressing station established by No. 5 Field Ambulance.* He saw his first psychiatric case a few days later. "An interesting patient on D + 3," he wrote, "was an English Commando who was suffering from hysterical blindness and aphonia. On the floor of a granary, hypnosis was used with spectacular success and the Commando returned to his unit happy that the frightening symptoms were not of serious consequence."[35] For that soldier at least Doyle's trip was worth the effort.

The 1st Canadian Division encountered only sporadic opposition in their battle initiation. Dispirited and badly led Italian garrisons gave up or disappeared into the hills, while German units were too far away to interfere with the Canadians. The major difficulties were the intense heat and the inhospitable terrain that had to be covered for the most part on foot by troops whose physical fitness had faded on the long sea approach.[36] As the infantry battalions marched inland off the coastal plain and into the hills Doyle made himself useful where he could. After a week he joined a British ccs which eventually moved into an Italian military hospital at Caltagirone where he improvised a neuropsychiatric ward primarily for British soldiers. When he could Doyle visited combatant units and consulted in forward medical installations. His advice to prepare facilities had been ignored and like other aspects of the Sicilian campaign the deployment of psychiatric treatment resources depended largely on local initiative and improvisation.[37]

Consequently Doyle's major problems were administrative rather than professional. He had an establishment of one – himself – with no transport and only the equipment he could carry: "a stethoscope, tycos sphygmomanometer, reflex hammer, tape measure, opthalmoscope, 2 lumbar puncture needles size 20."[38] More serious Canadian casualties were not evacuated through a central clearing unit. Instead they went directly to British rear installations in North Africa or Malta from a number of widely scattered points. As a result, Doyle was unable to see all psychiatric cases before they left Sicily. This anomalous situation was not corrected until the beginning of August when the short

---

* One Field Ambulance was allotted to each brigade. Deployment could be centralized at the divisional level or decentralized if a brigade was operating independently. The Field Ambulances were flexibly organized and capable of forming various sub-units: Casualty Clearing Stations (ccs), Field Dressing Stations (fds), and Advanced Dressing Stations (ads). They were responsible for evacuating casualties from battalion medical officers who formed Regimental Aid Posts (rap). Field Surgical Units (fsu) and Field Transfusion Units (ftu) could be attached to sub-units where and when they were most needed.

campaign was ending. By this time No. 5 Canadian General Hospital was functioning near Syracuse and Doyle moved there to take command of a Medical Rest Station that was part of the Base Reinforcement Depot. The centre's role was to limit otherwise routine and wasteful evacuation by holding wounded and sick cases who were expected to recover within a week.[39]

There were few psychiatric patients for Doyle to see but he was very busy with the malaria crisis that struck much of the Eighth Army, including the 1st Canadian Division. A large number of malaria cases in fighting formations can be an indication of psychiatric problems, but in this case there was a more straightforward explanation. As one British medical officer wrote, "when the Eighth Army landed in Sicily its conception of malaria prophylaxis was not two steps ahead of that which prevailed at the end of the last war." The result was that "Sicily witnessed a medical disaster which repeated on a small scale much-quoted episodes of previous wars."[40] The Canadians, who lacked medical intelligence about Sicilian conditions, also suffered from a lack of malaria control equipment (it had failed to arrive) and from the inexplicable decision to site much of the division in a malarious area when it was sent into reserve.[41] The long-term effects of malaria in Italy and its relationship to psychiatric casualties have not been studied but sickness in all its forms, not battle casualties, was the major drain on manpower in the Italian campaign, as it had been in the Middle East.

Doyle was disappointed professionally with his Sicilian experience because of his inability to insert himself effectively into the tangled evacuation stream. During the whole month he saw only 46 cases, a number he reckoned as about half of the 1st Division's neuropsychiatric casualties. Of these he reported 29 "returned to their units, 2 were so ill that histories could not be obtained." The remaining 14 he described as "chronic cases with long civilian histories of nervous disorder." These were reallocated to non-combatant duties.[42] Six of the 14 had previously been hospitalized for nervous or mental disorders.

Doyle remained confident that simple treatment provided well forward was practicable. "In view of the high percentage that can be returned to duty in a period of a week," he wrote, "it is felt that neuropsychiatric services should be maintained as far forward as possible. By and large, all that a recoverable patient requires is rest and reassurance, security from enemy action and some sedation. In a few cases special treatment such as hypnosis, was employed with success. No special equipment is required for such treatment."[43] He also made "occasional use in suitable doses of pentothal abreaction." Doyle believed that the field psychiatrist must establish his credibility with the commanders and soldiers who were doing the fighting and who were his potential patients. Consequently "The psychiatrist must visit and live and work with forward units of his formation. Only when he is accepted as a 'field officer' as distinct from a 'base wallah' will his opinions be desired or accepted, aside altogether from the fact that he cannot give sound advice unless he has thoroughly familiarized himself with the life and conditions under which forward units function."[44]

Doyle was the only division level psychiatrist in the Allied landing forces. A British psychiatrist eventually went to Sicily for a short time, but patients were evacuated to Tripoli or Malta for treatment. Reliable numbers are difficult to come by but psychiatric casualties were estimated to be at least 11 per cent of battle casualties. British commanders and medical staffs were still trying to formulate an acceptable approach to the problem. Lieutenant-Colonel S.A. MacKeith, who was appointed theatre adviser in psychiatry just before the assault, used his time to prepare a more comprehensive approach for the pending landings on the Italian mainland. In those assaults psychiatrists joined the participating Corps and improvised forward treatment facilities.[45]

The United States Army assigned its psychiatrists to forward evacuation hospitals that followed combat formations in their advance across Sicily. They encountered many of the same problems that had frustrated Doyle. Casualty collection was not centralized, so many bypassed the psychiatrists, being evacuated from the divisions directly to North Africa. There, Major Hanson had succeeded in establishing the 43rd Station Hospital at Mateur, Tunisia, as a psychiatric centre. A typical evacuation had a soldier first sedated by his unit medical officer. The dosage, six grains of sodium amytal, was maintained on the journey back through collecting and clearing stations. The objective of the continuous sedation was to give the patient from two to four days of enforced rest before treatment, a policy some doctors deplored because it sometimes delayed treatment and increased dependency. Psychiatrists at the 43rd experimented widely with chemical hypnosis, or pentothal abreaction, with mixed results. For the Americans, like Doyle, the Sicilian campaign served chiefly as a very useful field trial. The value of sending psychiatrists where they could provide rapid forward treatment was confirmed. It also became evident that new inexperienced troops were not the only or even the most susceptible candidates for breakdowns. There were more psychiatrist casualties among Tunisian veterans than in fresh divisions. This suggested that closer attention should be given to the situation in which the casualties were sustained.[46] While psychiatrists in all three armies had pioneered well they still had to establish their credibility and usefulness to commanders and staff officers, many of whom agreed with General Patton that soldiers who were "nervously incapable of combat" were to be branded "cowards."[47]

DOYLE HIMSELF had proven his value, and was given command of two sections of No. 9 Field Ambulance when the 1st Division invaded the Italian mainland on 3 September. After establishing a beach dressing station in Reggio, he opened a neuropsychiatric annex in an abandoned school. He and the 1st Division's senior doctor, Colonel C.H. Playfair, agreed on a common evacuation route. One Field Ambulance was centrally located to hold minor sick and wounded while the other two leap-frogged forward to maintain close contact with forward battalions. As they trekked over the hills Doyle stayed with the central unit through which all psychiatric cases were channelled. Thus he was able to consolidate his reception and treatment procedures.

As in Sicily, the early weeks of the mainland operations did not produce many physical or psychiatric casualties. While battalions marched through the mountains the Germans were at first content to slow them down by destroying roads and bridges. Until he moved to Campobasso in October Doyle had just a trickle of patients. In the meantime he enjoyed a "postgraduate course in the treatment of malaria, hepatitis, dysentery and desert sores."[48] From that time, however, as enemy resistance stiffened, and the soft underbelly of Europe transformed into a crocodile's back, medical officers referred sufficient numbers of neurological and psychiatric cases to keep him fully occupied in his specialty.

Doyle's initial observations on his operational experience are worth noting, bearing in mind the less than ideal conditions in which they originated. This was no well-paid psychiatrist seeing wealthy neurotics in comfortable surroundings with analyst's couch and dictaphone nearby. Administratively dependent on the handiest Field Ambulance for his personal and professional needs, Doyle travelled on a scrounged motorcycle, typed his own case and research reports on a liberated Italian typewriter, and spent much of his time on general medicine. He treated many of his patients where he found them in forward units and made considerable efforts to visit battalions to acquaint himself with their day-to-day concerns. They were all, at this stage, learning harsh realities about human behaviour under intolerable stress produced by battle.

Infantry commanders told Doyle that their main concern was to rid themselves of unstable, jittery soldiers who lost control of themselves in action. Not only were they a danger to themselves, they were also an operational hindrance, because good soldiers had to be diverted to look after them. According to Doyle, combat commanders judged that there were few malingerers among the exhaustion cases. "Though they frequently use such uncomplimentary terms as yellow they usually recognize that the soldier with an anxiety neurosis just can't help it," he wrote. All agreed that "the worst possible situation in the line is a body of troops led by a neurotic officer. Troops that have fought well under another break and run when under an officer they know to be himself abnormally nervous and vacillating."[49]

Doyle gradually elaborated his initial administrative and clinical conclusions. Psychiatrists, he thought, should be located at both the divisional and corps levels, the former to provide forward, common-sense treatment at Field Ambulances, the latter to act as specialist consultants in conserving and allocating manpower. Further, besides being clinician and administrator, the military psychiatrist had to be an educator, disseminating "sound psychiatric principles among medical officers and combatant officers." He also had to be a sound general practitioner able to handle a range of physical casualties. The inseparable connection between general and specialist practice was graphically demonstrated when several cases referred to Doyle turned out to be malarial not psychiatric cases. "Most of them," he wrote, "showed general nervousness, dizziness, weakness and ready fatigue and were apathetic and indifferent. These features, plus the fact that they had happened to be afebrile when seen by their MO accounted for the mistake in diagnosis."[50]

The psychiatrist had to persuade the sceptical that he was not creating a problem by his mere presence, but rather had an important role to play in responding to a collective problem that, if ignored, would seriously affect a formation's effectiveness. Doyle seems to have viewed himself as a link between the operational, medical, and administrative streams that cement any body of troops in the field. One of his British colleagues wrote later that "The Army psychiatrist must first know his Army, for his patient is the Army rather than the individual. Next, he must have a clear picture in his mind of what the ordinary soldier has to face and how he contrives to face it. Only when he has established his norms can he adequately assess the deviations from them."[51] Doyle's eclectic activities at this time suggest that he agreed. Establishing norms of battlefield behaviour and assessing deviations, however, was a complex and controversial matter.

The 1st Division's situation changed dramatically around the beginning of December 1943. Although very real to immediate participants, fighting generally was not heavy before then and casualties, including neuropsychiatric cases, were relatively light. But when the division reached the Sangro and Moro Rivers, just south of the Adriatic port of Ortona, battalions encountered first-class German formations determined to stop further Allied advance. On the other coast at this time the United States Fifth Army was similarly stopped before Monte Cassino, which blocked the Liri River valley route to Rome.

As it tried to take or outflank Ortono, the 1st Canadian Division was committed as a formation for the first time. The fighting took a terrible toll. All nine battalions were sucked in piecemeal. Progress was measured in yards not miles and German paratroopers contested each step. Once finally across the Moro River and the deep gully protecting the town, the division had to clear Ortona street by street and house by house. To Charles Comfort, the war artist who painted the scene, it was a "wild barbaric extravaganza of violence."[52] The battle for Ortona still evokes strong emotions. December casualties in the 1st Division leaped to 176 officers and 2,163 other ranks, most of them from the rifle companies of the infantry battalions.[53] A large number were platoon and section commanders, essential forward leaders. To place the casualty figures in perspective it may be noted that the effective rifle strength of a deployed infantry division – the teeth – was seldom more than three thousand riflemen. Reinforcements did arrive – 150 officers and 2,258 other ranks[54] – but some were ill-trained at best. Many joined their units in the midst of an action and were killed or wounded before anyone knew their names. Conditions were not appropriate for introducing inexperienced soldiers to combat. The Commander of 2 Brigade recalled talking to a new young subaltern one evening and uncovering his body next morning.[55]

Unit circumstances varied from day to day. It took just one or two well-sited machine guns or an ill-timed mortar concentration to maul an infantry company seriously in a few minutes. Luck and good fortune, as well as guts and leadership, played a large part in achieving success. All three battalions of 3 Brigade, for example, battered themselves in a series of fruitless attempts to cross the gully that protected Ortona on the south. Finally a company of the Royal 22e Régiment found a way and fought through to Casa Berardi. The company commander, Major Paul Triquet, subsequently received the Victoria Cross for his leadership. In contrast, the West Nova Scotia Regiment had been reduced to a quarter of its strength without having achieved any notable success.[56] The Carleton and Yorks were in no better condition. The brigade's intelligence officer reported that:

the battalion's battle administration was in poor shape, and after as tough a battle as could take place, both the WNSR and the Carlt & York Regt were pretty shaken. There was a definite minority in both battalions which couldn't take it much longer. One officer in the WNSR marched his platoon right back and a general loss of confidence was now experienced. By contrast the R 22e Regt, who were similarly shaken, had all the confidence in the world. They were now in a more favourable position for killing the enemy than ever before held, whereas the Carlt & York Regt were still pinned by machine-gun fire from their front and left flank. In general, reinforcements which were brought up were thoroughly scared by the stories they were told before they began to fight. Little care was displayed for the comfort of the troops. No rum or dry clothes were available and the men were unable to wash or shave. The forward companies bore the full brunt, and altogether battle administration had broken down.[57]

Doyle's case load directly reflected the increased severity of the fighting. When Colonel Van Nostrand visited him early in December just before the Ortona fighting intensified, Doyle recalled, he had been "complacent, felt that he knew the probabilities of Neuropsychiatric casualties from his past experience." Two weeks later he realized "that he had not before seen the effect of really severe fighting."[58] From 7 to 21 December he saw about 350 cases, the next week another 237, in one very long day 57, with more waiting. He urgently signalled the base hospital to expect at least 300 patients.[59]

Doyle established his treatment centre with No. 5 Field Ambulance and an advanced surgical unit at Rocca San Giovanni, a small town between the

Sangro and Moro Rivers on the main evacuation route. Within range of enemy guns, Rocca was surrounded by Canadian artillery batteries that were continually in action. While upsetting, the incessant roar and startle reactions helped Doyle to sort his patients. He retained "cases of excellent prognosis who only needed a forty-eight hour period of rest or at most very little treatment." They were sedated, rested, reassured, and returned. Those who might recover within a week with further care were diverted to a British corps exhaustion unit, the rest evacuated to a 200-bed neuropsychiatric wing of the No. 14 Canadian General Hospital which had opened at Caserta early in December.[60]

"Every sort of clinical picture was seen," Doyle recorded, "gross hysterias with mutism, paralysis, aphonia. Gross ticquers were common and the range went from these to the poor inadequate personality who showed little outward evidence of anxiety but said simply – 'I can't take it'." He returned just 20 to 25 per cent of the men to their units.[61]

Once the fighting stabilized for the winter, just north of Ortona on the next river line, Doyle moved his centre to San Vito, where he stayed until May. Cases continued at an average rate of 30 each week but for the first time Doyle was able to assemble a permanent staff, including an administrative officer, nursing orderlies, a clerk, a physical training instructor, and an auxiliary services officer. He was also able to compile some statistical analyses of incidence and clinical diagnoses. In the first compilation for the period 28 November 1943 to 12 February 1944 (see table 1) he compared incidence in the 1st Division's nine battalions by using a "neuropsychiatric ratio." He and his colleagues reasoned that it was meaningless to compare unit incidence without some indication of the stress each unit had experienced. Units out of action would naturally show low numbers compared to those fighting. Therefore Doyle took the number of battle casualties – killed, wounded, and died of wounds – as a stress level indicator and weighed the number of psychiatric casualties in relation to them.

Doyle commented that:

A number of factors entered into the cause of this large number. The first and most important was the fact that the majority of cases were really persons suffering from chronic psychiatric disorder, usually chronic neurosis or psychopathic personality, inadequate type. For the first time the whole Division was under fire and patients who could not carry on fighting had to be evacuated because there was no place in the rear echelons that was quiet or free from shellfire. Formerly it was well known that many patients who broke down fighting were kept in quiet areas and not evacuated. One unit, for example, had only 4 neuropsychiatric casualties up until 1 December. It was well known that people breaking down in this unit were not evacuated but existed somewhere between R[egimental] A[id] P[ost] and front line and in quiet times rejoined their companies. In action on the Moro [River] this inadequate method

Table 1

Percentage of Neuropsychiatric Casualties in relation to Total Battle Casualties, 28 Nov. 1943 to 12 Feb. 1944 (Includes Battles of Moro and Ortona)

	Battle casualties (killed and wounded)	NP casualties	Total	NP ratio
Royal Canadian Regiment	190	40	230	17.4
Hastings and Prince Edward Regiment	227	90	317	28.4
48th Highlanders	215	74	289	25.6
Princess Patricia's Canadian Light Infantry	185	56	241	23.2
Seaforth Highlanders	202	59	261	22.5
Loyal Edmonton Regiment	186	38	224	16.9
Royal 22ᵉ Régiment	223	62	285	21.8
Carleton and York Regiment	215	51	266	19.2
West Nova Scotia Regiment	228	100	328	30.5
Totals	1,871	570	2,441	23.7

Source: A.M. Doyle, "The History and Development of Canadian Neuropsychiatric Service in the CMF," NA, RG 24, vol.12,630.

of dealing with psychiatric casualties broke down and the unit mentioned was soon on a par with others in the number of casualties. Another unit had an abnormally high number of psychiatric casualties and in this action topped the list by a long way. In no small measure the high number of casualties from this unit was due to other factors than severity of battle, namely inefficient leadership and poor unit discipline. The regiment became practically demoralized in one action and the psychiatric casualties certainly reflected this fact.[62]

Doyle presented his second compilation to the 1st Canadian Infantry Division Medical Society on 6 April 1944. Perhaps the most remarkable feature of this report is the extraordinarily large number – 84 per cent of 1,509 diagnoses – that he categorized as chronic. He explained that: "By chronic, it was meant that the patient suffered from a neurotic condition *prior* to joining the Div[ision]. This usually meant *prior to joining the Army* and in most cases the condition had existed from any early age. Only those patients were called 'acute' when it appeared from their history that they had been stable individuals without neurotic tendencies prior to military experience. It thus appeared that by far a greater percentage of neuropsychiatric battle casualties are not really battle casualties at all but are persons whose personality make-up was such that they should have been selected for other than combatant duty."[63]

Thus when a very concerned British Corps Commander, Lieutenant-General C.W. Allfrey, visited Doyle in the midst of the Ortona fighting, when control of the division seemed to be slipping and morale was badly shaken, Doyle reassured him that nothing was untoward. The division had simply "had a good and overdue 'house-cleaning'" of its weakest and most susceptible soldiers.[64] At least half and perhaps 75 per cent of the chronically predisposed individuals, Doyle judged, could have been detected and weeded out beforehand. Unit and medical officers could have found most and a psychiatric consultation others. This, he maintained, "was highly desirable and would improve rather than impair the morale of any unit. The presence in units of such unsuitable personnel was far more deleterious to the unit's performance than bad ammunition."[65]

Doyle's diagnostic analysis is puzzling. Either the 1st Division had an unduly large proportion of non-effectives or he may have been a captive of his predilections. In the light of later studies Doyle's extraordinary emphasis on chronic predisposition may be questioned. Both formal studies and anecdotal literature are replete with examples of unlikely heroes and their opposites. Self-control and character, responding to unpredictable swings of morale, leadership, group cohesion, and bloody-mindedness, are infinite in their variety. Motivation was as unmeasurable as it was vital. Moreover, situations producing fear and panic vary with individuals; few riflemen and Lancaster tail gunners would likely have swapped their equally unenviable wartime occupations. With experience, psychiatrists focused much more on the environmental situation than on deep-seated neurotic weakness as the major factor precipitating breakdown.[66]

That said, Doyle's preoccupation is understandable. His response was well within prevailing diagnostic conventions. It was perhaps natural that he might perceive personality disorders in the frightened, disoriented men who presented themselves for treatment. Moreover his early military experience in weeding out the unfit in Britain must have reinforced whatever assumptions he may have had concerning the ubiquitous influence of neurotic predisposition. The 1st Division had been hastily recruited in 1939 from among 50,000 volunteers whose mere act of volunteering was presumed to indicate their fitness for soldiering. Not for the last time the premise was found to be unsound. The most rudimentary prudence might have detected, not marginal individuals, but mental defectives, psychotics, alcoholics, and former mental patients, whose potential usefulness to the army was questionable. Despite neat aphorisms to the contrary, not every recruit carried a Marshal's baton in his small pack.

This was particularly the case with reinforcements, who made up almost half of Doyle's patients.[67] Many of them had had no chance to learn, as one observer has remarked, "that combat was a lethal race to understand how to survive and function in a world organised for his death."[68] Complaints of inadequately trained replacements were commonplace. In one of those unintended quirks of army life a perceived need to maintain security may have contributed to the problem. Because of security demands, units called upon to supply immediate reinforcements were not told the reason or their destination. Some responded in familiar army fashion by posting to reinforcement units soldiers they wanted to be rid of for behavioural or administrative reasons.[69] Such soldiers were not the most suitable to be sent to an operational theatre of war.

Doyle's psychiatric colleague in Italy at this time, Major Charles Gould, saw some of the reinforcements both before leaving Britain and soon after arriving in the Mediterranean. In the spring of 1943 Gould had conducted a psychiatric out-patients' clinic at No. 8 Canadian General Hospital near Aldershot. Most of his 1,000 patients were soldiers from those dismal repositories of the unwanted – holding or reinforcement establishments. Many had been cast off from their original units because they were unable to complete their training successfully and they had drifted into menial jobs with little direction or purpose. Collectively they created a formidable disposal problem (see appendix 2).[70] An indeterminate number were dispatched to Italy as infantry replacements. One battalion commander has related that before leaving England for Sicily he "formed a list of those I called the physically, morally, mentally and temperamentally unsuitable, and tried to have them removed from the battalion; I said that I was not asking for them to be replaced. There were about twenty names on the list and eventually higher authority agreed to remove ten of them. The worst of these was a certain Private. When six or seven months later, having re-assumed command, I found myself in Sicily, who should be a member of the first reinforcement draft but the same private."[71]

By mid-December, when the Ortona fighting was at its peak, Gould was in North Africa. There he saw a number of incoming reinforcements who reminded him of his former patients. He reported to Colonel Van Nostrand that he had been asked by the reinforcement unit to advise on a draft that "was considered by the Company Commander, the Training Officer and the Medical Officer to contain [such] a significantly large number of men of inferior quality to make it questionable as to whether the entire draft was fit to send forward as Category 'A' reinforcements." After examining the men Gould concluded with some asperity that: "It is the opinion of many officers in this theatre and fully shared by [me], that many of the grossly inadequate men arriving in this theatre are drafted here simply because their inadequacy has become a burden to their commanding Officers.

"[I have] examined a relatively large number of men in this theatre whose army inadequacy and neuropsychiatric defect is of such glaring degree and of such long standing that it could not fail to be noticed in England. The posting of such men to a theatre of operations is, in [my] opinion, tantamount to sabotage of the war effort."[72]

These were strong words, but some of the 348 cases whom Gould saw in the month after Ortona may well have been soldiers from that same draft who had been sent to the front. "The great majority of these men," he wrote, "have proven inadequate under a degree of battle stress that in [my] opinion could be termed relatively mild."[73] He based this conclusion on information accompanying the soldiers in reports from their combatant or medical officers. Most were already labelled with the catch-all diagnosis of psychopathic personality – inadequate type, as they "have not only been found wanting in action, but have evidenced inadequacy throughout their lives, both in civilian and army spheres." Gould continued:

This same majority has evidenced inadequacy of an obvious degree throughout their career, as shown by their failure to complete route marches, assault courses, etc. during their training period. Many of them prior to coming to Italy (where they were employed in full combatant duties) had in Canada and England been employed as batmen, clerks, drivers, hut orderlies, and similar sedentary jobs simply because of their failure to stand up to full training conditions.

This same majority of inadequate psychopaths have not only become psychiatric battle casualties, but for some time prior to this event have been nearly, or even totally, useless as combatant soldiers. In many cases this uselessness dates back to when they first went into action ...

The number of cases of men who have an adequate past record, with successful completion of all training, but who have become psychiatric battle casualties, is encouragingly small.

The relatively high number of psychiatric battle casualties is occasioned by the relatively high number of men being sent to this theatre who are grossly inadequate from a neuropsychiatric standpoint.

The inadequacy of these men is of such a nature and such a degree that it could be detected by a routine neuropsychiatric screening process that could be applied in England, if not in Canada.

... the institution of such a process would reduce the number of psychiatric battle casualties to an encouragingly low level and increase the efficiency of the Canadian forces in action.[74]

Clearly something was awry. Assuming the veracity of their informed observations, the psychiatrists were not making fine distinctions about relatively trivial neurotic reactions but identifying individuals who were inadequately trained, prepared, and motivated to be sent forward to a combat unit. Gould recommended that soldiers whose training records suggested that they were grossly unfit should not be sent to Italy. Successfully completing military training was not an unreasonable criterion in selecting soldiers for combatant duties. Provided he was physically fit and proficient in handling weapons and living in the field, even a seriously disturbed psychoneurotic had a fighting chance of survival. In any army it is difficult to achieve efficient coordination between commanders responsible for operations, trainers preparing reinforcements, and personnel administrators. This appears to have been the case in Italy in 1944.

Increasingly, the psychiatrists found themselves caught in a dilemma, forced to make medical judgments on matters that were more properly the preserve of operational, training, and administrative staffs. This problem worsened as fighting continued.

CHAPTER FOUR

The D-Day Dodgers

Italy 1944

We heard all through the war that the army "was eager to be led against the enemy." It must have been so, for truthful correspondents said so, and editors confirmed it. But when you came to hunt for this particular itch, it was always the next regiment that had it. The truth is, when bullets are whacking against tree-trunks and solid shot are cracking skulls like eggshells, the consuming passion in the heart of the average man is to get out of the way. Between the physical fear of going forward and the moral fear of turning back, there is a predicament of exceptional awkwardness from which a hidden hole in the ground would be a wonderfully welcome outlet.

David L. Thompson, *Battles and Leaders of the Civil War*

One of the paradoxes of military affairs is that a unit needs battle experience to complete its training, but the inherent strain of operations begins a wearing-down process, which if not arrested, leaves the unit impotent. Accumulating casualties can easily shift the boundary between battle worthiness and ineffectiveness. Eventually the unit can become, as it were, a collective neuropsychiatric casualty. The 1st Division was on the brink in the weeks after Ortona. Heavy losses in rifle companies, especially of junior leaders, seriously strained battalions. "I am compelled to bring to your attention, therefore," the divisional commander, Major-General Christopher Vokes, informed his British Corps Commander, "that in my opinion the infantry units of this division will not be in fit condition to undertake further offensive operations until they have had a period of rest, free of operational commitments, during which they can carry out intensive training."[1]

In the circumstances the division could not be pulled out of line. The primary focus of the Italian fighting had moved to the west coast where the United States Fifth Army was similarly stalemated before Cassino some 100 kilometres south of Rome. In fighting as bitter as that at Ortona, the Americans, reinforced by the New Zealand Corps, battered fruitlessly against the Germans'

Gustav Line. The front stabilized for the winter across the shin of the Italian boot and except in local situations divisions could not be spared for major refit. They adjusted as they might.[2]

The aftermath of Ortona was as vicious in its own way as the bitter street fighting had been. German paras withdrew a few miles to just beyond the next river gully and dug in for the winter. Sunny Italy became cold, wet, muddy, and miserable. The Canadians' job was to keep the German units facing them from reinforcing Cassino. The stark, ugly reality behind these easy words was that battalions had to provoke fights. One task was to threaten an offensive; another to probe for information about German movements and identifications. In military terms the objective was to dominate no-man's land by seizing the initiative. Threatening an offensive means mounting diversionary or holding attacks, the least attractive of military options for those taking the action.[3]

Commanders sought information by patrolling. Patrols by small groups to find, observe, ambush, or raid enemy positions were nerve-wracking trials. "A patrol meant long hours of listening in the dark, often in cramped cover; crawling considerable distances through the freezing mud; negotiating trip-wires strung among the innocent cordage of the grape trellises; making one's way along paths or roads sown with mines which gave no response to the sweeps. Every ridge, every rubble pile, every reverse slope, offered hiding places to enemies who did not make many mistakes. It was terrain on which a careless step, an accidental noise, might spell disaster – in which the first error of judgment was apt to be the last."[4]

Patrols were not infrequent affairs. During forty days in the line one battalion sent out forty fighting patrols to raid or take prisoners, twenty-four reconnaissance patrols to gain intelligence, and sundry security patrols. On temporarily assuming command the battalion's new commanding officer cancelled all scheduled patrols except those intended to provide warning of an enemy attack. "The Company Commanders," he wrote "felt that the men were being driven into the ground by the patrol policy which seems to be that every platoon here has to be on the go, running in and out of the gullies all night ... [one] said that the only thing needed up here is traffic lights in the gullies to keep Canadians and Germans from bumping into each other."[5] Higher commanders quickly countermanded his instructions, however, and it was likely due to his eccentric candour that he remained a major for the rest of the war.

Unsurprisingly morale suffered. "There was a sense of futility in the air," one officer wrote. "A man told to capture [an objective] knew perfectly well that his success or failure would not lead to the capture of the massif on which [the objective] stood, let alone any advance on the part of the Allies." Another remarked that "day after day you sit looking at a hillside and you go out on patrol and get shot at time and time again. After a while the hillside seems to become almost impregnable. Stagnation set in; we weren't moving."[6] Yet another thought that "the horrible winter of holding a static line ... led to a deterioration in the morale of the Battalion. All units of the Canadian Corps went downhill during that winter."[7] The malaise that permeated the troops prompted General Vokes to crack down. "There is far too much 'belly aching' going on in this Division at the present time," he told his senior commanders. "One hears continuously 'belly aches' about the next higher formation – units 'belly ache' about brigade, brigades about division, etc. etc. The 'belly achers' in most cases 'belly ache' because some matter is not to their personal liking. This or any other army cannot be run on personal likes and dislikes. Policies are made and orders issued after due consideration and are for the good of the army, not of the few individuals with ideas of their own ... Most tactical plans fail not in their conception, but in their poor execution, because some individual fails to play his part with loyalty and energy."[8]

Generals may propose but their soldiers ultimately dispose – not always in intended fasion. Some were reluctant to risk their lives for little apparent purpose and "wanted to know their sacrifices really counted."[9] The full range of soldiers' reactions and behaviour on any battlefield is impossible to recapture. Soldiers have always found ways to relieve stress by avoiding the stressful circumstances. For example, if the need for patrolling was not readily perceived and accepted, it was a simple matter for soldiers to lay up short of their objective so as not to provoke a reaction. This must have been the case in at least some of the patrols described above. In none was an enemy ambushed or prisoner taken. It seems likely that prudence tempered an ill-conceived patrol policy, making life less stressful for some soldiers, if not for higher staffs.

Other soldiers took more direct action to avoid or escape their surroundings. Between December and February sixty-seven cases were categorized as self-inflicted wounds; an unknown number went undetected.[10] Soldiers deserted, went absent without leave, or otherwise breached military discipline and ended up in rigorous confinement. The 1st Division opened its own field punishment camp in the Ortona Castle in February 1944 for offenders serving up to twenty-eight days detention. In a few weeks it had two hundred prisoners. Soldiers serving longer sentences were incarcerated in Canadian and British military prisons that had been opened in Italy. They operated on the fundamental detention barracks premise that conditions should be sufficiently unpleasant to deter soldiers from casually choosing to endure them. The camp's War Diary remarks that: "of necessity initiation must be tough, or the whole camp would fail in its purpose, that of instilling a sense of discipline in soldiers who 'fall out of line'. It is hard to describe it – the soldier under sentence is not touched in any way, but he is kept so busy doing things, and being constantly shouted at by four or five sergeants, that he doesn't know whether he is coming or going, and soon he doesn't care." All movements in camp were at the double. There was a daily half-hour talking period and a one-hour Sunday reading period when prisoners would read mail and write one letter. They might also at this time eat one issue chocolate bar.[11] While conditions were undoubtedly tough, it must be kept in mind that prisoners were not being shot at by Germans.

In this period of shaken morale the arrival in Italy of I Canadian Corps Headquarters marked a significant change for Canadians in the theatre. Neither the headquarters nor its commander, Lieutenant-General Harry Crerar, were welcome. Responding to Canadian representations for the need to give their senior commanders high level command and staff experience, the War Office belatedly agreed to send the Corps and the 5th Armoured Division to Italy. Unfortunately they neglected to consult either General Alexander or General Montgomery. The latter, especially, made it quite clear that he did not want another Corps headquarters, particularly one commanded by an inexperienced Canadian, and had no need for an armoured division in the Italian mountains. Montgomery snubbed Crerar who, although underwhelmed by British assumptions of natural military omniscience, was placed in a difficult position. He had a mandate to command Canadian formations in the theatre and he had to tread a very fine line between his national and his operational responsibilities. These were not always compatible and differences compounded already tenuous morale problems.[12]

If the Eighth Army was less than hospitable to the newcomers many 1st Division veterans equally resented their arrival. The old Desert Army was by then a comfortable informal club under Montgomery's paternalistic guidance and General Vokes and others had taken kindly to its casual professional ways. Belying stereotypes of breezy Canadians and stuffy Brits, Crerar's Headquarters displayed a jarring concern for disciplinary forms. For instance the Eighth Army had cultivated an image of casual dress that appeared very unmilitary to the uninitiated. An apocryphal story circulates that Montgomery issued just one injunction on proper dress. After encountering a driver in baked Sicily naked except for a liberated top hat he ordered that in future top hats would not be worn in the Eighth Army.[13] In contrast Crerar insisted on more conventional dress and other restrictions that annoyed at least some veterans. General Vokes was one.

When the 1st Canadian Corps came into being, in the Ortona salient, in 1944, life became a sort of administrative hell on earth. [The staff] produced more useless paperwork containing more absolute bullshit than one could ever cover with an exploding No. 36 grenade. I felt, militarily, having just been separated from my competent British superiors, as though I was in the position of a boy whose loving mother had just died and who is then put under the control of a cold-hearted and ignorant step-mother. I didn't like it. [Crerar] stood for shining buttons and all that chicken-shit ... We had taken to British Corps Commanders and their staff officers. They were not only great extroverts but competent. They had great tact and understanding. If we were colonials still to some extent, they knew how to deal with us. We were proud to be a part of the British Eighth Army.[14]

"Belly aching" clearly was defined by the "belly acher" but despite Vokes's preoccupation with verbal fertilizer he had a point. Discipline and the way it is exercised and displayed affects morale, and morale was central to the problem of battle exhaustion. As one experienced senior doctor remarked, "The last stage in the failure of a man's personal morale, [is] the so-called neuropsychiatric casualty."[15] The soldier's psyche and character may have formed the core of his personal morale, but the support he received from his mates and leaders, his training and discipline, were also central in determining his behaviour on the battlefield. During that miserable Italian winter this became even more evident as commanders, doctors, and staffs tried to differentiate between the medical and disciplinary spheres of behaviour. As with the handling and treatment of venereal disease, they were unable to decide whether to hand the matter over to the psychiatrists or to the keepers of field punishment camps.

The static defence lines that Crerar took over that winter reminded him of the trench lines he had seen in France thirty years earlier. Unsullied by recent operational experience Crerar shocked his new Eighth Army colleagues by reminding them of these similarities, which in his view called for World War I tactics. Those who had been nurtured in the Eighth Army's mobile warfare in North Africa, Sicily, and southern Italy thought him an outdated old fogey. Crerar's successor, Lieutenant-General Tommy Burns, later wrote: "Not a few officers in the 1st Canadian Division and the 1st Canadian Armoured Brigade took a dim view of being placed under the command of fellow Canadians who had come to the battlefield over half a year after the vanguard had waded ashore on Sicily beaches. The feeling was not unnatural; the first contingent of Canadians in the theatre had had seven months' hard fighting and had been consistently successful up to and including the capture of Ortona. There was a certain disposition to assume that the history of modern warfare had begun on 10 July 1943, and that only the lessons which had been learned after that date had any relevance to the way the war in Italy ought to be fought."[16]

Crerar and his senior staff had developed their attitudes about soldierly behaviour in a simpler, less equivocal World War I setting. Times had changed, however, with behavioural nuances more freely acknowledged. As General Burns recalled: "Psychiatrists and psychologists in their attempts to explain human behaviour have made ... distinctions far less clear, insofar as the Army is concerned than they were, or seemed to be, in 1914-18. At that time a man did what he was told, encouraged by the kindly admonitions of his sergeant or sergeant-major – or else. If he reported to the medical officer with nothing visibly the matter with him, he was malingering, a crime under the Army Act."[17] In that war, it may also be observed, it seems plausible that at least some of the 25 Canadians and 346 British soldiers executed for cowardice or desertion were dysfunctional psychoneurotics.[18]

Crerar and his senior doctor, Brigadier E.A. McCusker, were taken aback when they learned about the manifestations of declining morale. "The pride that I have in our Canadian troops makes me hesitate to discuss openly such problems as the high incidences of SIW [self-inflicted wounds] and of neuro-psychiatric casualties during the past winter," McCusker wrote when the imme-diate crisis had passed.[19] Earlier he had relieved Colonel Playfair, the 1st Divi-sion's Assistant Director Medical Services,* for a time and had experienced the difficulties at first hand. Enemy resistance and bad weather had made things go poorly, he recorded, and "this has been the first real test of the stamina of officers and men and consequently the weaklings are being weeded out. The psychiatrists say that all, or nearly all cases are genuine. The OCs feel that they are a bad influence and must be gotten rid of as they upset their companies. The problem is what to do with them."[20]

However, McCusker was not fully persuaded that soldiers were not faking or malingering. Doyle found him upset, "ascribing [the NP casualties] to every-thing from poor leadership to the presence of a psychiatrist."[21] Doyle and Colonel Playfair had three long discussions with him, reviewing patient records and finally persuading McCusker to examine a group of patients himself. Doyle thought that he seemed convinced when he remarked, "There's not one who could make a soldier; the Corps Commander must see these men so that he will understand."[22]

McCusker was caught uneasily between his medical and his soldierly con-victions. A short time later they came into direct collision when an adminis-trative officer in his own Corps broke down under shellfire. A very awkward situation developed when McCusker "was extremely harsh with this officer, asserting that he would be given two alternatives (1) that of reverting to rank of private and going to Pioneer Company as labourer and (2), to go with the section in forward Field Ambulance."[23] Doyle intervened and found the officer other employment, but the rift widened between some 1st Division veterans, who by this time accepted the phenomenon of NP casualties as fatal-istically as they did the weather, and the newcomers who viewed the matter as an affront to their beliefs about proper soldierly behaviour.

It would be instructive to have a full record of the consultations between General Crerar and his medical staff at this time. Despite scanty documenta-

---

* The senior doctor at Division was the Assistant Director Medical Services; at Corps the Deputy Director Medical Services; at Army the Director Medical Services; in Canada the Director General Medical Services.

tion, however, it is possible to trace some aspects of their attitudes and policies. For example, conserving manpower was a compelling imperative, especially as planning for the Normandy landings matured in 1944, leaving Italy a neglected theatre. Reinforcements arrived, but for the most part the Corps had to regenerate itself from its internal resources. This meant severely limiting evacuations from the theatre for any reason. Wounded soldiers went back into trenches after the briefest convalescence. Crerar concluded that the "general problem concerns the natural but, in the circumstances of war, reprehensible objection of a small proportion of other ranks of 1 Cdn Corps to risk death, or serious injury, for their country. The 'angles' include such things as desertion, self-inflicted wounds, attempts to be diagnosed as 'exhaustion cases,' vD re-infection and so on."[24]

His solution was to tighten discipline, with rapid response to infractions and exemplary punishments. "By 'education' all ranks should be brought increasingly to the view that 'escapism' is a shameful thing." Unit leadership was the key. Crerar observed that "there is a general tendency amongst forward units and formations to take the easy way out of this difficult problem. If a man shows himself to be unreliable under fire, he is left behind in the case of a fighting patrol and left out of battle in the case of a unit action."[25] This was a natural reaction by those actually fighting under trying circumstances, but it established a natural selection process that separated reliable and willing soldiers from those incapable or unwilling.

The residue of unwilling and/or incapable soldiers presented the fundamental problem. Crerar thought not all of them were genuine medical cases: "Undoubtedly, a pretty high proportion of the cases which get back to General Hospital are real nervous breakdowns on the part of the unstable mental characters. On the other hand, as it is not considered any disgrace to be an 'exhaustion case' it is becoming increasingly tempting to 'lead swingers' and others, whose hearts are not in the war to seek this way out. While, therefore, the real 'shell-shock' must be regarded and treated as a casualty, I consider it very important that the mesh of the administrative sieve should be so close that the fake exhaustion case should be detected and held ... suitably punished and not allowed to get away with it."[26]

Doyle was also concerned with conserving manpower but his views were closer to those of combatant officers than to those of higher commanders. He fully sympathized with platoon and company commanders who wanted to be rid of unreliable soldiers. He discounted malingering as a serious problem, noting that "ocs and other officers of combatant units are almost unanimous in the opinion that the soldier hides his fear and his complaints rather than parades them. They rarely have any reason to suspect malingering." Those of suspicious minds, he thought, "surely have some psychological weakness in themselves," and cited a recent incident in one unit where "the only officer who was afraid of malingering in his company was one about whom his medical and his commanding officer had asked professional advice. His own weakness was betrayed by his lack of confidence in his men."[27]

Undoubtedly some soldiers malingered. Their numbers are debatable. Doubts about the endurance of fighting troops varied proportionally with the observer's distance from the front. Brigadier Rees has remarked that the "fighting soldier was in no doubt at all as to what kind of man he wants to have with him. The further you get away from the front line the tougher become the comments, the more hints there are that everyone is trying to evade the service, and that is a common experience of armies."[28] One much-decorated Canadian battalion commander cautioned that "persons who are not exposed to the bullets and shells in a slit trench situation or having to advance over open ground against a determined enemy should be very careful of using the words 'cowardice', 'yellow,' and 'malingerer'. Sooner or later, in those circumstances, we would all break down, some sooner than others."[29] Doyle was possibly disappointed but not surprised at the response when he spoke to the 5th Division Medical Society just before the battle for Rome began in May 1944. His first questioner asked: "Should some demoralized, malingering cases, cropping up whilst in action, be shot on the spot as an example?" Doyle replied that it was "purely a disciplinary problem. If we were to adopt this, we would be well advised to start our disciplinary measures from the bottom rung rather than off the top one."[30] He also might have pointed out that shooting men was hardly a means of conserving manpower.

Traditional attitudes about proper soldierly behaviour defined the problem in one way, professional psychiatric opinion in another. The premise that any individual regardless of character or circumstance could be made an effective soldier was not self-evident. The timid might be motivated and the recalcitrant disciplined up to a point, but, as General Burns acknowledged after the war, "it is difficult to fix the point beyond which disciplinary measures can have no good result, either exemplary, or in producing a reasonably useful soldier from indifferent material."[31] Burns noted larger implications:

The psychologists point out, and the Army must agree, that it is of no use training a man as an infantryman or for one of the more hazardous military postings if, in the first hours of stress, in combat, his weakness of nerve and brain will render him useless and, what is more, a bad example for others who do not have his excuse.

The difficulty is that it seems somewhat unjust that the brave and steadfast must be sacrificed, while the poor spirited are allowed to avoid hardship and to preserve their lives ...

It is obviously unfair that well-behaved and valuable citizens should have to risk their lives and submit to the restraints of life in the forces if criminals and psychopaths are allowed to be discharged to civil life. Furthermore, soldiers who are bored would be tempted to procure their discharge by bad behaviour.[32]

Unpalatable as it may have been, an increasing number of neuropsychiatric cases were accumulating around base hospitals and holding units where, left idle, they demoralized incoming replacements as well as themselves. Combatant units did not want them back, the psychiatrists said they should not go back, and command policy dictated they were not to be evacuated from Italy. One group of evacuees was removed from a ship about to sail for the United Kingdom. The solution to their disposal was to form them into a pioneer company for general labouring duties. Within a few months two more units were formed and their name was changed to Special Employment Companies (SECs). Each had a different function. Nos. 16 and 17 were located in the Corps area, the former acting as a reception centre for cases whose prognosis promised a quick return to their units, the latter for others who remained SEC labourers. No. 18 SEC was a base facility adjacent to holding units receiving soldiers discharged from hospitals. An NCO's school was attached to the base to evaluate the potential of NCO cases. The SECs were a Canadian innovation. Their soldiers loaded ammunition and fuel, worked as medical orderlies, and performed other useful work. They were freed from idleness and morale improved. The SECs were viewed as being something between a penal battalion and a rehabilitation centre. Doyle believed that these soldiers were treated harshly.[33] General Burns, however, then commanding I Corps, considered that he had to make a distinction between them and regular units: "It was felt that if troops were allowed to believe that evacuation because of nervous or emotional conditions was a passport for the United Kingdom or Canada, the weak and the wavering would be encouraged to let their pride go and take the easy way out. Whether or not it got to be known that instead of a ticket to Blighty, an evacuation only meant hard labour at the base, I do not know; but I imagine it did, and it may have encouraged some men to hang on, who otherwise might have given up. In any case, I never heard the frontline men complain that the special companies were being treated harshly or unreasonably."[34]

Medical channels were systematized in other ways during the spring of 1944. PULHEMS classifications were implemented and medical boards evaluated soldiers in SECs. Those given s5 gradings were repatriated for discharge; s4s were retained in theatre on non-combatant duties. Following British organization Doyle was promoted to Corps psychiatric adviser. Medical treatment of exhaustion cases was centralized in his Corps neuropsychiatric centre located with a Field Ambulance. Several handling stages were standardized. RMOs sustained patients as long as practicable. Forward medical units then held cases for twenty-four hours before evacuating them to the neuropsychiatric centre. Cases were labelled generically as exhaustion and categorized as sick unless traumatized in action, when they were recorded as battle casualties. None was to be sent beyond the Corps area before being seen by the Corps psychiatrist. The neuropsychiatric centre held those soldiers who might be returned after a few days of rest and reassurance, sent potential s3s to the SEC, and others to the psychiatric base facility at No. 14 Canadian General Hospital in Caserta. In addition, the unit practice of keeping their own soldiers in rear echelons was discouraged: "The practice of sending psychiatric cases to rest unsupervised at B [administrative] echelon is undesirable, since their condition tends to deteriorate. RMOs should recommend men for employment at B echelon only (a) where they are showing signs of stress but have not yet broken down, and (b) where there is a definite job available for them over a considerable period."[35]

WHILE THE CANADIANS held the line, patrolling and surviving, and their commanders debated manpower difficulties, yet higher commanders were grappling with the problem of breaking the stalemate in the Italian campaign. Since the Allies had invaded the mainland in September 1943 the British Eighth and United States Fifth Armies had been fighting separate wars. The latter had landed at Salerno south of Naples and slowly advanced north towards Rome, west of the Apennine spine of Italy. The Eighth Army had moved along the other, Adriatic side of the mountains. Little thought was given to coordinating their movements let alone to defining a strategic purpose for the commitment of such large military forces. Rationales changed with the seasons. The initial purpose of going to Sicily had been to clear the Mediterranean for shipping and to knock Italy from the Axis coalition. The objective of invading the mainland was to gain access to the Foggia Plains airfield complex, which air barons wanted in order to extend their strategic bombing campaign into Central Europe. Inadvertently they conceived *Catch-22* in the process. When the Germans decided to stay in Italy both armies were left, in Churchill's memorable phrase, to crawl over the mountains like harvest bugs against the grain. The final rationalization was that Italy became a strategic holding operation to prevent the Germans from reinforcing their defences in Normandy. It was not a stirring purpose to motivate fighting troops, especially as the tactical objective of driving Germans out was hardly compatible with the strategic aim of keeping them in Italy.

By Christmas 1943, while Canadians were fighting through Ortona, the Fifth Army had reached the mountains facing Monte Cassino. Ahead was the valley of the Liri River, the historic invasion route between Naples and Rome. In January a combined United States-British force mounted an amphibious landing at Anzio within marching distance of Rome. The outflanking movement got ashore with little difficulty but then bogged down. Churchill aptly summed up the situation when he remarked that instead of a tiger loosed in the enemy's entrails the expedition was a beached whale. The Germans regrouped with their customary skill and penned the bridgehead along the coastal plain. The result was that throughout the spring of 1944 three disconnected Allied forces sparred separately with well-entrenched Germans.

General Sir Harold Alexander commanded the two armies. In spring his staff developed a plan to concentrate both in the west for an assault along the Liri Valley. When it was underway the several divisions in the Anzio beachhead were to break out as the other pincer round the German defenders. D-Day was set for mid-May. Warned well ahead of time, the Canadian Corps began training its two divisions, 1st Infantry and 5th Armoured, in mobile warfare. The Canadians were to breach the second German defensive barrier anchored on Monte Cassino, the Adolph Hitler Line, and exploit towards Rome.[36]

General Burns, who succeeded General Crerar as I Canadian Corps Commander in March, knew that any military plan was only as good as the number and quality of the troops who ultimately had to implement it. He briefed his senior commanders accordingly in May, informing them of a looming reinforcement problem. They were facing an equal number of German divisions albeit weakened, he said, and the campaign would be one of attrition where the "vital factor might be termed the conservation of trained soldiers. This is particularly important in the infantry and armoured corps, which are the assaulting arms, and on which the brunt of battle casualties must fall." Replacements for losses were in scant supply – "325 men in the case of infantry battalions and proportionately less in the case of other arms." If casualties occurred at expected intense rates the Corps would be completely out of reinforcements by July, except for those returned from hospital. One major difficulty in obtaining replacements was that s3 category soldiers, exhaustion casualties in SECs, were partially counted against reinforcement establishments authorized in London. Most of them were infantrymen. Burns proposed remustering soldiers such as anti-aircraft gunners as infantry but that would take time. Battle casualties had to be expected but, Burns pointed out, "it is equally obvious that a man evacuated on account of disease and other avoidable cause is just as much lost as if he were a battle casualty, except that he may return to the unit sooner than a wounded man. But in the meantime a reinforcement has been needed." Avoidable disease and wastage, therefore, had to be reduced. Much sickness was preventable, especially malaria, dysentery, and venereal disease. "The elimination of wastage from these causes," Burns told his officers, "is therefore a matter of organization and discipline." Moreover, he cautioned, "the wastage rates are a direct indication of the efficiency of the unit and its commander in these matters. The medical officers can be relied upon to do their part, but nothing they can say or do will be effective unless the co takes proper disciplinary measures to enforce the hygienic regulations and sees that his officers all follow out his directions."[37]

Battle exhaustion cases represented another category of wastage that Burns thought preventable. But it was a peculiar, more intractable, less definable condition. While discipline could be used to limit disease by ensuring that soldiers took mepacrine to suppress malaria, and by policing those indiscriminately urinating in public areas, it was less helpful with exhaustion cases.

General Burns thought that "the incidence of this type of disability varies directly with the state of discipline, training and man-management in the unit." He elaborated: "Basically, the cause is the inability of man to control his fear, and while most men are afraid, they overcome it by the example of others and by the feeling that they are safer, better off and happier while enjoying the respect of their fellows in their section, platoon or regiment. They will only have the feeling where 'esprit de corps' is high, and 'esprit de corps' can only be high where discipline, training and management are good."[38]

Officer psychiatric casualties presented the most difficult problem of all. They were a danger to their men when they broke, but it was difficult to decide what to do with them. General Crerar had decreed earlier that officers judged unfit for service in the field should not be employed on staff, administrative, or instructional duties. With evacuation ruled out because it set a bad example, not many alternatives remained. If an officer became inefficient he could be given a customary adverse report and sent away for other employment. However, if he acquired a psychiatric tag as well he was in limbo. Doyle described one case: "I have just examined an officer who is anxious to lead his men. He is just not a leader though he could render good service elsewhere. I hesitate to label him with a psychiatric diagnosis but will do so rather than allow men to be entrusted to him in battle. He has done his best in a situation to which he was not suited and I fear that the psychiatric diagnosis will prejudice his chances of getting a fair opportunity of success in other work ... There is no sense recommending a rest or treatment and return to duty because the man, put back into the same situation will again develop symptoms of stress."[39]

Officers with lowered s categories were ostracized – not only those who were unable to accommodate themselves to battle stress when they first met it but also those worn out through long and perhaps distinguished combat service. Moreover the s factor was an all-encompassing one, another psychiatrist recorded, "used for a great many widely differing types of personality disorder and psychiatric illness." He continued: "Under the same label are included such serious reactions as insanity, drug addicts, sexual abnormalities, psychiatric criminal tendencies, and also such mild abnormalities as tendencies to general nervous tension under stress, marked swings of mood, symptoms related to overmeticulous rigid thinking, mild depressions, etc. States of anxiety, depression and fatigue developing with battle stress are graded under the s but the grading often doesn't differentiate between the timid immature officer who had broken down with little battle experience and the steady mature leader who has developed disabling psychiatric symptoms only after very prolonged severe stress."[40]

Rank did not immunize an individual from breakdown. An inexperienced officer might well panic when introduced to the chaos of battle. Many did, although the challenge of leadership doubtless helped some control their fear, at least outwardly. As a British subaltern recalled of his experience in North Africa:

We were all afraid now. Before an attack fear is universal. The popular belief that in battle there are two kinds of person – the sensitive, who suffers torment, and the unimaginative few who know no fear and go blithely on – is a fallacy. Everyone was as scared as the next man, for no imagination was needed to foresee the possibility of death or mutilation. It was just that some managed to conceal their fear better than others. Officers could not afford to show their feelings as openly as the men; they had more need to dissemble. In a big battle a subaltern had little or no influence over the fate of his platoon – it was the plaything of the gods. His role was essentially histrionic. He had to feign a casual and cheerful optimism to create an illusion of normality and make it seem as if there was nothing in the least strange about the outrageous things one was asked to do. Only in this way could he ease the tension, quell any panic and convince his men that everything would come out right in the end.[41]

Burn out from long exposure was almost inevitable, although timings varied. One very experienced Canadian battalion commander has remarked that it was the accumulated stress of responsibility in command as much as battle itself that wore commanders out.[42] A young man in the last months of the war in Germany found himself commanding his company, after eight months of combat during which his platoon had been shot out five times. He had to report to his commanding officer but, "instead of furnishing a coherent account, I simply stood in front of him weeping inarticulately, unable to construct a sentence, even to force a single word out of my mouth. He approved my release from front-line platoon-leading, which I had requested of him three weeks before, when it had really begun to break me ... I am too tired out to care."[43]

Not only combat commanders were seriously affected. One of the most trying jobs was that of conscientious chaplains who had to mind the "aftermath of battle ... sorting the personal effects of the dead, making burial returns, writing letters to next-of-kin."[44] One padre who was evacuated as an exhaustion case described how his reactions evolved when he returned to a front line unit:

During my first afternoon with the forward infantry I had to harden myself to battle over again. Jerry was putting some shells down around a house four hundred yards away. I had intended going over to it but was deterred, and, telling myself that they were not expecting me anyway, I actually turned to go the other way. Then I realized what had happened to me and I was ashamed. In the months of summer fallow I had begun to count on surviving the war and now here I was taking care of myself. I went over. When I was a hundred yards or so from the house a shell hit it and sent a cloud of dust with pieces of rubble into the air. There were two casualties, one wounded and one mental. The first was sent back on a stretcher. The lieutenant in charge was a recent reinforcement and asked me what to do with the mental. I advised him to put him in a sheltered place and send him back with another on the next carrying job.[45]

He acknowledged his foreshortened stamina and limited his forward visiting. "As long as I was not tired out the shelling did not bother me; the brain analyzed the noise quickly enough for the nerves to be controlled. When I was tired, though, the process was slowed down and I found myself wincing before the rational faculty took control."[46] Even more difficult than willing himself to go forward when rational calculation told him not to was the increasing strain of trying to comfort the afflicted. "Now come the interviews. In England a considerable number of these had concerned girls. Now it was trouble at home, lost love, ill health, death, financial difficulties, children becoming a problem, and through it all the heartache of separation, the emotions of the soldier mangled and raw by battle tension, death and weariness ... Listening to these men [the chaplain] must in his own way bear their griefs and carry their sorrows. I now found one interview more wearing than a day's shelling at Cassino. I never had any serious carry-over from shell fire, I am thankful to say, but interviews produced tensions that stayed day and night."[47]

These honest officers recorded experiences that might have happened to anyone in such circumstances. The chaplain was very concerned to have the "gratifying assurance that no marks to my detriment would be put on my medical record," and thus avoid the stigma of psychiatric disability. A formal psychiatric label would have left him, like others, with the lingering stigma of a lowered s category. One must be very careful when treading the minefield of battlefield behaviour lest underlying nuances explode.

General Burns, a reflective, humane man and a rare intellectual soldier, was in an onerous position. He wrote:

It is obviously also very important that if men are to be treated [firmly] officers shall have no preferential treatment.

At present, a certain number of officers are dealt with by adverse report, generally to the effect that the officer is unfit to lead men in a fighting unit. I presume that this procedure is only resorted to when it has been found impossible to make the officer do his duty after repeated and vigorous admonition and reproof. It must be made clear to all officers that to be sent back in this way is a great disgrace. It might be more just if any officer so found unfit were stripped of his commission and obliged to serve in the ranks in this theatre. If standards are strict for men, they must be more than strict for officers. But present regulations do not permit this. The trouble is that it is not fair to the men under him that an inefficient officer should continue to serve as such, and at the moment I do not see any entirely satisfactory answer to this problem.[48]

The limits of discipline set up another Catch-22. If an officer acknowledged that he was less than an exemplary model on the battlefield he was disgraced; if he failed to acknowledge that reality he was a menace to his troops. It was an insoluble dilemma.

General Burns had little choice but to place the responsibility for performance on unit commanders. He instructed his brigade commanders to compile weekly records of " 'avoidable wastage' so that they can assess the state of man-management of their units. If any unit shows a high rate of wastage from these avoidable causes, it means that it will eventually be under strength and there will be no more reinforcements for it, and it will represent from all points of view, a weakness in the formation concerned. The remedy is obvious."[49] It was unexceptional for commanders to be held responsible for their unit's performance – that is why they were commanders. But realities of command impose limits on any commander's influence or authority. Judging their own performance by the number of their unit's neuropsychiatric casualties placed them in an impossible position. Forbidding breakdown by fiat and punishing those who disobeyed may have been perversely satisfying but ultimately it was as futile as pushing a rope. External discipline alone could not dictate battlefield behaviour. If so, then presumably the fabled discipline of the British Brigade of Guards would have prevented breakdown in their battalions. But when Doyle visited V British Corps its psychiatrist informed him that their 1,300 neuropsychiatric cases in May included a large number of guardsmen. Doyle noted that "The so-called 'Guards neurosis' idea was exploded by Major Patterson. It has previously been stated by a number of psychiatrists and physicians that in the Guards Regiments, because of their excellent training and severe discipline, a soldier does not break down except under exceptional stress and when they did break down it was only after hanging on to the last and breakdown showed very bizarre gross characteristics. Major Patterson said that neuroses appearing in Guards was the same as other Regiments and that frequently personalities had been of very inadequate type, although physically very good specimens."[50]

Units whose collective esprit and morale were soundly based on more than strictly imposed discipline – leadership, professional competence, concern, training – were more capable of limiting psychiatric problems even if they were inherently unable to eliminate them altogether. At the core were the incalculable factors of individual motivation and group cohesion.

Discipline was tightened before the Corps fought in the Liri Valley at the end of May. Whether by medical conviction or perceived military necessity Brigadier McCusker, in Doyle's view, "appeared to believe that [exhaustion casualties] could all be prevented by discipline; that they were due partly to bad leadership on the part of officers and partly to laxity on the part of MOS."[51] McCusker ordered medical officers and units on the evacuation chain to hold exhaustion cases. None was to be sent rearward until personally examined by the commander of a Field Ambulance. He also prevented the psychiatrists from directly intervening. Doyle's neuropsychiatric centre was removed from a forward Field Ambulance, where he was well positioned to provide rapid forward treatment, and banished to the Corps maintenance area well away from the front.[52]

The more tightly controlled system was tested when the Canadians moved west across the Apennines to assault through the Liri Valley. This first Canadian Corps operation since 1918 had several phases. The first was an advance to close with the main German defences in the Hitler Line; the second to stage a major or set-piece attack to breach them. Both phases were the 1st Division's responsibility. The 5th Division's task in phase three was to move through the breach and pursue what was hoped would be a beaten enemy. Simultaneously, Polish, British, American, and French troops attacked along the flanks.[53]

Opposition was desultory in the early stages of the advance, as the Germans withdrew deliberately. Taking relatively light casualties, 1 Brigade leapfrogged its battalions forward on the left. On their right 3 Brigade moved rapidly until they reached the Forme d'Aquino, a deep-sided wide gully meandering across their front. When they moved across and approached the Hitler Line one battalion, the Royal 22ᵉ Régiment (R22ᵉR), came under particularly severe German fixed defensive fire. They were stopped with heavy casualties.

A three-day pause followed to allow staffs time to arrange the battle. Guns were registered, ammunition dumped, reconnaissances completed, and troops moved into assembly areas. The Hitler Line was a formidable military obstacle. Its Liri Valley segment was anchored at either end on the towns of Pontecorvo and Aquino. Irregularly spaced along a lateral road connecting them were several steel and concrete emplacements with 88 mm anti-tank guns, which out-ranged and out-hit our own tank weapons. They were supported by nests of mobile anti-tank and machine-guns. In front were minefields and barbed wire obstacles which, when they slowed attackers down and forced reserves to telescope, created ideal killing grounds.

After much to and fro-ing and not a little indecision, in the early morning of 23 May General Vokes sent 2 Brigade supported by the Carleton and York Regiment of 3 Brigade into the assault. Preceding them was a massive artillery barrage fired by more than 800 guns. When the leading battalions moved forward, however, Princess Patricia's Canadian Light Infantry (PPCLI) and the Seaforth Highlanders were slowed by wire, and their supporting tanks by mines. They were very badly mauled by fixed German weapons, as was the reserve battalion, the Loyal Edmonton Regiment, when it advanced into the same maelstrom. Unfortunately artillery fire support became separated from the infantry, who were left with only their own limited weapons.[54] The fog of war displaced the usual May ground mist as the battle followed von Moltke's dictum that no plan survives first contact with the enemy or, less elegantly, that Murphy's Law will prevail. "Liaison officers and runners go forward and do not return. There is nothing to see; walking wounded bring back black tidings but only in vague terms – map locations, enemy dispositions, everything definite – has escaped them. Everyone knows the attack has failed; no one is prepared to accept failure as final. Reinforcements are moving up, new fire programmes are in course of organization, calls for help are being sorted out and accorded proper priorities. Fresh units of Eighth Army are being deployed for a new blow. That three battalions have been dispersed, are pinned down and perhaps destroyed, is regrettable. But they no longer count – the battle belongs to others."[55]

The PPCLI, had a fighting strength of 77 when it consolidated in the evening. The brigade's casualties were its worst single day's toll of the campaign: 162 killed, 306 wounded, and 75 made prisoner.[56] The battalions had hit at the strongest part of the Hitler Line, manned by German paras who had just withdrawn from Cassino to a location immediately beyond the rectangular bounds of the moving artillery barrage. Fortunately for the overall attack the German defences weakened towards the west, and the Carleton and Yorks found a hole, which the West Novas and R22ᵉR then widened. Once the line cracked, the Germans withdrew and next day the 5th Armoured Division went through the breach.

In the three weeks of the Liri Valley operations 789 soldiers of the I Canadian Corps were killed and almost 2,500 wounded.[57] Four thousand sick and injured patients were admitted to medical units in the same period. A major medical effort was needed to handle what was the equivalent of a major disaster gutting a moderate size city. Battalion doctors with a few paramedical assistants provided first-line care to casualties carried in by soldier stretcher bearers. They diagnosed, sedated, labelled, and prepared them for evacuation by ambulances sent forward from the next line of care. Supporting Field Ambulances distributed cases to their own and other medical facilities, which collected, sustained, and evacuated further. Field Dressing Stations with surgical and transfusion facilities deployed advanced surgical centres five to ten miles apart along the main evacuation route, some within range of enemy guns. Surgeons working alternate eight-hour or twelve-hour shifts operated on 205 critically injured men. Post-operative mortality was 16.5 per cent.[58] When surgical teams moved to keep near forward troops patients were kept in dressing stations staffed with doctors and nurses. One visiting surgeon wrote of them: "It was most gratifying to see several post-operative abdominals, chest and compound fractures, most of which had been operated on within 12 hours, now comfortably placed in good beds with mosquito nets, intravenous fluids being given, duodenal suction, and indeed practically every post-operative care, including expert nursing. Too much praise cannot be given to these sisters who work unceasingly, oftentimes with little sleep, and giving their best at all times, not only in post-operative care but in assisting the surgeons of the Field Surgical Units."[59]

Regardless of prior injunctions and despite tighter forward screening about 400 soldiers drifted back through the system to the neuropsychiatric centre. Categories were identical to those identified earlier. The major difference from previous practice was how they were disposed. Doyle sent 68 soldiers back to their units after rest, evacuated 90 to base, and sent 249 to the SECs (see table 2).[60] During the action Doyle wrote that he found "himself at great tactical disadvantage at the Corps level." Nevertheless he kept in touch "with the Intelligence Branch and with operations and obtained a clear picture of the nature of the stress and action undergone by each unit." He also had incomplete numbers for the 5th Armoured Division, which had just one infantry brigade at this time. Its armoured brigade suffered markedly fewer casualties. Doyle attributed this to both operational and human differences. Operationally, tankers had few men in direct contact with the enemy, and spent less time in static positions. Moreover, their tanks offered protection from mortar and shell fire. Echoing his now familiar theme of human differences, he thought the "most important factor is that higher standards of intelligence and personality are required for recruits in armour. The high percentage of skilled tradesmen makes this fact obvious."[61]

There are a number of inexplicable aspects of Doyle's numbers and unit comparisons. The numbers themselves are as suspect as most others that take psychiatric incidence as an accurate reflection of diverse battlefield behaviour. Consider, for example, three soldiers who lose their self-control and run around in the open under shellfire. One is killed, one physically wounded and the third is evacuated as a psychiatric casualty. Each becomes a different statistical entity. Doyle's numbers indicate only those soldiers who were admitted to the neuropsychiatric centre. Doubtless many more, randomly scattered throughout battalions, were comparably affected but did not become medical statistics. There were ways for soldiers to merge with the ground and rejoin their units later. Stragglers are not uncommon on any battlefield.[62] The outcome of many if not most military clashes is eventually determined by only small numbers of soldiers who actually close with their enemy. In the Liri Valley, for instance, the Eighth Army's attack on the formidable Hitler Line actually disposed just three infantry battalions forward. When deployed, this meant about one infantryman every ten yards across a 2,000 yard front. Fewer by far actually got forward. One 5th Division report after the action commented on the difficulty in distinguishing stragglers from genuine casualties.

Table 2
Percentage of Neuropsychiatric Casualties in relation to Total Battle Casualties,
25 Mar. to 17 June 1944. (Includes Battles of Gustav and Adolph Hitler Lines)

	Battle casualties	NP casualties	Total	NP ratio
Royal Canadian Regiment	69	14	83	16.9
Hastings and Prince Edward Regiment	82	25	107	23.4
48th Highlanders	113	39	152	25.7
Princess Patricia's Canadian Light Infantry	166	45	211	21.4
Seaforth Highlanders	160	31	181	17.1
Loyal Edmonton Regiment	152	26	178	14.6
Royal 22ᵉ Régiment	144	66	210	31.4
Carleton and York Regiment	152	65	217	30.0
West Nova Scotia Regiment	193	59	252	23.4
Totals	1,231	370	1,601	23.1

Source: A.M. Doyle, "The History and Development of Canadian Neuropsychiatric Service in the CMF," NA, RG 24, vol.12,630.

One difficulty experienced was the control of so-called neuropsychiatric cases. The true neuropsychiatric cases, ie, the completely demoralized and hysterical cases, were, in the main, collected at Regimental Aid Post and/or Field Ambulance car posts, and thence evacuated through Advance Dressing Stations to the Corps Neuropsychiatric Centre. There were, however, a number of cases which wandered into unit B echelons [rear areas] in the Divisional Maintenance Area. These cases were not neuropsychiatric. This matter has been discussed with Officers Commanding combatant units and we feel that such cases which are not checked through forward medical establishments must be treated as deserters. For future operations it is proposed to establish a collecting centre in the B echelon area to which all men returning to the B echelon without written authority from their unit medical officer or a unit officer, will be collected. If such men are not clear-cut neuropsychiatric cases it is proposed that steps will be taken to ensure that the full facts are brought to the attention of the unit commander in order that he might decide regarding the necessity of taking disciplinary action.[63]

Differences of NP ratios between battalions and within the same battalions in the two periods reported are equally puzzling. Battalions certainly differed in their character and their competence both from others and within themselves over time. Battalions are much like an organic family. They are held together by intangibles – leadership, comradeship, motivation, morale – that defy quantification or even easy description. In good units, soldiers feel – know – they are in the best section in the best platoon in the best company, in the best battalion.[64] Many veterans cite the character and capability of the commanding officer as vital factors shaping a battalion's collective character. A commanding officer who cared for his men while leading them intelligently, humanely, and honestly was more likely to motivate and influence them positively than another who did not. His concern could permeate the remotest reaches of a unit in strange ways. One mystery is how battalions retained their distinctive characters while being continually depleted by casualties and refilled by replacements. It is like the old story of having the same axe in the family for generations, with only three handles and two new heads. Somehow, it seems, there was a nucleus around which battalion traditions and responsibilities cohered.[65] Unlike soldiers in some other armies, Canadians did not seem overly affected by lofty ideals or patriotic rhetoric. Perhaps their firm belief in the justness of their cause did not need open display. The slit trench or section or platoon formed the most immediate boundaries. "These were your brothers; you could not let them down," one recalled. Another added that "with nothing to look forward to but pain, deprivation and death, life becomes so intense and so utterly stripped of pretense, cant and falseness, that we were all bound as brothers in the real sense of the word."[66] Battalions provided the vital external support systems which frail humans needed. A British psychiatrist in Italy reflected that "In a force overseas the morale structure builds itself on clear cut, traditional, hierarchical lines, affording, for short-term purposes, great internal strength, resiliency in the face of communal misfortune, and considerable support to the individual officers and men who make up the force. If it were not for the 'immunizing effect' in the psychiatric field of this well-braced morale structure, half the expeditionary force would become psychiatric casualties, or desert, however harsh the disciplinary regime might be; and the psychiatrist's job would be impossible."[67] Some battalions, of course, were more cohesive and thus effective than others. Battle exhaustion rates were directly affected by the state of the unit's morale, leadership, competence, and esprit.

Other variables affected unit NP ratios. Sick rates and common complaints often masked psychiatric dysfunction. So did desertion, absence without leave, self-inflicted wounds, and military crime generally. A quite different variable was the nature of the battle. A winning, successful unit was more likely to have high morale, which in itself can sustain the shaky, than one experiencing defeat. This may be especially important if the battalion feels itself misused. The case of the R22ᵉR in the two battles possibly illustrates the point. In the first, at Ortona, where it fought a very tough but inspiring battle at the Casa Berardi, the battalion's NP ratio was 21.8. The battalion covered itself with military glory, symbolized by the Victoria Cross awarded to Major Paul Triquet. In contrast, the battalion fought for no apparent purpose in its inconclusive probe of the Hitler Line. Lacking support, the unit got nowhere, took heavy casualties, and resented what it considered its misuse. The NP ratio was 31.4. Its commanding officer reflected with some asperity many years later:

The day had been a costly one. We had more than 50 dead and wounded and still had not managed to effect a breach in the fortifications presented by the Hitler Line. I felt that my regiment had been the victim of the recklessness of the High Command, which had sent it on a dubious mission on the basis of relatively limited information and without artillery support to surprise the defenders ... Nor had the division shown much imagination in assuming that the Germans would abandon such well built fortifications ... As a former staff college instructor, I was left with a bad taste in my mouth about the whole affair. I looked on those who had analysed the intelligence reports as ill-advised bureaucrats. And, after this event I retained serious doubts about the competence of our commanders, who had blindly made the decision to hurl us, without preparation, against lines supposed to be abandoned shortly anyway.[68]

Doyle did not attempt to account for the unit differences in his report. He pointed to the utility of the NP ratio as a means of comparing overall battle stress, and noted that 2 Brigade battalions had constant ratios despite having new medical officers and many replacements. But it was not clear why the Royal Canadian Regiment and the Loyal Edmonton Regiment had the lowest incidence. Nor did Doyle speculate on the few sharp increases, remarking only that "in the units where a great increase in ratio incurred, it is suggested that there must be a good reason for this increase, which could be readily ascertained."[69]

There is a defensive tone in Doyle's after-action report that betrays a certain bitterness at being shunted aside and having his medical emphasis on the neuropsychiatric phenomenon overridden. He felt vindicated by the constant divisional ratio of 22 per cent, concluding that the hard-nosed disciplinary and screening policy imposed between the two periods had no effect in reducing incidence. Nor had restrictions imposed on evacuation. Commanding officers of forward medical units had been ordered to hold cases but, Doyle wrote, "the whole effort broke down within two days time ... To some extent this effort had good results. Two of the Field Ambulance Commanders were new to the Division and were rather skeptical about psychiatric casualties. They became excellent supporters of psychiatry in the Corps after a few days attempting to treat these cases."[70] Doyle's view of the aetiology of the psychiatric problem also remained constant:

These figures indicate what has long been clinically believed by the writer, namely, that the most important factor resulting in NP casualties is the presence in the unit of unstable people most of whom could be recognized as unsuited to combatant duties. It is unnecessary to say that excellent discipline and training are necessary to produce a good soldier out of a perfectly stable, normal man, but it is time for universal recognition of the fact that there are some human beings who will not become combatant soldiers however good their discipline and training and leadership may be. It is the belief of the writer that the units which have shown consistently high NP ratios are those units which have had in their ranks too many inadequate, neurotic, or mentally defective personnel. This has been a far more important factor than variations in discipline and leadership as far as NP casualties are concerned. It is well known and we have seen actual instances where good soldiers failed and even fled under poor leadership but they did not become NP casualties and they returned to fight well again under efficient leadership.[71]

One of those who received Doyle's report was the ADMS of the 5th Armoured Division, Colonel Ken Hunter, who disagreed with much of what he had to say. Hunter was a Permanent Force medical officer who had given some thought to the matter of psychiatric casualties. While stationed in London, Ontario, in 1937 he had responded at length to a query on the subject from the DGMS. As his paper foresaw much of what he experienced a few years later in Italy it is of interest.[72]

Hunter thought that the neuropsychiatric problem had been much more significant in World War I than the generally accepted estimate of 2 per cent of battle casualties. He suggested a three-stage policy to handle psychiatric cases in the coming war. In the first preparation period, medical officers would be trained and the army educated about the problem. Also, special handling units staffed by qualified neurologists and psychiatrists would be organized. In the second stage, during mobilization, the medical service would involve itself actively in selecting soldiers, using physical criteria for the most part, because medical histories were suspect and "any assessment of general appearance had little chance of detecting those men who will break down and suffer from functional nervous disorder."[73] The weak would be weeded out during training through the closest liaison between trainers and doctors who could refer doubtful individuals for psychiatric examination. These could then be channelled to non-combatant units. During this stage all soldiers would be taught the psychology of fear to prepare themselves for battle. Finally all should be medically boarded by a panel which included a psychiatrist before going abroad to fight. The last stage would be in the field: "It is in the field that the measures advocated for the pre-mobilization and mobilization periods will reach fruition. A large number of units will have been weeded out, potential nervous cases will have been transferred to posts less arduous but nevertheless essential, troop NCOs and officers will have some knowledge of the ways of preventing breakdown, the unit MOs will be trained to spot early signs of breakdown, units will be especially trained to handle nervous cases, and returning many of them to duty in the shortest period of time."[74]

Once in operations the unit medical officer was the key to controlling psychiatric casualties. His role extended far beyond the bounds of narrow clinical professionalism to include the fullest consideration of the soldier's behaviour, training, and place in the unit. Breakdown was to be expected, but on no account should its onset allow the soldier to escape from the war. Treatment should be given well forward and convalescent care follow normal military routine. Shell shock and similar disabling terminology should be avoided. Recovered soldiers should be returned to their units or, if clearly unable, given constructive work in the rear. Finally, Hunter recommended, "practically no discharge for functional nervous disease should be permitted."[75]

Hunter followed his own prescription in the 5th Armoured Division. Unfortunately his first two stages had been only imperfectly implemented, but he was compelled to face the implications of the final operational stage. His view of the problem and of how it should be handled was different from Doyle's. To begin with he disagreed with Doyle's conclusion that the 1st Division's NP ratio was constant "in spite of the increased severity of disciplinary handling." Rather, Hunter maintained "that if such is the case the NP ratio must be relatively higher in the latter battle than in those of the winter, since he [Doyle] points out ... that a lesser number of milder cases were permitted to go back as far as the Neuropsychiatric Centre."[76] Hunter had a point. If all the milder cases in the Liri Valley had gone straight to the neuropsychiatric centre it seems very likely that 2 Brigade's incidence would have been somewhat higher than it was. It is ironic that both Doyle and Hunter were able to find justification for their differing views in the same set of numbers.

Hunter also disagreed with Doyle's "theory that selection of personnel is the primary factor in reducing NP casualties." He agreed that the quality of troops was important, but he placed "even greater importance on the maintenance of discipline in units. Another, and probably the most important factor is the attitude of the RMO. If the line of least resistance is taken by the RMO and unit officers then the NP casualties will increase." While pre-selection would eliminate many potential casualties, Hunter continued, "I think it must be accepted that battle will eliminate more completely the weaklings that will pre-selection ... I point this out only to emphasize the fact that I feel that Major Doyle emphasizes too greatly the importance of pre-selection and does not attach sufficient importance to the factor of unit discipline and RMO inflexibility."[77] His conclusion closely followed the views he had expressed seven years earlier:

1 Good pre-selection during recruitment and training will eliminate a large proportion of NP breakdown under battle stress.
2 Once a campaign is entered by trained units the NP incidence can only be kept to a minimum by the exercise of strict discipline and man management. Attempts at large scale weeding out during a campaign will produce the idea of a "way out" (possibly subconscious) in the borderline cases who otherwise would carry on.
3 No neuropsychiatric casualty should be evacuated beyond the RMO or, at the most, the ADS [Advanced Dressing Station] unless he shows a most concrete picture of inadequacy. This throws a very definite and clear cut responsibility on the RMO and the regimental officers. This method is being used in 5 Cdn Armd Div and

I feel the results shown in the Liri battle justify the procedure.

4 The Corps Neurospcyhiatrist Centre and the Pioneer Companies are both valuable parts of our organization.[78]

The perspectives of Colonel Hunter and Major Doyle offer an intriguing contrast. One was a regular soldier, medical generalist, and senior staff officer, the other an amateur soldier, medical specialist, and line officer. They agreed on some matters, for example that the quality of their soldiers was important. They differed on how best to respond to the immediate problem of psychiatric dysfunction in the field. Hunter insisted that at that stage severe discipline was the only feasible means of maintaining firm control and limiting the increasingly serious loss of men. Doyle remained persuaded that the fundamental cause of losses was the presence of too many unstable soldiers who should be continually culled from combatant units. To a degree their difference was whether to emphasize quality or quantity. Both doctors accepted the utility of the SECs as a mechanism for employing those men who clearly were unable to function effectively as fighters but who could provide useful service in non-combatant jobs.

Throughout this period Doyle maintained contact with his British and American peers. He exchanged visits with Lieutenant-Colonel MacKeith and British Corps psychiatrists, filling in for the British XIII Corps.[79] There he found British patients indistinguishable from his own in the 1st Canadian Division.[80] He also visited forward and base psychiatric facilities in the Fifth United States Army. While the Canadians fought at Ortona, American and British soldiers had an almost identical experience facing Cassino and along the west coast at Anzio. Heavy fighting in bad weather produced very heavy battle and psychiatric casualties. Individual and unit reactions to battle were comparable, as was the basic aetiology of battle exhaustion. Psychiatrists in all three armies also met a range of attitudes from indifference to downright hostility when they were damned for being the bearers of unwelcome news. The main difference between them was the manner in which the three armies disposed of their combat non-effectives.

The British had about twenty psychiatrists in Italy. Their four-level handling system began with RMOs who sorted, sedated, labelled, and evacuated cases to a Corps psychiatric centre. Those with favourable prognosis, on average about one-third, were held there for up to five days and returned to their units. The rest were evacuated further to an advance psychiatric centre. A minority of these patients, including "all the psychotics, the gross psychopaths, and those neurosis cases likely to be sent home to England," were directed to base hospitals with psychiatric wards. The majority of men stayed for secondary treatment at the advance psychiatric centre and were then channelled to a rehabilitation camp for reallocation to non-combatant duties. Lieutenant-Colonel MacKeith put most of his resources in the advance centre where psychiatrists employed "abreaction, prolonged narcosis, modified insulin, and a few psychiatric interviews for each patient." Otherwise patients were kept busy with physical training, games, and hospital work. MacKeith was pleased with the result. "The contrast between our clinical findings there, and our findings at Algiers during the North African campaign, was immense. Thanks to earlier evacuation, sedation for their journey, and contact with a psychiatrist (in the corps exhaustion centre) at an early stage, practically none of the patients were severely 'regressed.' The psychiatric syndromes they displayed were much milder and more 'embryonic' in type; there was less fixation of symptoms, no new symptom formation, little general deterioration, and amazingly little 'secondary gain.' Continuous narcosis was less frequently needed, and abreaction much less often employed. Treatment was, in general, much less specialized."[81]

The United States Army placed its greatest emphasis on establishing psychiatry at the divisional level. This took some time. Although the War Department authorized the program in November 1943, it was not until four months later that a psychiatrist joined the 3rd Infantry Division in the Anzio bridgehead. Until then, and during the Cassino fighting, casualties were handled through battalion aid stations, divisional clearing stations, and the Fifth Army neuropsychiatric centre. Treatment – rest, sedation, abreaction – resembled Canadian and British procedures. The case load through the 1943-44 winter was heavy and the numbers of soldiers returned to combatant duty few, but the active group of psychiatrists at the centre collectively developed a pragmatic approach that prepared them for the divisional program. The major thrust of that program was to return the maximum number of soldiers to combat as quickly as possible. In those terms the divisional psychiatric emphasis worked. In November 1943 the return rate was less than 20 per cent; a year later it was more than 80 per cent. The psychiatrists' emphasis on conserving manpower by getting soldiers back into battle may have been one reason for their increasing acceptance by the army. As one of them wrote later, psychiatrists "became familiar with problems of manpower, organization, informal and formal channels of communication, and other milieu characteristics of a combat army, and soon became identified with its values and objectives. In turn, many senior line and medical officers came to learn that most psychiatrists were not odd, impractical do-gooders, who spoke a strange language and were only interested in protecting the 'weak' and the unmotivated, but constituted a professional resource which could be depended upon to apply technical skills for the solution of specific individual problems or to recommend and implement practical programs of reducing manpower losses due to psychological causes."[82]

By the end of the Battle for Rome procedures for handling exhaustion cases were similar in all three armies. The evolving system in the 5th Canadian Armoured Division might have applied to all, except for their different organizations and terminology. "The general principle of handling such cases was as follows: The RMO evacuated those cases which he thought to be unsalvageable at his level. Other cases he retained in his Regimental Aid Post, prescribed sedatives and rest and then returned to duty. A similar procedure was followed at the Advance Dressing Station, with the result that all neuropsychiatric casualties passed through two filters before they were evacuated to the corps level. At the Corps Neuropsychiatric Centre a third filtration took place and a proportion was returned to duty whilst others were reallocated to other branches of the service, or transferred to the base Neuropsychiatric Centre for down grading or long term treatment."[83]

Treatment was also similar. For an inexperienced soldier especially, his mates, NCOs, and officers were the first line of support when self-control faltered. After that, forward medical intervention was simple and basic: rest, relative security, comfort (food, drink, clean clothing), and reassurance that reactions to fear were normal and understandable but could be overcome. Individuals were first met as soldiers rather than as patients. Medical intervention followed successive evacuations: sedation, prolonged narcosis, abreaction, hypnosis, electroshock. The further a soldier was removed from the cause of his reaction the less change there was of retaining him for either combat or noncombatant duties.

While the three armies handled and treated their exhaustion casualties similarly, they disposed of them differently: the Americans returned maximum numbers to battle; the British reallocated most of their casualties to noncombatant jobs on an extensive line of communication; the Canadians found an outlet through SECs. This was partly the result of a need to maintain national administrative control over Canadian troops functioning as an autonomous formation in a larger Allied force. It was unacceptable and impracticable to disperse Canadian non-effectives throughout widely scattered British support establishments. Besides, the SECs directly supported the Canadian Corps. Their War Diaries record some notable examples of twenty-hour days in supply points, loading fuel and ammunition vehicles. They also worked in field hospitals, not always without difficulty. One twelve-man detachment was arrested when it refused to follow orders to leave a rear hospital for a forward medical unit. The parent SEC complained that such treatment "defeats the purpose of these Companies which is to rehabilitate the men and bring them back to the Front line by stages." In another instance four stray heavy artillery shells dropped behind a working party. The unit reported: "The men were badly shaken up, and it was almost impossible to start them working. Many ran away and hid under the culverts. Three or four were actually prostrated and about a dozen left with their small packs." Twenty-seven bolted, some being caught thirty-five miles back. When rounded up, the examining psychiatrist sent some along the medical chain and referred others for disciplinary action because they were "deliberately taking advantage of the excuse to disappear."[84] On balance the secs struck a reasonable institutional compromise which, however uneasily, acknowledged the gulf between preconceptions of proper soldierly behaviour and reality.

We are the D-Day Dodgers, out in Italy,
Always drinking vino, always on the spree,
Eighth Army skivers and the Yanks,
We live in Rome, we laugh at tanks,
For we are the D-Day Dodgers in sunny Italy.

Author unknown

CHAPTER FIVE

If This War Isn't Over . . .

Battle Exhaustion and the Manpower Problem in Italy, 1944-1945

Oh, what with the wounded
And what with the dead.
And what with the boys
Who are swinging the lead.
If this war isn't over,
And that goddamn soon,
There'll be nobody left
In this bloody platoon.

Author Unknown – Italy, 1945[1]

There was a two-month interlude between the Liri Valley and the next major operation, which was against the Gothic Line on the Adriatic coast south of Rimini. It was a period not without interest. The Eighth Army Commander, General Sir Oliver Leese, first tried to sack General Burns and, when that failed, moved to break up the Canadian Corps. General Leese preferred a homogeneous army untouched by national identifications and like many other senior British officers wanted Canadian troops, but not their senior commanders.[2] For a time, consequently, the 1st Division was detached to the newly stabilized front on either bank of the Arno River, where Canadians and Germans prowled around the Ponte Vecchio as Florence quivered with apprehension. Fortunately much of the city was spared and the division soon rejoined the Corps at rest.

There they met, in Colonel Hunter's apt phrasing, "the deplorable off-spring of Venus and Bacchus," – a scourge of venereal disease. From 68.8 per thousand in June, a combat period, the disease rate doubled to 145.8 in July when troops were able to sample the ambiguous pleasures of leave. In August when they went back to fighting the rate fell to 76.8.[3] As has been noted, Generals Crerar and Burns grouped venereal disease with psychiatric cases and military crime in the overall category of avoidable manpower wastage. All were seen as straddling the imprecise line between medicine and discipline. One medical study linked the problem with morale, observing that "promiscuity, like drunkenness and absenteeism, is a matter of morale rather than morals." It concluded that "ethical judgement of neurotic problems has not proved helpful in the past."[4] The staff of I Canadian Corps also determined that, ethics aside, the "disgracefully high" incidence of venereal disease was a reflection of unit morale, which, in turn, was a function of leadership. It decreed, that "Regimental Officers, including commanding officers, have been in some cases inclined to thrust the entire responsibility for the control of Venereal Disease upon the Regimental Medical Officer and/or Padre. They have, therefore, failed to accept or exercise their full responsibility for this aspect of unit administration. *The institution and enforcement of measures for the control of Venereal Disease within the unit is the responsibility of the Commanding Officer.* Experience has shown that in units where discipline is good and where Company and Platoon Officers take a personal interest in this problem, the Venereal Disease rate is considerably lower than the average."[5]

Such demands on the young men heading these battalion families, added to their operational responsibilities, may explain why commanding officers wore out so quickly. There were severe limits to the capability of any individual commander in controlling the sexual proclivities of 500-1,000 men short of locking them all up. They put most towns out of bounds, but this also adversely affected morale. They tried education. Graphic illustrations of ravaged syphilitic organs possibly helped curb the urges of some soldiers. A disciplinary club remained poised for others. Soldiers contracing VD who were unable to produce a certificate from an early treatment centre or prophylactic station, issued immediately after exposure, were arrested and subjected to "severe disciplinary action."[6] Habitual offenders were tried by field general court martial. In time official policy abolished penalties but local commanders often imposed their own restrictions and punitive measures, including publicity, which tended to discourage reporting of the disease. Unfortunately, a British study noted, "no penalty has yet been devised, or is likely to be, which is effective in controlling the disease, and all are unjust in practice ... Venereal disease is a penalty of war."[7]

It was penicillin not punishment or moral stricture that eventually brought VD under control. Penicillin saved a manpower equivalent of 1,000 soldiers a day among British troops alone. "If the figure for Dominion and Allied troops were added, the total would be truly staggering."[8] The Canadians in Italy had the dubious distinction of having the highest incidence of VD among Commonwealth contingents, (or the most accurate statistics) followed in order by the Africans, British, New Zealanders, and Indians.[9] Before sufficient supplies of penicillin to eliminate the need for prolonged treatment became available a soldier hospitalized for VD was as lost to his unit as one diagnosed as a psychiatric case.* Unfortunately no one discovered a comparable cure for battle exhaustion.

The lull between battles ended in August. In the meantime Allied commanders considered ways to break the tactical stalemate and drive the Germans from Italy. On maps their situation seemed favourable. Coloured green on maps, the open spaces of the Romagna beckoned, just over the Apennines beyond Florence. They were very enticing to staffs hankering to loose their overwhelming numbers of tanks on a weakened enemy. But the notion of mobile armoured sweeps over clear ground arose from monumentally careless wishful thinking. Attracted to green, staffs neglected the equally abundant blue on maps, indicating an endless succession of rivers and canals that impeded vehicle movement as effectively as mountains. Nonetheless the vision took hold and a two-handed thrust emerged from an extensive planning process. The Eighth Army concentrated around Ancona on the Adriatic and prepared a full-scale assault north along the coastal plains, through the Rimini gap and past the Apennine shoulder of San Marino into the valley of the Po. Once the assault was launched, General Mark Clark's Fifth United States Army was to mount a left hook along the Florence-Bologna axis. The Eighth Army's D-Day was 25 August.[10]

The Corps' assault against the Gothic Line defences began the last six-month phase of Canadian operations in Italy. While tactically varied, with the two divisions fighting and resting intermittently, the continuous operations had an internal unity. Their aim was to blast through the fixed German defences and get behind the mountains into the plains before autumn rains restricted movement. Initially the Canadians had great success, bouncing the Gothic Line on the Foglia River before the Germans could man it in strength. Then the battle stalled.

The Eighth Army's reserves were misdeployed and unable to exploit early gains. The Germans regrouped with their familiar professional competence and forced a battle of attrition until the weather broke and rain bogged the countryside.[11] Ghosts of Coriano, San Martino, San Fortunato, Rimini, the Savio, Lamone, and Senio Rivers, Ravenna, and Valli di Comacchio still haunt regimental folklore. Their unit battle honours were not bought cheaply: almost 4,000 were killed or wounded in September, the heaviest monthly toll during

---

* VD and NP casualties were not the only causes of diminished manpower resources. The mean monthly rate of hospital admissions for June 1944 (all troops under British Command, North African and Central Mediterranean Forces) was 80.13 per 1000. The VD rate was 5.12, psychoneuroses 2.75, malaria 7.31, diseases of the digestive system 9.75. Injuries due to enemy action accounted for 15.48 while injuries due to accidents (not enemy action) added 8.32 to the total.

the campaign. The Canadians were less intensely involved in the battles of October and November but in the last month of 1944, 2,500 battle casualties were added to the grisly total.[12]

The incidence of neuropsychiatric casualties during the last six months followed predictable paths, in step with the intensity and duration of the fighting, weather conditions, and intangible pressures on morale. By then their inevitability was accepted and several screening levels attempted to ensure that only the most intractable cases filtered through forward medical units to the psychiatrists. Doyle was promoted to lieutenant-colonel as Canadian psychiatric consultant in the theatre, his Corps neuropsychiatric centre finally being acknowledged in the order of battle with the ungainly if descriptive nomenclature of No 2 Canadian Exhaustion Unit (No. 2 CEU). Major A.E. Moll succeeded Doyle in command.

Moll was a no-nonsense professional, fully conscious of his dual and potentially contradictory responsibilities to his individual patients and to the collective needs of the army. While an area psychiatrist in England in 1942 he had outlined some of his operating assumptions in a review of cases referred to him. The report made it clear that Moll was disinclined to tolerate slackers, including doctors who took their jobs casually. Regimental medical officers, he thought, were vital parts of any unit. Unfortunately, some assumed their jobs began and ended with morning sick parades, relying too easily on routine specialist referrals "when a careful physical examination together with an even superficial knowledge of psychiatry would eliminate the presence of organic disease, the symptoms being obviously of a functional nature." Moll reckoned that "psychiatric problems in a unit appear to run parallel with the confidence the men have in their MO and with the interest the MO has, not only for the well being, but also for the welfare of his unit." He cited one example of under-effort and over-use when a medical officer referred twenty of his unit's two-hundred men for psychiatric consultation. Moll concluded acidly that "in such circumstances one cannot but wonder whether there is not a definite aetiological factor within the unit itself responsible for the high number of cases requiring examination."[13] In other words more than the psychology of individuals was involved. The sociology of the group – its leadership, morale, cohesion – was flawed.

During training, Moll wrote, it was advisable to "eliminate from a unit cases which to date have not shown adequate adjustment to Army life and which no doubt would break down in active warfare when a firmer attitude will have to be adopted." With this in mind, he concluded, psychiatrists also had to adapt their practice to the needs of the army and the rigours of war. They would have "to take a much firmer attitude ... such attitude should permeate throughout the unit, with 'toughening of the mind' as well as of the body, with the enforcement of Army discipline, a more rigid attitude by the RMO towards sick parades, a lesser interest in individual problems of maladjustment and in general a more severe outlook on life."[14] After all, there was a war on.

Moll's approach to the practice of battlefield psychiatry suited the stringent screening system adopted earlier. Soldiers were supposed to be looked after first in their companies, then by their battalion medical officers, then in forward divisional treatment facilities, and finally by Moll in No. 2 CEU. During the battle of the Gothic and Rimini Lines in September, Moll sited his unit just behind the front, barely out of enemy artillery range. He saw about five hundred patients. At any of these handling stages they "presented a rather monotonous and anything but dramatic picture – dejection, fatigue, and apathy being the outstanding features, with varying degrees of tremors, unshaven faces, dull eyes and muddy uniforms completing the 'beat-up' appearance. The complaints were also stereotyped – 'I just can't take it anymore; I can't stand those shells; I've had it.'"[15] Most had notes from medical or combatant officers:

Evacuated from the front line by his company commander as useless and demoralizing to other men ... became so confused that he didn't know what he was doing.

Was evacuated from the front line because mentally confused under shellfire.

Evacuated from the front line because shaky and weak in action. Froze to slit trench.

He was sent out of action by his officer because he became completely demoralized and was unable to do anything except shake and cry. Mentally retarded.

In a defensive position in a slit trench; the area came under intensive shelling ... about an hour later ... this soldier reported to platoon headquarters in a terrible state of nerves. He was screaming and crying and shaking like a leaf ... in his present state he is absolutely of no use to the platoon.

During mortar shelling he became shaky, ran out of his trench into a house, could not think ... trembling, crying, jumpy at every noise. Kept at RAP, phenobarb. 3grs. given. Made to work – no apparent results.

His first time in action, nerves have been bad. Was sent back this morning by company commander because he was jeopardizing the lives of other men in the platoon. Stays in slit trench all the time, except during shelling, when he runs around everywhere.

This soldier has been a member of my platoon ... he has already been evacuated as an exhaustion case after the Hitler Line battle ... On both the 6th and 7th of September during this last battle, he broke completely under the constant shelling and lost his equipment and weapon on both occasions. In my opinion he is and will be unfit for front line duty, and his retention in a rifle platoon would endanger the lives of other men.

Evacuated from the front line because he was no jittery in action that he shot at his own patrol wounding three men.[16]

Moll had to diagnose quickly, label men from a lexicon of imprecise terms, and treat or evacuate them. The vast majority he diagnosed as either psychoneuroses (anxiety state, anxiety-hysteria, hysteria, unspecified psychoneurosis) or psychopathic personality – inadequate type. He frankly acknowledged the inadequacy of these labels. For instance, he noted that differentiating between anxiety-hysteria and anxiety state "rests mainly on the brief description by the RMO of the soldier's behaviour under shell fire," which the RMO received at second hand. Moll continued:

The differential diagnosis of psychoneuroses and psychopathic personality inadequate type is also open to discussion. Generally speaking the diagnosis of psychoneuroses has been used in the case of an individual showing obvious symptoms of autonomic dysfunction having good motivation and reported by his unit to have made an honest effort to carry on in battle notwithstanding his neurotic constitution.

This differential diagnosis is fairly clear cut at the extreme levels and becomes more apparent the longer the interval between the time of interview and the time of evacuation from the front line. Hence perhaps the greater ease in diagnosis at the Neuropsychiatric Base as compared to that at Corps level, where the patient more often than not is interviewed within twenty-four hours from his evacuation.

The mixed states are much more frequently seen at the exhaustion Unit and the diagnosis of "Anxiety state in an inadequate personality" or of "Psychopathic personality inadequate type with anxiety": is more descriptive and accurate in a fairly large number of cases ...

The incidence of psychosis has been small, a total of only 14 cases, three belonging to the group of toxic psychoses. A diagnosis of schizoid personality has been used in 15 cases, some of them definitely prepsychotic.[17]

Soldiers did not spend long at the exhaustion unit, an average of just two and a half days. They washed and shaved, were given hot drinks and a change of clothes, and rested. Those showing marked tension were sedated with phenobarbital, but Moll found that most did not neet it. A 400 grain supply lasted three months, and he had no occasion to induce continuous narcosis. Removal of the patient from the stress of shell fire, even if only temporarily, was the best form of psychotherapy. Symptoms of anxiety frequently disappeared within twenty-four hours of admission. Even more striking was the rapid lifting of the patient's mood when he heard that he was not going to be returned to his unit and "the persistence or aggravation of symptoms when he suspects he is going to be discharged to full duty."[18] Despite their reluctance, Moll sent about 40 per cent of his patients back to their units, while a slightly larger number went directly to SECs. The relatively large number returned was probably deceptive, as Moll cautioned: "A certain proportion of these will probably be returned to this unit as ineffective in battle, the policy followed to date having been to RTU individuals of doubtful prognosis and yet considered to be worthy of a further trial at full combatant duties. Relapses are to be expected and cannot be prevented, particularly when one tends to err on the side of retaining the man in the field."[19] Unfortunately the recidivist rate was not recorded.

In the midst of his very active practice Moll wrote another paper reflecting on his immediate field experience.[20] First, he noted that the popular conception of "bomb-whacky" soldiers was misleading. "The incidence of psychosis (insanity) is to my knowledge not higher in the Army in active warfare than one would expect in a similar group of individuals in civilian life." Moreover, he wrote, "battle conditions may be a precipitating factor of mental disorder, but more often than not the seed of that mental disorder has been present all the time." He categorized his cases into three groups: first, "antisocial and incorrigible offenders" who had to be treated with severe discipline; second, those who had displayed in both civilian and military life "some constitutional inadequacy ... who have been restless and unstable all their life [sic], who have never been able to face difficulties, who have always evaded the issue, and who when faced with shell fire react poorly," third, soldiers "whose nervous mechanism is such that they can only stand up to a certain amount of stress." He continued:

They are usually individuals who are conscientious, over sensitive, of a somewhat unaggressive nature, good citizens in civilian life and keen soldiers who have made an honest effort to stand up to the stress and strain of battle conditions. They have given all and finally they have been unable to carry on and have required evacuation.

These cases come to us with a note from their Company Commander, Platoon Officer or RMO, with such statements as: "this man has been through some very heavy action and has done an excellent job. Since the last attack he has undergone some very heavy shelling and has now reached the point where he requires rest and treatment." Or "this man is a very good soldier. Stood up to five days of hell, under heavy concentration of mortar, HE and MG. No sleep. Comrades killed and wounded. Now requires treatment."[21]

Fear was doubtless the most common shared emotion on the battlefield. "Fear," Moll observed, "is not only a normal reaction but actually a useful emotion as it speeds up our mental processes and reactions in time of stress." Controlling and channelling fear was the key to acceptable battlefield behaviour. "It is only when fear is naked, when it is no longer controlled by the higher emotions such as sense of duty, loyalty to the unit, and ideals for which we are fighting that fear has to be condemned." It was loss of control that gave Moll his patients. The result was that by the time they reached him "lack of will power is probably [their] most striking feature ... the necessary result of a severe blow to the man's self-respect." The psychiatrist's task was to help the soldier regain his self-respect, and the best way to restore that "deflated ego" was to give him productive work. Consequently Moll returned as many men as possible, and found the SECs to be an invaluable alternative for those who, unable to withstand battle stress, were still able to contribute to the common cause.[22]

Moll's perspective reached far beyond the confines of individual psyches to embrace the widest context of the soldier's unit life on a violent battle-field. Echoing earlier views, he emphasized the significance of the man's unit in supplying the external support that frail humans needed when under trial.

Sound management within the unit is of the utmost importance in preventing nervous breakdown. All other factors being equal, the comparative incidence of Psychiatric Casualties may be safely considered as reflecting the state of morale of the unit. A good Company Commander or section officer is at all times well aware of the mental state of the men under his command and of their ability to stand up to the strain both physical and mental of battle conditions, and of the measures necessary to present a breakdown. A good MO feels the pulse of his unit and with sound judgement is able to prevent the occurrence of an unnecessary number of Psychiatric Casualties. Twenty-four hour rest at Echelon level is often all that is required to fortify the individual and to rebuild his physical and mental state.[23]

Moll's "good MOs" were sternly tested as the character of the Canadians' war changed. Winter recalled unpleasant memories of Ortona. Once more, static positional fighting followed mobile battle. It was much harsher on nerves. Moreover, expectations about the Gothic Line fighting remained unfulfilled. The Eighth Army Commander, General Leese, had claimed that they would all end up in Vienna; instead they were just a few miles up the Adriatic with Germans behind every obstacle. Expecting relief after reaching Rimini, both Canadian divisions went back to the line. They spent November in reserve but December brought them into a new offensive, where rather than ranging freely in tanks infantrymen had to crawl through sodden bog from one river line to the next canal.[24]

With due respect to supporting gunners, sappers, and others, it was an infantryman's war. The romantic image of the Queen of Battle, however, was more appropriately the PBI – poor bloody infantry. Infantry soldiering is one of the most peculiar of occupations. It is one of the few in the army without some vague socially acceptable civilian equivalent. The infantryman's job was to kill other infantrymen. But, as with the sex act, the final furious spasm of activity usually comes only after lengthy preliminaries: patrolling, being shelled, simply enduring in miserable weather and appalling terrain. An infantryman spent most of his time training, marching, waiting – a lot of waiting – and digging whenever he stopped. He had little except apprehension to occupy his mind and less to anticipate. One veteran infantryman of both wars described the dismal prospects:

Only those who have some first-hand knowledge of it can begin to appreciate the incessant dangers and discomforts, as well as the cumulative stresses and strains, which the front-line soldier is called upon to endure for weeks and months on end, often without the proper rest. The demands made upon the fighting troops proved so heavy that few men over 40 could withstand the burden, and the average age for commanding officers in the "teeth arms" units was only 35.

In the Second World War, as always before, the heaviest battle casualties occurred amongst the infantry soldiers and few of them managed to survive a year in action without being wounded. Such a steady strain on their fighting manpower kept nearly all infantry battalions permanently under strength as battle formations. They were further handicapped by the fact that many of their men, sent as replacements, tended to be imperfectly trained, and were new to the conditions. All these factors put further strain on those who remained to carry on ... for most of the front-line soldiers, the bleak rule was that you normally continued to fight on; either until you were killed or so severely wounded as to be unfit for further active service in the line.[25]

Circumstances converged to exert enormous pressure on morale over the 1944-45 winter. It is impossible to quantify the state of morale because it constantly shifts – individual to individual, unit to unit, day to day. Nor does morale lend itself to easy generalization. When he visited in the autumn of 1944 Colonel Van Nostrand thought morale was reasonable: "not as high as one would gather from enthusiastic officers at Corps level, nor as low as is suggested by the material passing through No. 2 Reallocation Centre."[26] His impression was that it was better in combat than in static units, but it may be doubted that forward infantrymen were as "keen to get into battle again," as the new Corps commander chose to believe.[27] Infantrymen are seldom as bloodthirsty as distant commanders.

Van Nostrand sensed that there was considerable war weariness and resentment about being neglected in a forgotten theatre. A company commander reported that weariness, an understandable reluctance to risk death in the closing stages of the war, lack of NCOs, and the dread of another winter combined to drive morale down. He found his men less reliable than they had been. Four of his scarce NCOs had recently been wounded "because they had to go back, or expose themselves unduly so as to force their men to come with them."[28] A platoon commander recalled that when he rejoined his battalion after convalescence its spirit was not what it had been. "There seemed to be a profound change in attitudes toward the war – cynicism of the grandiose schemes and plans of the generals; contempt for the 'bumph' of the staff from whom all troubles flowed; resentment over the mounting casualties; surliness because of the appalling weather and tortuous terrain; intolerance of the mistakes of others; a feeling of injustice due to the lack of reinforcements and equipment; above all, a weariness of the war."[29]

When his battalion was ordered to repeat a failed assault over a wide, fast-flowing river he sensed "the disbelief among the members of the [Orders] Group that higher authority are persisting in their suicidal plans ... But god-dammit, the general wants his lousy bridge and he shall have it even if it takes us all winter." A few weeks later he recoiled in horror at the "failure and slaughter of another fine Regiment ... so typical of the way troops were thrown into battle, day after day, month after month, with so little thought given to proper recce, or careful, intelligent planning."[30]

This officer's comments on questionable tactics and deployment were neither idle nor isolated. A commander's competence and his use of available resources profoundly affects confidence and morale. Criticism was common among junior combat officers who, when they returned to England, completed detailed questionnaires about their battle experience. One of their echoing themes was that over-optimistic higher commanders drove morale down by persistently committing too few troops against tough objectives. When an under-strength battalion failed another equally weak battalion would be sent to do the same task with equally dismal results. Another theme was that by continually changing plans and countermanding orders while troops were deploying, battle leaders were usually left with no time to brief their soldiers. Often junior commanders themselves had only a vague knowledge of their tasks.[31]

Cynicism about higher commanders and contempt for their staffs is common among fighting troops who have to implement their tidy plans. Commanders themselves, however, were in a difficult position, faced as they were with the unpleasant task of persisting in a gigantic holding operation in Italy designed to keep German divisions away from other fronts. But the more they drove their troops forward in dismal tactical circumstances the more they drove down morale. General Burns was removed from command when he was trapped between pressure from the army commander and resistance from his subordinates. His successor, Lieutenant-General Charles Foulkes, lacked the fire to inspire his new command. When he spoke to his assembled battalion commanders, instead of winning their confidence he discouraged them. "I watched the faces of his audience as he spoke," Foulkes's chief operations officer has remarked, "and it was obvious to me that he had failed to win their enthusiastic support ... He missed a great opportunity."[32] When yet another assault crossing of the Lamone River was staged, Foulkes's own regiment was decimated. Foulkes outraged one of its most gallant officers by accusing his men of failing to fight.[33] Those who were fighting held a different view. As that officer scathingly recalled: "The Lamone debacle had been a bitter episode in the Regiment's history. Even the rear rank privates knew that they had been pushed into a 'killing ground.' They therefore still believed that our newly appointed brigade, divisional and corps commanders either didn't know what they were doing, or didn't care. It certainly looked that way, as there was very little humanity noticeable behind Battalion Headquarters."[34]

Individual character and small group loyalty kept most soldiers going. Many writers have commented on the difficulties of defining soldiers' motivations.[35] For some the fear of fear itself was enough, for others the fear of letting down mates in their section or platoon – the physical and emotional boundaries of most infantrymen. These intensely felt ties between men sharing common threat were inherently vulnerable. When a bonded section of, say, six men was badly hit, the survivor(s) were left stranded. "Some men with long service in action state they do not want to return because all their friends are killed or wounded. They feel lost. There is no way of completely overcoming the personal loss of a friend in battle."[36] Moll weighed the grim balance of strengths and tremors in such closely knit groups: "Courage is more a mass than an individual phenomenon [he reflected after the war]. Indeed, one may state that the capacity for group identification is perhaps the best gauge in determining the threshold of intolerance towards battle stress. The more intense the attachment and loyalty to chums and leaders, the higher the threshold of breakdown, and for the same reason the higher the vulnerability in the case of excessive loss through death or wounding of companions or of efficient leaders."[37]

Leadership was vital. "As long as there is hope," a veteran platoon commander thought, "even just a glimmer, a man will usually accept the risks, if he is well led. It is only when there is no hope at all that the average man will falter."[38] Sometimes, when a soldier served under a trusted and exceptional leader, his loyalty spread farther than his slit trench but this became increasingly difficult as strangers replaced worn-out unit veterans.

The lack of trained infantry reinforcements became a quiet national scandal. It was noisy enough in Canada where political lives were at stake, but quiet in Italy where soldiers died during that last corrosive winter because their ranks were depleted.[39] Part of the problem lay with the country's manpower policies, which produced an over-manned airforce and two distinct armies, one of them for service in Canada only. Part lay with the army's sloppy manpower allocations, which trained too few men for the fighting teeth and too many for a lavish administrative tail.[40] For example, the formal establishment of an infantry division's 18,000 men had 8,000 to 9,000 infantrymen, including specialists like machine-gunners. A battalion's establishment was 850. Its four rifle companies had 125 each, the rest were headquarters and support troops. Of course they were seldom if ever able to put that many in the field during operations. Soldiers were killed, wounded, sick, on leave, or left out of battle to provide immediate reinforcements. At this stage of the war rifle companies rarely mustered 75 men. Not infrequently battalions went into action with three rather than four companies, each with no more than 50 riflemen.[41] Consequently, of the division's total strength of 18,000 it might deploy 2,000 to 3,000 fighters. They took more than 75 per cent of the casualties.

Full discussion of the manpower problem in the Canadian Army during the war is beyond the scope of this study. Some indication of its impact on fighting troops is necessary, however, because it affected morale, behaviour, and the incidence of battle exhaustion. The most charitable description of the replacement system at this time is that it remained inadequate. A fault line ran from the front, where battalions lacked the time and conditions required to absorb new men properly, through reinforcement units in Italy and England, to Canada, where political exigencies masked the source of the problem.

That problem was clear enough to fighting soldiers. There were too few replacements and those who arrived were often ill-trained. Rear echelon organizations and redundant units like anti-aircraft gunners were combed for soldiers who could be given a crash course in infantry survival and sent forward.[42] They were prime candidates for early burial or hospitalization as physical or psychiatric casualties. So were men hastily reallocated in England and shipped to Italy. For example, in September General Burns urgently asked London for additional reinforcements. Canadian Military Headquarters (CMHQ) found 500 men in Royal Canadian Ordnance Corps depots and other static units and added them to an already scheduled draft. At least nominally they were medically fit but, CMHQ advised, "if you require them as infantry General Duties you must remuster and retrain them on arrival. To facilitate such retraining we will send by bomber mail the standard four week syllabus of remustering training which is designed to produce duty infantry soldiers trained to minimum standards. I would request you pay particular attention to weapon training and assessment of this draft in respect of training before despatch and many may be unfamiliar with some platoon weapons or in need of refresher training. Hardening training will also need special stress."[43]

A British sergeant aptly remarked in similar circumstances that "the battlefield is no place for experiments in euthanasia."[44] Readers may share a sense of outrage on reading this abject confession of bureaucratic impotence. It is as bereft of commonsense as it is of military competence. Commanders and senior administrators had had time to prepare reinforcements since 1939.

This abhorrent situation placed intolerable burdens on battalions receiving untrained men. Seventy-five per cent of one draft of 113 soldiers were unable to pass their basic tests of elementary training on infantry weapons when they reached Italy.[45] A Loyal Edmonton veteran recalled that he "saw reinforcements who could not handle a rifle. They knew what it was – but to aim it and kill the enemy at 400 yards away – impossible. They had only the barest working knowledge of the Bren [light machine-gun] and the anti-tank weapons."[46] When Colonel Ralston, the Minister of National Defence, visited Italy in October the regimental sergeant-major of the 48th Highlanders told him that only seven men in his recent draft of 72 reinforcements were ready to go into the line.[47] The commander of the base reinforcement group confirmed that he was receiving untrained men and lacked time to train them before sending them forward.[48] It helped morale not a whit when soldiers knew that there were trained and trainable men in Canada whose presence in Italy might have made the difference between living and dying. A padre wrote:

Among the wounded we tended and the dead we buried were lads whose physique was not equal to war. They had been urged into the army by the recruiting advertising of which we saw some specimens in the newspapers from Canada. This advertising worked upon fathers of families who should have been kept at home. It worked on boys in their teens, It did not work with thousands of able-bodied young men who might well have gone into battle. Now we were burying lads who had the stuff to go into battle but not the physical stamina to recover from their wounds. And during these battles in the Gothic Line we read in the Canadian papers about the Canadian hockey players and their well-fed and well-publicized summer training with the reserve army. "O Canada we stand on guard for thee." Presently in Canadian arenas crowds would cheer them as they skated out on the ice to play hockey under floodlights. In Europe other Canadians went into battle and died in the darkness.[49]

The wonder is that there should have been any surprise when the results of this chronic mismanagement became tragically obvious. One officer commented wryly that "Since my batman, who is kind of dumb, knew all about the reinforcement situation a couple of years ago, it is strange that it has come as a shock to the Minister and Chief of Staff."[50] It is to his credit that Colonel Ralston left the government when it persisted in trying to wish the matter away, but in the meantime the tragic burden was left with worn-out men like the soldier whom General Foulkes visited in hospital on Christmas Day "who had been wounded, evacuated, returned to his unit and wounded again during the operations taking place between 1 and 25 December."[51] He was not alone. Foulkes acknowledged that "undoubtedly some soldiers were wounded several times and the convalescent depots were watched most particularly to ensure that all fit personnel were despatched forward with a minimum of delay," but he claimed there was "no indication" that unfit soldiers were being returned to the line.[52] On Boxing Day the officer commanding one of the reinforcement battalions informed Foulkes's senior doctor that "reinforcements were arriving from Convalescent Depots ... with open wounds, limitation of movement and unfit for duty."[53]

As might be expected, the circumstances of the winter war increased the psychiatrists' practice. No. 2 CEU received 703 cases during the last quarter of the year and another 269 in the first five weeks of 1945.[54] The peaks coincided with the worst actions and the onset of winter. Moll's doubts about his earlier high RTU rate proved to be sound and it now declined to II per cent. He sent more than half his patients to the SECS. Colonel Hunter described the evolving pattern of incidence: "Neuropsychiatric casualties have been encountered in about the same general proportions as we have come to expect. As a rule these casualties appear among the most susceptible individuals very early in action. Following this initial influx, the incidence becomes gradually greater according to the length of time a unit or formation is in action, the weight of enemy shelling, the state of physical exhaustion of the personnel, the magnitude of the casualties suffered by a unit and the discomforts from bad weather conditions."[55]

The most significant changes noted by the psychiatrists were an increase of physically exhausted cases and, as Moll noted, "an increase in the incidence of psychiatric casualties among individuals of long service and good motivation."[56] Colonel Van Nostrand observed the same phenomenon during his visit, remarking that "as the campaign progresses, we are all noting the increasing number of soldiers with good histories who are breaking down under the cumulative effects of service."[57] Lieutenant-Colonel Doyle was more expansive in his December report on conditions. He also noticed that "an unusually high per cent of the neuropsychiatric casualties were soldiers who had originally been stable and good men."[58] The psychiatric rate, Doyle wrote, reached 35 per cent of total casualties and 50 per cent of wounded in the worst period. He remarked that the situation had been much the same in the Ortona winter, and related incidence to morale lowered by casualties, weather, and interminable, inconclusive operations, "Neuropsychiatric casualties," he reported, "rose sharply to the extent that DDMS, I Canadian Corps, warned the GOC, I Canadian Corps, that the indications suggested the troops were about at their limit as an efficient fighting force." Doyle speculated that "for Canadian troops it is probably safe to say that when the neuropsychiatric casualties reach 20% of total battle casualties, (killed, wounded, PWs and missing) the formation concerned is tired and morale is dropping seriously."[59]

Burnout from long exposure became more common as the campaign went on. Earlier, Colonel Van Nostrand had written that "normal soldiers may develop severe psychiatric disease after being subjected to weeks, months or years of stresses which have no parallel in civilian life;" and he remarked on cases of officers, many with "excellent military records and no previous history of instability ... wearing service decorations," who had broken down from cumulative physical and mental stress.[60] This point was made by Lord Moran in his classic essay, *The Anatomy of Courage*. Lord Moran concluded that every soldier had his breaking point because "courage is will-power, whereof no man has an unlimited stock." He compared the supply of courage to an individual's bank account. "A man's courage is his capital and he is always spending. The call on the bank may be only the drain of the front line or it may be a sudden draft which threatens to close the account."[61]

In the 1944-45 Italian winter withdrawals outpaced deposits. Sudden drafts could come in infinitely varied forms to topple soldiers over the edge: a close shell burst, the death of a particularly close friend, some inexplicable terror in the night, or incremental loss of hope. Each had his own fears and preferences. One platoon commander recalled how he "deliberately left the bandaging of the wounded to stretcher-bearers and my sergeant: my job was to fight and I did not with to impair my ability to do so by more horror than I had to see." He went on to say that "on my worst occasion of all (when a shell landed among five of my men and I was the closest to them, three yards away) I handled the shell dressings, the morphine, and gathering the limbs and flesh alone: I had already seen it all and I decided that it would be better if no one else in my company saw it all too."[62] One courageous senior commander deliberately stopped visiting his wounded men in hospital after an especially disturbing incident that moved him so deeply that he feared a similar experience might affect his ability to command.[63] Yet another well-decorated platoon commander remembered that "if you had something to do it was not so bad, but lying in a slit trench during a shelling, the thought would occur to you that putting one foot up in an exposed position might be a sensible thing to do."[64]

More ordinary events could be equally devastating. "Marital problems I think are the chief of these," one psychiatrist wrote. "One man last week received a letter from his wife, who had previously told him she was finished with him, stating that she was sure God would find a way of permitting her to marry her new found mate. The subject said: 'the only conclusion I can draw is that she is praying for me to be killed.' He had been a good soldier but now he is depressed, anxious and without that intangible something which makes a man actually want to live in mud and cold and risk his life hourly for $1.50 per day. The men who have married in England and whose wives are pregnant don't do too well."[65]

Mail from home was not always a blessing. One soldier recalled the 1944 Christmas:

I remember we were in a school house just south of Bagnacavallo and the Christmas present we all received was on our minds. We poured [sic] over that Christmas mail like hungry dogs, I can tell you. We got some rum. A good friend of mine was reading his mail when all of a sudden I heard a whimper and he had just learned that his mother had died some weeks back. We continued to read through the pile and he let out another cry; this time he learned his father had died. After five years of tension he just went to pieces, yelling and crying. We got some rum. We were all his friends – it was Christmas. We were more than friends; we were brothers now and you know, we got him quiet and he didn't have to go to the Medical Officer for his nerves. In our group we handled it – we solved our problems. It made it all the tougher when you lost someone. I couldn't have felt worse if my own brother were to die.[66]

That unit looked after their own, the best means of looking after soldiers on the brink. So did others at the same 1944 Christmas: "On Christmas Eve a company-sergeant-major who had seemed a reasonable sort of chap up until then, arrived at the stone hovel where I was set up, in a state of near hysterics. He wept like a broken-hearted child, saying he could not go on, that we were all being murdered and for no good reason. It was difficult not to agree with him, but of course that could never be. I had him bundled off to 'B' Echelon for a 'rest'. Had he not been gotten safely out of the way in this manner he most certainly would have ended up with a court-martial. Also, his effect on the morale of the Junior NCOs and men could have caused complete demoralization."[67]

Most units did what they could. Officers and NCOs observing behavioural changes in dependable men could get them back to the company kitchen for a few days rest, but cooks could use only so many potato-peelers and some soldiers ended up in the medical stream. Each case was unique. At about this time one of Moll's colleagues described the difficult professional dilemma the psychiatrists faced in diagnosing and handling worn-out men.

This is exemplified by the man who was evacuated in an acute anxiety state. He was unable to sleep properly or eat his meals. He displayed marked objective signs of autonomic disability, i.e., tremor, tension, wet palms, fast pulse. His civilian record is good. He gave excellent service in offensive action for a period of months. After convalescence he has no complaints, shows no signs of sympathetic over-reaction. The problem is, should he return to duty when he frankly states "I can't go back. I know I can't stand it. I have lost my desire to kill Jerries."

Such a man has proven his ability to withstand front line service. He is a dependable type. There is no question of doubting his belief. There is always a temptation to regard such a man as one who has given his share of service. "Others have done less – let then have a crack at the front lines. Downgrade him."

However, this solution is not fair to the man. It is a dangerous precedent for him. One defeat is no reason for giving up. He has to remember that he will have to overcome difficulties in army and civil life. His self-respect demands that he return again, when he is fit ...

In individual cases the decision may be hard. But there is no room for sentiment since victory is the first requirement of the army.[68]

Combing convalescent depots and converting non-combatants could not balance the deficit in men, however, and commanders tightened discipline. In that second Italian winter of discontent the invisible boundary between medical and disciplinary alternatives blurred even further. With little to look forward to except misery, mutilation, or death, more soldiers crossed the line into military crime. There were 2,088 field general courts martial in Italy in 1944, and another 936 in the first months of 1945.[69] The 1st Division's historical officer reported in December that "at the present time all Brigades are busily occupied with Courts Martial, chiefly desertion and AWL charges."[70] One officer has described his experience in defending a soldier charged with hiding away while his section assaulted a farmhouse. The defending officer suggested that his man plead guilty because the combat-wise court president would probably understand fully how a soldier might not always behave courageously. However, unknown to him, a new non-combatant president appeared along with a lawyer from a distant Judge Advocate General's office. The latter informed the defending officer that "it appears that too many accused have been getting off with light sentences or even scot-free. I've been sent down to make sure the court is properly advised on the conduct of the trial, the interpretation of the evidence and the appropriate sentence."[71]

The court "threw the book at the accused,"[72] conforming to a general policy of meting out exemplary sentences to deter soldiers from behaving in unsoldierly ways. In World War I exemplary punishment was death by firing squad; in World War II it was three to five years imprisonment at hard labour, along with dishonourable discharge.[73] Sentences of two, three, or five years were awarded for a number of offences related to unbecoming conduct while in contact with the enemy. They included absence without leave for a few hours, desertion, cowardice, or leaving a reinforcement draft proceeding to the front.

Whether a soldier ended up in prison rather than in his company kitchen, Moll's exhaustion unit, or an SEC was largely a matter of chance. Aside from extremes, many cases could legitimately have ended in any of the alternatives. The no-man's land between courage and cowardice was broad, as an Eighth Army report acknowledged in some detail:

Some deserters were genuine cowards – men who deliberately set out to avoid action; their number, however, was probably no greater relatively than in any other campaign. The most serious aspect of the problem in Italy was the number of soldiers with good records who eventually broke down under the strain of prolonged action.

One of the principal causes of such collapse was the need to return men again and again to the line after evacuation for wounds or exhaustion. Men felt that they would go on being sent back into the line until they were killed, totally incapacitated by wounds, or broke down and deserted. The absence of any prospect of home leave, and the long period of overseas service greatly strengthened the feeling, to which many succumbed, that it would be better to spend the time in the safety and comparative comfort of a military prison rather than to return to the line with so little hope of final relief.

Some cases of desertion, moreover, were genuinely due to matrimonial and family troubles arising from long service overseas. Infidelity or suspected infidelity on the part of their wives at home led men to desert from the feeling that they had nothing left for which to fight.

Wastage from casualties and other causes resulted in a turn-over of personnel within units amounting in some cases to almost 100 per cent within a period of three months. As a result man-management inevitably suffered since officers and NCOs were often strangers to their men, and a fresh reinforcement might be drafted into a unit and committed to battle without his section or platoon commander even having the opportunity of knowing him by name and sight. Junior officers, again, were often inexperienced and failed to recognize the early signs of battle exhaustion, so that men sometimes remained in the lines when they should have been evacuated for rest or for psychiatric treatment.[74]

The increasing numbers of non-effective soldiers in Italy indicate the scope of the problem. When I Canadian Corps moved to Holland in the spring of 1945 to join the rest of the First Canadian Army for the last months of the war, Lieutenant-Colonel Doyle surveyed the residue of soldiers remaining in Italy who were inmates of the Eighth Army's military prisons. There were 1,033 scattered among one Canadian and nine British detention facilities. Another 100 were awaiting trial or sentence and there were 500 deserters at large. Doyle had detailed records of 584 of those detained. Eighty per cent were serving sentences of from one to five years hard labour. Almost half were first offenders. The great majority "had previously been well-behaved soldiers and usually their first offence had to do with their conduct in the face of the enemy or in anticipation of enemy action." Doyle diagnosed 32 per cent of them as psychiatric cases – "among those were a number who had previously been evacuated or had been treated in their unit echelons for exhaustion and had been returned to duty after treatment. All of this neuropsychiatric group had been guilty of being AWL or desertion usually at the time the unit was in action or when action was imminent. Many of them had appealed to their officers ... Among this group were a number who had previously been wounded." Eighty-two per cent of the soldiers were infantrymen.[75] The numbers are significant. Along with about 1,300 soldiers in SECs they totalled almost 3,000 – close to an infantry division's fighting strength.

This pattern of behaviour, which blurred medical and legal distinctions, was not solely a Canadian phenomenon. British deserters and absentees hovered around 1,000 a month during the 1944-45 winter. "Of these, 600 cases occurred in one division which had a distinguished fighting record, had been considerably reinforced in the Middle East and on return to Italy went straight into the line and remained there throughout the winter. This division was not engaged in any major operation for four months, but was subjected to the strain and tedium of holding the line in arduous conditions without substantial relief.''[76] Eleven British military prisons, detention barracks, and field punishment camps incarcerated more than 5,000 soldiers at their grim fullest. The equivalent of another division's resources was needed to accommodate them.

In the United States Fifth Army, "Perhaps the major daily preoccupation of the 'veteran' division psychiatrists during this time (November 1944-April 1945) was the examination before court-martial of disciplinary offenders who had been charged with desertion, misbehavior before the enemy, or similar military offences generally subsumed under the informal category of 'AWOL from battle' ... During this inactive period, each division psychiatrist saw literally hundreds of such offenders.''[77] At least 5,000 American soldiers were imprisoned. Most were judged to have some psychiatric impairment.[78] For soldiers in all three armies the Italian campaign was one of unlimited liability. There was no rotation policy worth the name. Soldiers fought until they were killed, wounded, luckily found an honourable way out, or took their own evasive action.

Looking round the mountains
   in the mud and the rain,
There's lots of little crosses,
   some which bear no name.
Blood, sweat and tears and toil
   are gone,
The boys beneath them slumber on.
These are your D-Day Dodgers,
   who'll stay in Italy.

Author unknown

CHAPTER SIX

Normandy

The Battle Exhaustion Crisis of July 1944

Operation Overlord, the invasion of North-West Europe in 1944, was one of the most complex military operations ever undertaken. Between the spring of 1943, when planning began, and June 1944, thousands of staff officers prepared reports on almost every aspect of the scheme. It was not, however, until February of 1944 that 21 Army Group, General B.L. Montgomery's Anglo-Canadian invasion force, allowed the appointment of a psychiatric adviser. Even then Montgomery's senior staff, including the DMS, Major-General E. Philips, were reluctant to commit resources to treating psychiatric casualties. Philips did not fully abandon his view that psychiatry was "a new form of witchcraft until the front had stabilized in Normandy and battle exhaustion presented a very serious situation."[1]

Lieutenant-Colonel Tom Main, the psychiatric adviser, firmly believed that a carefully screened division would develop few psychiatric casualties and he seems to have shared the prevailing view that battle exhaustion would not be a major problem in the British Liberation Army.[2] The system of treating neuropsychiatric casualties that 21 Army Group was prepared to accept for the invasion of North-West Europe was embodied in standing orders issued in April 1944. The regulations required that psychiatric casualties be classified as sick and labelled "exhaustion."[3] All men sent back from the regimental aid post were to be sedated and accompanied by a responsible person. If a Corps exhaustion centre had opened all casualties would be sent there, otherwise they would enter the general evacuation stream. RMOs were told that during battle acute cases were to be treated with: "i) sound sleep under general sedation; ii) restoration of an individual sense of security; iii) reintegration with their original fighting group."[4]

During quiet periods RMOs were to ensure that men and especially officers got enough rest. "Sleep reserves should be stored up, especially in key men. Officers should be encouraged to learn to snatch short periods of sleep during the day whenever possible in order that they may visit posts during the night without gross fatigue. Unreliable men should be sent to the Unit 'B' Echelon. Officers should be made aware that fatigue is the biggest single threat to the morale of their men and that during a lull even of 30 minutes, all who can should take advantage of it for a rest."[5] All of this was a considerable advance on the planning for any previous campaign[6] but the assumption that the RMO would be capable of handling exhaustion casualties in the midst of battle must have been based on the belief that there would be few such casualties.

The British approach was in sharp contrast to American ideas about the probable incidence of psychiatric casualties in Overlord. Under the direction of Colonel Hanson the United States Army had carefully monitored neuropsychiatric casualties in Tunisia, Sicily, and Italy. The Americans discovered that approximately 16 per cent of their non-fatal battle casualties were neuropsychiatric. This level rose to as much as 35 per cent during intense fighting. It was further shown that battle experience "provided no prophylaxis against breakdown."[7] Indeed in Sicily veteran troops had shown the highest rates of combat exhaustion. The United States Army had been working hard to develop a system of forward psychiatry that it hoped would limit such casualties and result in a high rate of return to combat. Each US division was to have a psychiatrist on staff and medical officers were to be thoroughly trained in prevention and treatment of neuropsychiatric casualties. This system was to prove its worth in Normandy.

The Canadian medical and administrative staff found themselves in an awkward position. Van Nostrand knew from Doyle's reports on Ortona that neuropsychiatric casualties might form as much as "10 per cent to 15 per cent of all battle casualties"[8] and he wanted to maintain the system of divisional psychiatry that Doyle had pioneered in Italy. Canadians would, however, be serving in a combined British-Canadian force* and he was informed that the psychiatric organization must "follow as closely as is practical that of the British Army."[9] Van Nostrand interpreted this mandate in his own way. He decided that it was essential to maintain a separate system for the treatment of Canadian psychiatric casualties and promptly appointed psychiatrists to work with each Canadian division. He also insisted on the closest possible liaison with the United States Army, which was appointing divisional psychiatrists and training them at a new school of military neuropsychiatry.

---

* 21 Army Group, the Anglo-Canadian force for North-West Europe, consisted of the Second British Army and the First Canadian Army. Until 23 July when the First Canadian Army became operational, the Second British Army controlled the Canadian as well as the British troops in the bridgehead. The 3rd Canadian Division served in I British Corps until 15 July when it combined with the 2nd Canadian Division to form II Canadian Corps.

Dr Robert Gregory[10] was Van Nostrand's choice for the 3rd Canadian Infantry Division, which was to land in France on D-Day. Gregory took up his position in March 1944 and immediately began a program of talks to RMOs outlining a procedure wherein all but the "mildest" exhaustion cases would be sent to a specially designated Field Ambulance. Only the divisional psychiatrist would be authorized to evacuate men beyond that level. Gregory wanted medical officers in each Field Ambulance to be "trained in the ordinary mechanical end of the treatment" and urged that "courses for two officers from each Field Ambulance be arranged with the American Army hospital of Psychiatry at the earliest possible time."[11] The Division's senior medical officer, ADMS Colonel M.C. Watson, endorsed Gregory's work and in April space was found for the Canadian doctors at the American school. Gregory attended the sessions and reported: "The course includes ... the outline of treatment of combat exhaustion in its different forms and actual demonstrations of how the cases should be handled. It was suggested that, insofar as possible, the exhaustion cases should be kept separate from the wounded principally for reasons of morale. The three MOs, one from each Field Ambulance in the division, were extremely pleased and interested. They will be expected to act as aids to the Divisional Psychiatrist should conditions be such that treatment may be established at the Field Ambulance level. If treatment of the cases is further back they will be expected to check all exhaustion cases for proper sedation ... so that in evacuation they will be quiet and not upset the morale of the others."[12]

Gregory also noted that copies of the American guidelines on exhaustion had been obtained and would be used in the talks that the RMOs were to give to the officers and NCOs of their units. "These are men who will be in direct contact with the soldiers in the fighting and will be the ones who have the best chance of observing early symptoms. If the predromal symptoms can be recognized by these it may be possible to get the exhaustion cases early enough to treat them within unit lines and avoid having them 'crack'."[13]

Preparations for forward treatment of battle exhaustion occurred in conjunction with a screening of the division. Gregory had read Doyle's reports from the Mediterranean and was quite willing to assist units in getting rid of neurotics and "inadequates" who were "apt to give trouble in action,"[14] but during a three-month period in which all units were carefully "weeded" only 127 men were removed on psychiatric grounds. Gregory was more concerned about the reinforcement units that would supply the division where "there is much to be desired in the training of replacements and the keeping up of their morale."[15] The 3rd Division as a whole, Gregory reported, was in fine shape. "The general morale throughout the division is excellent. The troops are relaxed and in the highest spirits. Some of the officers and practically all other ranks feel that our troops will go twenty-five miles in one day, that they have the fire power, the naval support and air superiority. There seems to be no talk of hazard."[16]

The Canadian troops that landed on D-Day were the best-prepared, best-trained body of men that the Canadian Army had committed to battle during World War II. All but a few however, were new to combat and they suffered the agonies of uncertainty common to all "green" soldiers.

Experience in other campaigns had suggested that battle exhaustion would be quite low in the initial days of fighting.[17] Psychiatrists had been forced to note this fact, but they had great difficulty in explaining it. The most common assumption about battle exhaustion – predisposition – provided little insight into this situation. Some psychiatrists suggested that soldiers with a poor history were able to keep their anxiety under control for a short time through an effort of will. A rise in exhaustion casualties, they assumed, would begin after such individuals had been exposed to a longer period of stress.[18]

Gregory reached the battle zone on the evening of D-Day + 2, 8 June.[19] Overall the landings in the Anglo-Canadian sector had been far less difficult and costly in terms of casualties than had been anticipated, but neither the Canadians nor anyone else had gone "twenty to twenty-five miles in one day." Instead the bridgehead was scarcely more than four miles in depth. The Canadian 9 Brigade had been struck by a sharp counter-attack on 7 June and had withdrawn to a "brigade fortress." Its advance guard, the North Nova Scotia Highlanders, lost 242 men, half its combat manpower. The supporting armoured regiment, the Sherbrooke Fusiliers, had 21 tanks destroyed with 60 crew casualties, 20 per cent of its strength.[20]

The 7 Brigade had reached its initial objective and had dug in astride the Caen-Bayeux highway. By the afternoon of 8 June it was under heavy attack, and this continued through the night. The Royal Winnipeg Rifles, which had suffered 128 casualties on D-Day, were overrun during the day losing a further 256 men.[21] With two-thirds of the riflemen in the regiment on the casualty list, the battalion was, for the moment, a spent force. Losses in other units were on a smaller scale, but no one in the bridgehead had escaped a baptism of fire.

Units of the 3rd (British) Division on the Canadian left and the 50th (Northumbrian) on the right had similar experiences in the first days of the invasion, but as far as can be determined the number of exhaustion cases everywhere was quite small. Gregory used 22 Canadian Field Ambulance to deal with patients from the four Canadian brigades and treated approximately forty men with forty-eight hours of sedated rest.[22] Weekly figures for the two British assault divisions and the 6th British Airborne are not readily available but medical officers reported that there were "no exhaustion cases on the day of the assault."[23]

The initial bridgehead battles were over by 11 June. The British-Canadian forces spent the next two weeks holding the perimeter under continuous shelling and mortaring. Offensive operations were confined to relatively minor probing attacks designed to hold the Germans on the eastern flank. Battle exhaustion casualties remained well below the percentages reported in Italy. On the American front, where the priority assigned to the capture of Cherbourg required continuous attacks, exhaustion ratios were similarly about half the number indicated by the experience of heavy fighting in Italy.[24] Differences in diagnosis and reporting made all these psychiatric numbers doubtful, but everyone in the bridgehead agreed with Major D.J. Watterson, the 2nd British Army's psychiatrist, when on 24 June he described the "ratio of exhaustion as lower than expected, probably 10 per cent or a little more."[25] (In North-West Europe the terms NP ratio or exhaustion ratio expressed the relationship between psychiatric casualties and all *non-fatal* casualties, including psychiatric ones). Watterson reported that the initial psychiatric casualties included large numbers of men who were "unfit for front line duty" and who had been weeded out by "a process of natural selection." This factor, as well as the high rate of breakdowns among "unit residues"[26] (those brought over from other units as immediate reinforcements), would, he believed, begin to diminish in importance leaving only the true battle exhaustion cases for psychiatrists to deal with.

True battle exhaustion cases, according to Watterson, were those men of normal personality who broke down when their personal morale failed. This, he maintained, was usually the result of a collapse in unit morale. He noted that the importance of good leadership in limiting psychiatric casualties "had been brought out clearly again and again" during the June battles. The cause of a rise in the NP rate, he wrote, could only be understood in the context of the battalion: "Is the unit well led? Are its welfare needs attended to? Is the post coming up to scratch? Do the men know the latest German weapons? Does the unit need resting?"[27] These and other similar questions had to be answered if battle exhaustion was to be understood.

Canadian medical officers agreed with Watterson. Gregory was confident that everything was under control. He reported that the low incidence of exhaustion in the 3rd Canadian Division was evidence of the successful "weeding" of the division while the 200-odd breakdowns were proof "that a division cannot be completely weeded." He added that "the numbers and percentage of NP casualties bears no relation to the daily total casualties but bears the usual relation to the conditions of troops (fatigue etc.), the tactical situation and the stiffness of resistance e.g. the greatest number of NP casualties occurred when the troops were very tired, very static, dug-in and under heavy counterattack. Fully 80 per cent of the NP casualties complained bitterly of mortar fire and 88 mm. artillery."[28]

These optimistic views were not fully shared by senior British and Canadian officers. An NP ratio of 10 was acceptable, but not if almost all such casualties were evacuated to England instead of being returned to unit. Psychiatrists kept saying that if exhaustion casualties were treated quickly, and near the front, the return to unit rate would be dramatically increased. Yet they were evacuating thousands of men[29] who apparently needed longer treatment than forty-eight hours, the maximum period any type of casualty was to be held in the narrow Normandy bridgehead.

Major-General Philips, the DMS for 21 Army Group, went to Normandy in early July to find out what was happening. "Psychiatry," he reported, "is getting out of hand." The Second Army needed a senior consultant psychiatrist to come to Normandy "with a view to tightening up."[30] In fact a good deal had been done to try and stop the flow of psychiatric cases to the UK. On 14 June XXX Corps* had opened its exhaustion centre and was able to keep a small number of promising cases for further treatment.[31] The operation of the other Corps exhaustion units was delayed a week because of the narrowness of the eastern bridgehead but two casualty clearing stations were designated for exhaustion cases. On 25 June the 200-bed advance section of No. 32 Psychiatric Hospital opened on "Harley Street" near Bayeux.[32] By 4 July, a rest centre for psychiatric and medical cases in need of further treatment (up to fourteen days) had been established.[33] All of these measures, some planned, some improvised, were intended to tackle the problem of the low return to duty rate experienced during the June battles. No one was anticipating the enormous increase in exhaustion casualties that occurred in July.

On 24 June General Montgomery launched the first of a series of major offensive operations designed to capture the City of Caen and break out into the open country to the south. By mid-July the small infantry component of 21 Army Group, less than 15 per cent of the total manpower in the bridgehead, had suffered enormous casualties. On average one in every four of these casualties was due to battle exhaustion.[34] On the western flank the United States Army, pressing toward St Lo, in the difficult boccage country, was experiencing even heavier total casualties with a similar NP rate.[35] In retrospect it is possible to argue that the battles of late June and July wore down the German defenders and precipitated a major collapse of enemy morale, but this was not apparent to anyone at the time. During July the Allied armies were too concerned about their own crisis in troop morale to wonder about the enemy's problems.

The battle exhaustion crisis began to appear during Operation Epsom, General Montgomery's first all-out offensive since the landings. On 23 June troops of the 51st (Highland) Division, veterans of the Eighth Army in North Africa and Sicily, launched a preliminary attack that met fierce resistance followed by a sharp counter-attack from a 21 Panzer Division. Exhaustion

---

* The Second British Army was composed of XXX Corps, VII Corps, XII Corps, and I Corps. I Corps became part of the First Canadian Army 23 July.

casualties accounted for 30 per cent of their losses.[36] The 51st Division had been engaged in unspectacular but intense "contact with the enemy" for two weeks. Regimental War Diaries for June record a steady stream of casualties, largely from mortaring.[37] Their lack of success in the attempt to hit back may have had some effect on the numbers evacuated for exhaustion.

At the other end of the British-Canadian zone, 49th (West Riding) Division's part in Epsom began on the morning of 25 June when two of its brigades attempted to force their way through a position held by elements of the 12 ss Hitler Youth Division and the German tank division known as Panzer Lehr. The 49th was a "green division" which had been in action for several weeks without signs of difficulty. In Epsom more than 200 exhaustion cases appeared in the first two days, accounting for 30 per cent of the casualties. After Epsom exhaustion casualties continued to be a problem in the 49th Division accounting for 25 per cent of non-fatal casualties in July.[38] At the end of the month the divisional commander instituted a board of enquiry to investigate the causes and to explain the widely varying figures between units.[39] In the same period the 3rd and 50th British divisions, the other British infantry divisions that had been in action throughout June, were also subject to rapidly rising exhaustion ratios, as was the infantry brigade of the 7th Armoured Division.[40]

For the 3rd British Division the battle that marked this turning point was Chateau de La Londe, 27-29 June, an engagement the British press described as the "Grimmest Mile in France."[41] Here its battalions had fought for control of a two-square-mile area until most of the officers and NCOs were casualties and rifle companies were reduced to skeletons. After 29 June the 3rd Division's NP rate skyrocketed and during July more than one in every three casualties was due to battle exhaustion. By the end of that month, the division had treated almost a thousand men as NP casualties.[42]

The 3rd Canadian Division fought in two phases – the battle for Carpiquet on 4 July and Operation Charnwood, the capture of Caen, 8 July. The 8 Canadian Brigade attacked Carpiquet village with what appeared to be overwhelming fire support. In addition to a Canadian armoured regiment, and two squadrons of specialized armour from the 79th Armoured Division, fire from the 16-inch guns of a Royal Navy battleship as well as from twenty field, eight medium and one heavy artillery regiments (a total of 432 guns) were linked in a fire plan that seemed certain to saturate the defences with high explosives. Nor was air power neglected. Attacks on pre-arranged targets were planned and Brigadier K.A. Blackader, commander of 8 Brigade, had two squadrons of Typhoons on call. The right flank of the brigade was extended by the Royal Winnipeg Rifles (7 Brigade), who were to capture the south hangars at the airport, while to their right troops of the 43rd (Wessex) Division were to move forward to prevent a counter-attack.[43]

Carpiquet village and airport were defended by several platoons (40 to 60 men) of young Panzer Grenadiers from the 12 ss Hitler Youth division.

Well dug-in, or entrenched in concrete bunkers, they survived the Allied barrage. Their own artillery and mortar fire, which had been registered upon every square metre of the mile-long expanse of grain fields crossed by the Canadians, devastated the brigade. Carpiquet village was captured but the Winnipegs were twice turned back from the south hangar area. It proved impossible to send the reserve battalion forward to the second objective. The troops in Carpiquet dug in under a deluge of artillery shells and mortar bombs. Carpiquet, so the Régiment de la Chaudière War Diarist wrote, had "become a true inferno."[44]

The events of 4 July involved five battalions, but the reserve battalion, the Queen's Own Rifles, was not heavily engaged and the 10th Armoured Regiment listed just eight killed and twelve wounded. The other three infantry battalions lost 105 men killed and 223 wounded. Approximately 50 additional men were treated for battle exhaustion on 4 July and almost as many the following day.[45] The medical War Diary of the 3rd Canadian Division described exhaustion cases as "the outstanding problem for the ADMS" and reported that he had urged units to keep "a reserve of left-out-of-battle personnel so that physical exhaustion cases could be sent out for rest and replaced by fresh reinforcements." The next day battalion officers were described as "co-operating wholeheartedly with this recommendation" and the ADMS expressed the hope that "the true battle exhaustion cases" would be sent to a Field Ambulance only after a rest within their unit.[46] Colonel Watson believed that this would alleviate some of the strain on medical units, but it did not really address the problems exposed by Carpiquet. The attack on Carpiquet was, in fact, the beginning of a month-long crisis for the 3rd Division, a crisis closely paralleled in most British and American divisions where the strain of the Normandy battle and the steady stream of casualties taxed human resources beyond capacity.[47]

For the Canadians the initial consequences of the "failure" at Carpiquet were demands for the removal of Major-General Rod Keller from command of the division. Both the Corps Commander, Lieutenant-General John Crocker and the Army Commander, Lieutenant-General Miles Dempsey wrote to Montgomery immediately after the battle, noting that the Canadians were not performing well and asking for Keller to be removed.[48] This was a delicate business for British officers, who were well aware that the Canadians did not take kindly to interference with their units, and Keller was not replaced until he was wounded in August.[49]

Before any further postmortems on Carpiquet could be conducted the remainder of the division was committed to the battle for Caen, which opened on the night of 7 July with the first use of the RAF's heavy bombers in direct support of a ground operation. The intended relationship between bombing "four map squares on the northern outskirts of Caen"[50] and an infantry attack on a ring of fortified villages outside the target zone has never been made clear.[51] The bombing had no immediate effect on German resistance. Canadian War Diaries do, however, report an enormous boost to morale at the sight of hundreds of seemingly invulnerable bombers streaming across the skies over Caen. It might reasonably be supposed that this demonstration of Allied power had the opposite effect on the German soldier, but if so it was not yet a sufficient blow to his self-confidence to reduce his will to resist the Anglo-Canadian advance.

For the people of Caen and for the soldiers who fought towards the city 8 July was a day of terrible bloodletting. Over 600 battle casualties were suffered by 9 Infantry Brigade, which led the Canadian attack. The total for the division was 1,194 of which 330 were fatal.[52] About 100 additional men were treated for battle exhaustion.[53] It was also a very difficult day for the 3rd British Division and nothing short of a nightmare for the newly arrived 59th (Staffordshire) Division, which lost well over a thousand men in its first twenty-four hours of combat.[54] Carpiquet and Caen were to be followed in ten days by Operation Goodwood, which would produce another 386 battle casualties for the 3rd Canadian Division. By 21 July the division had been in combat for six weeks and had casualties almost equal to its total strength in riflemen. Indeed, 75 per cent or more of these casualties had occurred in rifle companies of the division and the losses of officers and NCOs had been, as expected, proportionately very high.[55]

The experiences of the 3rd Canadian Division's individual battalions, however, had varied during June and July, making generalizations about divisions very difficult. Take the case of 7 Brigade. The Canadian Scottish Regiment's total casualties for the two months were 136 killed and 421 "wounded." These casualties meant that of the 37 officers and 751 other ranks who landed on D-Day only 15 officers and 321 other ranks were still with the unit in late July. Twenty-two of the original thirty-eight officers had become casualties in the seven-week period. The overall casualty rate had not increased (287 in July to 284 in June) but battle exhaustion evacuations climbed from 31 in June to 86 in the following month.[56]

The Canadian Scottish were, by the standards of the Allied armies, a well-trained, well-led unit. The commanding officer in Normandy, Lieutenant-Colonel F.N. Cabeldu, was a highly regarded officer who was promoted to command a brigade at the end of the Normandy battle. Both Cabeldu and his RMO approached the question of battle exhaustion with a genuine concern for the men in their care. During the seven weeks twenty-four men had been sent to "Corps Rest Camp, and a large number (approx. 36) withdrawn from the front line during periods of relative quiet." These men, "in the opinion of the Company Commanders and the MO required 24 or 48 hours rest,"[57] and were not included in the battle exhaustion figures. The Canadian Scottish was not the regiment it had been in early June but it remained a well-led cohesive unit.

Such detailed information is not available for other 3rd Division battalions but approximations can be made. The Royal Winnipeg Rifles, with more than 250 killed and 300 wounded by 6 July (reliable exhaustion figures are not available), were in such bad shape that they were used very sparingly for the remainder of the month. The Winnipeg co was, by July, unable to lead effectively and the company commanders had to do the best they could until he was relieved in October.[58]

The D-Day losses of the Regina Rifles, the third regiment in the Western (7) Brigade, had been similar to those of the Winnipegs but most had occurred in a reserve company that had encountered mined beach obstacles. In fierce battles on 8 and 9 June the "Johns," as the Regina Rifles styled themselves, had taken the best that the 12 ss could give and had maintained their position with a consequent boost in morale. Lieutenant-Colonel F.M. Matheson, who was to stay with the Reginas throughout the campaign, seems to have been a good co in a well-organized unit and battle exhaustion casualties were quite low in the Reginas.[59] Nevertheless, like the Canadian Scottish, the Reginas required rebuilding after the battle for Caen. Integrating the replacements would be a major challenge for Matheson and his remaining officers, but overall 7 Brigade was in comparatively good shape.

By contrast, 8 Brigade was seen as a problem throughout much of the war. One of its battalions, Le Régiment de La Chaudière, would show consistently high rates of battle exhaustion, self-inflicted wounds, desertion, and absence without leave.[60] These problems, added to the constant shortage of French-speaking reinforcements left the "Chauds," who displayed great bravery and endurance in a number of battles, almost always seriously understrength. After Carpiquet the regiment had to be used with care, mainly in a supporting role.[61]

The North Shore (New Brunswick) Regiment had performed well on D-Day, seizing St Aubin-sur-Mer and pressing inland at a cost of just over 100 casualties. Between 6 June and 4 July it had suffered the steady drain of losses that holding a defensive perimeter entailed. Then came Carpiquet, which the first generation of North Shores called the "graveyard of the regiment."[62] Major J.E. Anderson provides a chilling account of that day: "I am sure that at some time during the attack every man felt he could not go on. Men were being killed or wounded on all sides and the advance seemed pointless as well as hopeless. I never realized until the attack at Carpiquet how far discipline, pride of unit and above all, pride in oneself and family can carry a man, even when each step forward meant possible death."[63] "Pride of unit, pride in oneself and family" were reservoirs of strength that could quickly be depleted. The North Shore, during July, was a regiment that had lost too many leaders. Its exhaustion ratio was second only to that of the Chaudières[64] in the 3rd Division and their continued effectiveness was seriously in question.

The third battalion in 8 Brigade, the Queen's Own Rifles of Canada, could trace its history back to the mid-nineteenth century and the regiment had been active ever since. In the pre-war years when militia soldiering carried little prestige, the Queen's Own were able to draw upon a strong regimental tradition in Toronto.[65] But tradition could not prevent their taking the heaviest casualties of any Canadian unit on D-Day and one company had been virtually wiped out while supporting an early attempt to use the armoured brigade as an offensive weapon.[66] The Queen's Own were, however, virtually unscathed by Carpiquet or the battle for Caen. Their exhaustion ratio was above the divisional average but there is no indication that they shared the malaise that affected their sister regiments in 8 Brigade.[67]

On D-Day 9 Brigade had been in reserve. One battalion, the North Nova Scotia Highlanders, had been devastated while advancing along the road from Beny-sur-Mer to Carpiquet on 7 June. Casualties (84 dead, 128 men taken prisoner, and 30 wounded) put the regiment in a reserve role for the rest of June. It was also involved in the battles for Caen, 8 and 18 July, and on both occasions encountered heavy resistance.[68]

The other two battalions of the brigade, the Highland Light Infantry of Canada and the Stormont, Dundas, and Glengarry Highlanders, spent most of June holding the defensive perimeter in front of Caen.[69] On 8 July the Highland Light Infantry fought their bloodiest battle of the entire North-West European campaign with 62 fatalities and 200 men wounded.[70] The Glens had significantly fewer casualties and greater success in their operations that day and may be said to have survived into mid-July in relatively good shape. All three battalions had similar battle exhaustion ratios close to the divisional average.[71]

On 25 July the North Novas were ordered to capture the village of Tilly la Campagne as part of an offensive known as Operation Spring. The task was beyond the capacity of the fittest battalion and the North Nova attack collapsed in disarray. Major-General Keller attempted to push the attack, pressuring the North Novas and ordering a second battalion, the Glens, to reinforce them.[72] To their credit both battalion commanders refused and the officer commanding 9 Brigade, Brigadier D.G. Cunningham, supported them. Keller and Lieutenant-General Guy Simonds, the Corps commander, promptly replaced all three men and ordered an enquiry into the failure of 25 July.[73]

Fortunately Colonel Watson, the division's senior medical officer, had a much better grasp of reality. He pressed the case for withdrawing the division from the line. He later described his intervention in acceptable military language. "At the end of a period of seven weeks continuous over the top type of warfare, in which the 3 Canadian Infantry Division had been involved in every type of fighting ... the officers and men generally were beginning to show signs of war weariness and physical tiredness. The ADMS Col. M.C. Watson was aware of a considerable degree of lowered fighting efficiency in some individual units and by the end of seven weeks there were indications that this situation was affecting the division as a whole. The AMDS drew the attention of the GOC to the situation by a letter which he in turn discussed with brigade commands who strongly supported the request for a rest period of seven to ten days for actual physical rest for the troops and reorganization of the units on a strong company basis. Relief commenced on 27 July 44."[74] The experience of the 3rd Canadian Division was in no way unique. All of the Allied divisions that had been in action since early June were in need of rest and varying degrees of reorganization by late July.

Not only veteran troops were caught up in the crisis of July 1944. On 12 July, the 3rd Canadian Division and 2 Armoured Brigade were joined in the bridgehead by the 2nd Canadian Division. This division had been to France once before when it had been launched against German defences at Dieppe in 1942. While every unit that had participated in that disastrous raid still included men who had been at Dieppe, the vast majority of officers and men in the rifle companies arriving in Normandy had never been in battle.

The division had undergone extensive retraining in 1943. During 1944, as Operation Overlord approached, planning had concentrated on the division's role in a breakout from the Normandy bridgehead. Particular emphasis was placed on preparing for an "assault crossing of the tidal river" which, it was assumed, would take place after the Germans had retreated to the River Seine. Long practice in cross-country movement and wide-river crossing was, no doubt, of considerable general value, but the division was never given the opportunity to train with an armoured brigade and no special measures were taken to prepare the 2nd Division for the stalemated Normandy battlefield.[75] By mid-July every Allied infantry soldier in Normandy knew that the Germans were capable of contesting every yard of that battlefield. Allied advances were possible, the artillery could shoot you on to a position, but once there you were largely on your own, subjected to endless mortar fire and sharp counter-attacks led by enemy tanks. Normandy had turned into a battle of attrition, in which victory depended on endurance and the rate at which replacements arrived.

Lieutenant-General Guy Simonds, the commander of II Canadian Corps, was a serious and knowledgeable student of war with some concrete experience in Italy. He had warned his divisional brigade and battalion commanders about the "battle of counter attacks," insisting that everyone understand German methods. In his directive on operational policy, Simonds wrote that "the effect of mortar fire makes mopping and reorganization on the objective a most difficult task for the infantry. The Germans do not hesitate to engage a position on which their own troops are still holding out ...

"The way in which the Germans support their infantry in the counter attack must be clearly understood. They move tanks or self-propelled guns to within close range of the objective they are trying to retake. They do not support by neutralizing fire, in the ordinary sense, but with aimed shellfire directed through telescopic sights at a range in which infantry dispositions can be picked out. The morale and material effect on our own troops of this type of fire is considerable."[76]

Before Overlord, Simonds had argued that the solution to this problem lay in having anti-tank guns up with the forward troops or Allies, bringing tanks "close behind the leading infantry." In Normandy the lightly armoured, undergunned Sherman tanks and the thin-walled m-10 self-propelled anti-tank guns had proven incapable of performing these tasks and the infantry was largely dependent on its own weapons and the vital radio link with the artillery regiments provided by the foo or Forward Observation Officer.[77] The evidence suggests that these lessons learned in the first weeks of the Normandy campaign were not understood by Simonds or Major-General Charles Foulkes, who commanded the 2nd Canadian Division. This ignorance had a profound effect on the fortunes of the division in its first weeks in battle.

The senior officers of the Corps and the 2nd Canadian Division had decided that psychiatric casualties were largely the creation of psychiatrists and had refused to integrate such services into the corps or divisional medical system. Van Nostrand had selected Dr John Burch as the psychiatrist for the 2nd Division in May 1944, but Burch was simply ignored.[78] Van Nostrand had also planned a corps exhaustion centre on the British model with a war establishment of two psychiatrists and eight other ranks who had been trained at Basingstoke. No. 1 CEU was supposed to be attached to a specially selected field dressing station that would provide additional staff and administrative support for a combined venereal disease and exhaustion unit.[79] The co did not much like this role for his field dressing station, but Corps Headquarters was prepared to accept an exhaustion unit so long as the division psychiatrists were reassigned. Burch and Burdett McNeel were both sent to 10 Field Dressing Station (FDS) in early June where they began to train the nursing orderlies in the rudiments of battle exhaustion treatment.[80]

British practice also called for the appointment of an adviser in psychiatry to each Corps and Burch was re-assigned to this position with Captain T.A. Fraser replacing him at the exhaustion unit. In a letter to Van Nostrand, Burch described his role as adviser to II Canadian Corps: "I was called down to Corps hurriedly and informed I was to do sick parades, but for the moment no psychiatry. Such consultations were now off and if there were any weak sisters left, the army would look after them and they were coming along – psychiatrists or no psychiatrists. And so it remained until sometime after we landed here [in France] ... when the drive over the river [Orne] was going on, McNeel had more to do in the exhaustion unit than he and Fraser could handle, and asked for me."[81]

The introduction of II Canadian Corps into the bridgehead brought the exhaustion unit to France on 9 July. Two days later McNeel was told that the exhaustion unit was no longer attached to 10 FDS and that he and his men were to report to another FDS and get ready to receive casualties. The officer commanding 6 FDS knew nothing about the exhaustion unit and showed no interest. McNeel described the situation he confronted on the eve of battle in a report written in the fall of 1944: "The opening and early function of No. 1 CEU was beset with administrative difficulties. Higher medical authority failed to appreciate the fact that psychiatric casualties would be numerous, that the facilities and equipment of both the FDS and the EU were seriously limited, and that adequate arrangements would have to be made for the evacuation or rehabilitation of men following short treatment. Repeated suggestions and requests with reference to these matters were ignored."[82] In 1983 after re-reading his wartime reports, McNeel recalled the details of one of his attempts to overcome the administrative difficulties: "I went up to Corps Headquarters and saw the DDMS. What is going to be the line of evacuation, I asked. He replied, 'there is not going to be any evacuation in this Corps'."[83]

On 18 July II Canadian Corps, composed of the 2nd and 3rd Divisions, plus 2 Armoured Brigade, began its first offensive as part of Operation Goodwood, Montgomery's attempt to "loose a corps of armoured divisions in the open country about the Caen-Falaise road."[84] The task assigned to the Canadian Corps was to capture the industrial suburbs of Caen south of the River Orne and to be prepared to advance south seizing the high ground overlooking Caen, including Verrières Ridge. The 3rd Division attacked first with 8 Brigade leading. A long day and a longer night of confused fighting in the ruins of Colombelles and Vaucelles followed, and all three brigades were drawn into the struggle. By the night of 19 July their part in Goodwood was over at a cost of 89 killed and 297 wounded.[85]

The task of the 2nd Canadian Division in Goodwood was not nearly as clear-cut as that assigned to the 3rd Division, for it was hoped that this fresh formation could be used opportunistically in an exploitation role following the success of the British armoured divisions. The uncertainty as to precisely what the battalions were to do and where they were to do it added to the very considerable strain these troops were already experiencing. The division had entered the "line" on 11 July. Under continuous mortaring it had immediately begun to suffer relatively large numbers of exhaustion cases, who in the absence of any divisional centre were evacuated to the Corps exhaustion unit.

McNeel's War Diary for the period includes the following entries:

13 July 1944: The first twelve patients arrived at 1200 hrs. The majority of these were from the RRC (Royal Regiment of Canada) which had been in action two days ... Histories were taken, each man was given three grains of Sodium Amytal and put to bed.

14 July 1944: Forty-one patients were admitted today. About 15 of these are cases which have been out of the line for about a week ... cases seen yester-

day and today have shown chiefly anxiety symptoms ... The precipita-
tion factor in most cases is said to be blast – mortar more frequently
than shell.

15 July 1944: Twenty-six patients were admitted today and with a top accommodation of 110 beds, it is apparent that our plan of two days sedation and
three days rehabilitation will not be practicable ... As we are now
discharging patients, psychotherapeutic talks to groups about to be discharged have now been instituted. These consist of simple explanations
of psychogenic symptoms "exhaustion versus shell shock" etc. ... Many
of the men understand the mechanism of their trouble alright, and most
are ready to admit that the origin is emotional rather than physical but
many are without any incentive to carry on further.

16 July 1944: Twenty-three patients have been admitted today and our bed strength
is now eighty-four.

17 July 1944: hope of adequate and rehabilitation will have to be abandoned ... The
treatment cases are without pyjamas and the convalescents have to wear
their dirty and tattered clothes.

18 July 1944: We were awakened this morning by a terrific roar of gunfire ... rumour
is that "This is it" and that the show should soon be over. So far our
admissions have not exceeded the usual level: about twenty-two today
... We face a serious shortage of sedative.[86]

One hundred and sixty patients, the large majority from the 2nd Division,
had been evacuated to the CEU in a six-day period preceding the division's
first major battle. These numbers seriously taxed its resources. This was not
a very good beginning and did not fit with preconceptions about how and
when exhaustion cases would occur.

On the morning of 18 July 4 Brigade's Royal Regiment led off with an attack
to the River Orne that was intended to determine if the river could be crossed
in force. In the course of the campaign the Royals were to be transformed
into an effective fighting unit, but in July in memory of their virtual destruction at Puits on the north side of Dieppe haunted the battalion. Their first
battle was a confused halting affair that did little for anyone's confidence.
The Corps commander decided not to push an assault across the Orne and
instead transferred the weight of the attack to the left where 5 Brigade could
cross the river into the newly-won southern edge of Caen and move directly
south towards Falaise.

For 5 Brigade, 19 July began in tragedy. Le Régiment de Maisonneuve missed
the assigned start line and instead formed up within the zone of their supporting
artillery barrage. The two companies caught in this fire were completely demoralized and had to be evacuated. Fortunately the CO organized the remaining
companies and pressed on with the advance. Both of the other units in the
brigade, the Calgary Highlanders and the Black Watch (Royal Highland

Regiment) of Canada, reached their objectives in good order and as night fell on 19 July, it was possible to think that the 2nd Division, after a bad start, was finding its feet.

There will never be an adequate explanation of the decisions made by the commanders of II Canadian Corps and the 2nd Canadian Division on 20 July. Operating Goodwood had been planned as a British *blitzkreig* and had been welcomed by the army commander, Lieutenant-General Miles Dempsey, precisely because it would take some of the pressure off the long-suffering infantry divisions. The infantry replacement crisis was already apparent to Dempsey and he insisted "that it was no part of the Goodwood plan to get drawn into a costly (infantry) struggle."[87] By the afternoon of 19 July Dempsey recognized that Goodwood had failed to create a breakthrough and that it was British not German armour that was in danger of being "written down." For 20 July he ordered the 11th and the Guards Armoured Divisions to withdraw with the infantry divisions taking over their areas. The one intact armoured division, the 7th, was to try to occupy the high ground around the village of Verrières before handing over to Canadian infantry of the 2nd Division.

Dempsey's plans and his concern for avoiding an infantry battle seem to have been misunderstood by Simonds, who ordered the 2nd Canadian Division to advance south to seize the same objective assigned to the 7th Armoured Division. This confusion was only resolved after an initial attack by the 7th Division had been repulsed. Simonds reached agreement with the British Corps commander that the Canadians would take over with the support of British tanks functioning as artillery.[88] The attack could not begin until 3:00 p.m. The four battalions assigned to the operation had been moved across the Orne during the night of 19 July, reaching their forming-up places during the morning of 20 July. Prepared for a 12:00 noon start, they were left waiting, under intermittent fire, for four to five hours.

As the troops of 6 Brigade finally moved across the start line rain began to soak the battlefield. The initial objectives were reached by the three assault battalions but "devastating mortar and artillery fire"[89] immediately descended on them, directed by observers on the high ground to their right. Attempts were made to dig in and bring the towed, six-pounder anti-tank guns forward, but the Germans launched a counter-attack with self-propelled assault guns and Panther tanks. No armour had accompanied the Canadians forward and a brave attempt by the M-10s of the 2nd Anti-tank Regiment to intervene was stopped cold by the arrival of more German armour from the direction of Verrières. The infantry had been ordered to attack a position that had been strongly reinforced by battle groups from the I and II ss Panzer Corps. As night approached and the rain continued 6 Brigade was cut off and out of touch with its headquarters. The men who were still alive lay hiding in the wheat grass until there was an opportunity to escape.

The Essex Scottish Regiment, which had been borrowed from 4 Brigade to act as reserve battalion, had been ordered forward when the lead units had reached their objectives. Their move up the slope was interrupted by a stream of soldiers abandoning the battle and then by enemy tanks. Two companies of the Essex broke and ran, discarding much of their equipment. Casualty rates in the four battalions for 20 and 21 July varied; the South Saskatchewans, who had borne the brunt of the armoured attack, lost 245 men, the Essex, 244. The Queen's Own Cameron Highlanders, who had gone to ground in the village of St André, reported just 81 casualties and the Fusiliers de Montréal, who had been unable to advance on Verrières village, lost about the same number. Overall, the 2nd Canadian Division had 249 men killed and 900 wounded in its first operation.[90]

Battle exhaustion on a very large scale was an inevitable consequence of this disaster. The War Diary of No. 1 CEU records something of the pattern:

21 July 1944: Yesterday fifty-nine patients were admitted. Today has been heavy. We have admitted over eighty patients and they are still coming in. Our routine sedative Sodium Amytal, is exhausted and most of a bottle of Medinal which we borrowed is gone. However, the day has been saved by the arrival of 2000 capsules of Sod. Amytal.

22 July 1944: One hundred and one cases of exhaustion were admitted ... our convalescent ward and the "morgues" are filled. Those in the morgue have had to sleep on blankets spread on the ground. The rain has been pouring down and the majority of the men are wet and muddy.

23 July 1944: Total bed state 175 ... treatment will have to be limited to a one or two day period. Today has been spent in sorting and evacuating as many as possible.[91]

Brigadier Farmer, the Corps senior medical officer, who had so vehemently opposed preparations for psychiatric casualties, came to see McNeel to find out what the exhaustion unit needed and to warn him that a new operation, code-named Spring, would soon be underway and "the unit should expect another increase in admissions."[92]

Spring, the battle that finally forced the decision to rest and refit the 3rd Division, was primarily a 2nd Division operation. On 22 July Montgomery had issued orders for the attachment of two British armoured divisions to II Canadian Corps. These formations, together with the two Canadian infantry divisions, were to attack by 25 July to secure the original objectives of Operation Goodwood. Montgomery's directive was passed to the Second British Army, which still commanded II Canadian Corps, and an outline plan was sent on to Lieutenant-General Simonds on 23 July.

The Canadian General was later to maintain that Spring was a "holding action," a battle designed to attract German reserves away from the American front where the decisive battle was to be fought. Whether or not this was so (the contemporary documents do not support it), it is clear that at brigade and battalion level Spring was portrayed as a major breakthrough battle requiring an all-out effort.[93] Simonds's detailed plan for Spring called for moving by night, in an attempt to overcome the problem of seizing a strongly-held ridge overlooked by German artillery on still higher ground. The troops had not been systematically trained for night attacks and after the events of 20 July only half the division would be available. But in less than forty-eight hours everything was set – at least on paper.

On 25 July, one of the blackest days in the history of the Canadian Army, a disaster of near-Dieppe proportions struck the 2nd Division. By nightfall 450 men were dead and more than 1,000 wounded, missing, or taken prisoner. The Black Watch battalion had 121 killed, 119 wounded, and 82 taken prisoner. Battle exhaustion during and immediately after this trauma added several hundred more casualties to the toll.[94] The division, after only twelve days in battle, had produced almost as many serious exhaustion cases as the 3rd Division had suffered in six weeks.

The Canadian battle exhaustion problem was fairly typical of the overall Allied experience in Normandy. NP ratios of 35 were not uncommon in battalions exposed to exceptionally adverse battle conditions. The average for the Allied armies was certainly in excess of one in every four non-fatal casualties during July. Of the three Allied armies in Normandy only the Americans were prepared to deal with thousands of exhaustion cases. Every American battalion aid station had been organized to provide primary treatment and every division had trained personnel on its medical staff. The 3rd Canadian Division had developed its psychiatric services along US lines and Gregory's divisional centre worked reasonably well. The 2nd Canadian Division and all British divisions found themselves ill-equipped to deal with the large numbers of psychiatric cases and were forced to improvise new approaches to forward psychiatry.

ON THE OTHER SIDE of the battlefield the German Army was attempting to cope with its own exhaustion crisis by tightening the disciplinary screws. German military psychiatrists had long insisted that stress breakdowns were a leadership problem not a medical one.[95] In the early years of the war, with the Germans everywhere victorious, such casualties were few. It was satisfying to attribute this to the army's emphasis on group cohesion and the responsibility of junior officers and especially NCOs for the welfare of their men.[96] But even in the days of triumph the new Nazi-inspired code of military law was dealing out death sentences and long terms of penal servitude, thus profoundly influencing military behaviour.

By 31 March 1943 more than 1,500 death sentences had been carried out, most of them for the crimes of desertion and "subverting the will of the people to fight." (Only 48 German soldiers were executed in World War I.) By mid-1944 107,000 German soldiers had been tried for absence without leave, 49,000 for disobedience, and 46,000 for contraventions against guard duty. The more serious crimes of desertion and subversion had led to between 13,000 and 15,000 cases each. More than 7,000 German soldiers had been executed for these crimes by June 1944.[97]

Battle exhaustion became a significant problem after the German Army was forced onto the defensive. Some psychiatrists tried to intervene, urging recognition of the psychogenic nature of stress reactions in battle. A script for a film about treating such casualties was completed and the office of the surgeon-general issued a statement advocating early forward treatment.[98] No doubt many German army units were already using short rest periods and "comradely comfort"[99] for stress casualties. The alternative was to allow soldiers to be caught up in a legal system that was "underpinned by its compliance with Nazi war aims and ideology." With new crimes added almost monthly in 1944-45, "death sentences rained down faster and faster each year."[100]

For most Allied soldiers in Normandy battle stress symptoms that could not be relieved at a regimental aid post meant evacuation to the rear, medical treatment, and reassignment away from combat if necessary. A diagnosis of battle exhaustion carried no stigma and held no threat of severe punishment. The German soldier breaking under severe pressure could hope for sympathy and protection from his comrades or he could allow himself to be captured. The Allied armies took more than 200,000 prisoners of war in Normandy. Many of them had surrendered in a condition suggesting complete physical exhaustion and serious nervous fatigue. McNeel, who saw many such prisoners in late July and August, was convinced that most remaining German soldiers were battle exhaustion cases by the end of the battle of the Falaise Gap.[101]

CHAPTER SEVEN

Proximity, Immediacy, and Expectancy

Forward Psychiatry in Northwest Europe, 1944-1945

The battle exhaustion crisis was just one aspect of the stalemate that developed on the Normandy battlefield that summer. The battlefield forced the British, American, and Canadian Armies to re-examine and revise many of their assumptions about the nature of modern warfare. This chapter examines the development of Canadian policy on battle exhaustion from the July crisis to the end of the war.

The Canadian experience can be examined in unique detail. The Canadian forces in North-West Europe, unlike those of the British and United States Armies, were concentrated in one sector of the battlefield. They were also relatively few in number and subject to a highly centralized system of military administration, which generated extensive records. The Canadians were, however, fighting as part of Montgomery's 21 Army Group and their approach to all facets of military enterprise was influenced by British ideas and developments. American influence was far less significant on operational military matters, but Canadian and American neuropsychiatrists had a long-established relationship that was carried forward in North-West Europe. To be understood, therefore, the Canadian approach to battle exhaustion must be considered in the context of both British and American practices.

American policy towards neuropsychiatric casualties had been firmly established before D-Day and on the whole the United States Army Medical Corps stuck to it throughout the Normandy campaign. "Combat exhaustion" was described as a function of the intensity of battle closely related to the overall casualty rate. Exhaustion was treated as a medical emergency and rapid sedation (narcosis) for up to seventy-two hours was employed as far forward as possible. This regime was designed to save a minimum of 50 per cent of all exhaustion cases for further combat.[1] The Americans accepted high exhaustion levels and concentrated on seeking better return to unit rates.

The United States Army was confident that it had provided the facilities and training needed to carry out this program and there was a strong commitment to making it succeed. In July, the First United States Army dealt with 9,101 neuropsychiatric admissions, not including "a sizeable group of cases which were treated and returned to duty at the battalion and station level." Official statistics suggest that 77.8 per cent of those admitted were "returned to duty." The balance were "evacuated to the rear of the Army."[2] The Third United States Army entered the battle as the stalemate in Normandy was ending. The standard forward treatment policies were employed and a very high return to unit rate was reported.[3]

During 1944 the US 12th Army Group and its medical corps appeared confident that its neuropsychiatric program was working well. Many infantry divisions created rest centres in their rear echelon to allow larger numbers of exhaustion casualties to recover within the division.[4] This was seen as a rational extension of the principles of forward psychiatry and was quickly institutionalized. During late August and September, as the First and Third Armies advanced rapidly across France, casualties and NP ratios declined dramatically. So did return to unit rates, because it became impossible to keep casualties within the division. Combat exhaustion patients, once evacuated to the rear, were not viewed as capable of returning to combat in large numbers and apparently lived up to this expectation.

A very different pattern emerged in the Seventh United States Army, which served in southern France. Its veteran divisions, brought from Italy, had high rates of incidence and low rates of return. Overall just 31 per cent of its neuropsychiatric casualties went back to front line duty in 1944.[5] This pattern had gradually been accepted in Italy. Most American psychiatrists accepted the reality of the "old sergeant syndrome" and held a generalized belief that "burnout" would occur among all soldiers who survived prolonged exposure to battle. There was no formal agreement on when this would occur, but if a man had been in combat for 90 to 120 days there was thought to be little chance that he could return to the line after a breakdown.[6]

The contrast between the experiences of the various United States Armies was perhaps not as sharp as these return to unit rates would suggest. After Normandy the First United States Army undertook a comprehensive follow-up study which shored that "[r]eports received on 708 men, many of whom were returned to duty during July and August, were as follows: Still on duty with their units, 217; killed in action, 21; wounded in action, 84; evacuated for medical disabilities, 108; and evacuated for neuropsychiatric disabilities, 278."[7] Most of the men officially evacuated with a "recurrence of combat exhaustion" had not lasted seventy-two hours. This was not quite what the proponents of a high return to duty rate had expected, or have subsequently claimed.

The study was not available in 1944 and most of the United States Army remained firmly committed to a policy of maximum return of exhaustion cases through immediate forward treatment. After the war it became clear that the United States Army's extraordinarily high rate of hospital admissions for other diseases concealed a "significant incidence of psychiatric disorders."[8] It also became evident that the frequency of non-battle injuries, including the trench-foot epidemic of late 1944 concealed the same problem.[9]

Canadian contact with the United States Army was episodic[10] but throughout the European campaign a close relationship with the British Army was an operational necessity. Canadian troops frequently served under British command and British troops were always an important part of the First Canadian Army. The reaction of the Second British Army and 21 Army Group to the problem of battle exhaustion must be examined in greater detail.

When the exhaustion crisis began in July, Major Watterson and his Corps psychiatrists were taken by surprise. However Watterson, a man of considerable ability, responded quickly and efficiently. His actions during July reflect a coherent and consistent view of the problem and its resolution. He described the general trend of the period in his monthly report for July:

The high optimism of the troops who landed in the assault and early build up phases inevitably dwindled when the campaign for a few weeks appeared to have slowed down. Almost certainly the initial hopes and optimism were too high and the gradual realization that the "walk-over" to Berlin had developed into an infantry slogging match caused an unspoken but clearly recognizable fall of morale. One sign of this was the increase in the incidence of psychiatric casualties arriving in a steady stream at Exhaustion Centres and reinforced by waves of beaten, exhausted men from each of the major battles. For every man breaking down there were certainly three or four effective men remaining with their units.

Swings of morale often tend to overshoot the mark and this happened during the first half of July. Thereafter men settled to their new appreciation of this War of Liberation, discarding their notions of marching through welcoming and gay French villages, replacing them by more realistic appraisals of a brave and skillful enemy, of battered towns and of necessary days, perhaps weeks, of grimly sitting down and holding on under mortar five, cloudy skies, rain and mud.

Finally in the last week of the month a noticeable steadying and bracing of morale occurred so that the subsequent breakthrough South of Caumont by our own army, the long strides of the Americans into Brittany and the pursuit of the enemy by the Russians through Poland and the Baltic states caused no sudden inflation of false optimism but rather a sober satisfaction that the hard fighting ahead would bring its own similar rewards. With this background the incidence of exhaustion and neurotic breakdown in the army may be assumed to have reached and passed its peak.[11]

This interpretation of battle exhaustion, with its emphasis on battlefield conditions and general morale, was accompanied by comments on the aetiology of exhaustion that pinpointed a high rate of breakdown among replacements:

One factor mentioned frequently by combatant officers and RMOs is the greater frequency with which reinforcements break down. Apart from the general quality of reinforcements, three points stand out. The first is that a unit that has suffered a very large number of casualties consists almost entirely of reinforcements and can hardly be considered a coherent body of men. For example, the 1st Hampshire battalion were visited on July 17th. They had lost 686 killed, wounded and missing since D-Day. Sixteen officers and two Commanding Officers had been killed, and the battalion was then waiting for its third CO. When such a battalion goes into action a very high break-down rate must be expected, since the emotional ties among the men, and between the men and their officers (which is the single most potent factor in preventing breakdown), barely exist. Having reached this state a unit needs several weeks out of the line (at least two) to reform.

The second is that reinforcements should be integrated into their new units in sizeable bodies, sections at the least, preferably platoons. The Reinforcement Group set up by 59 Div is a valuable step forward here in that it gives fresh reinforcements a few days to acquire a feeling of attachment for the formation they are going to.

The third point is that untrained reinforcements frequently become psychiatric casualties. Stories of clerks, cooks, storemen and the like being sent forward as riflemen reinforcements are all too frequent. Such men, apart from breaking down themselves, can be a real menace to their units. For example 4 RWF were visited in the line on July 29th. A few nights previously an NCO had scurried back with his section to Coy. HQ with the information that they had been surrounded by Germans. What had happened was that an enemy patrol had passed them nearby. The NCO had not broken down[12] or lost his head. He merely did not know the job of Section Sgt. He had always been a CQMS in charge of a store.

These arguments, which further emphasized the historical and situational basis of battle exhaustion, were paralleled in the comments of other psychiatrists.[13] For example, a report from VIII Corps, dated 17 July 1944, focused on specific patterns among the 928 cases examined so far that month:

The general morale seen from cases from 43 div was low. Very few indeed showed any desire to return to their units. This was quite in marked contrast to what occurred in units of 15 (S) Div. It was also apparent that, from the number of cases arriving in groups – from some companies, platoons or sections, often accompanied by NCOs or even officers, that not only had individual morale gone, but group morale as well. In 53 Div, most cases came from 115 Welsh; they were very poor personality types, chronic neurotics, men of low average intelligence, etc. These should obviously have been eliminated from the regiment long ago. An impression one gained, after chatting with a large number of men admitted to the Centre, is that they were not really in the picture from an operational standpoint. Their officers had not given them a clear idea of the plan or objective of the action in which they were participating.

When this is the case, morale is bound to crack easier, because the man feels insecure, becomes extremely anxious about all that is happening around him.

I have been very impressed by the large numbers of MOs – chiefly from 11 Armd Div & 15 (S) Div – who have visited the Centre to enquire about patients they have sent in. It is obvious that they are keenly interested and have been making every effort – even under difficult circumstances – to rest their men within their own battalion area. A number of FDS, too, have been retaining men for periods 36-48hrs rest in the divisional area.

Enemy Weapons. It is obvious that the most frightening weapon has been the mortar. In quiet periods it would be advantageous to use captured German mortars as a method of battle inoculation.

A rumour which appears to be prevalent is that the Germans are using wooden bullets impregnated with *poison*. Steps should be taken to dispel this or give our men the true reason why they are being used.[14]

The British system for treating exhaustion had not been able to deal with the numbers occurring at the Normandy battlefront.[15] In mid-July two divisions, 50th (Northumbrian) and 49th (West Riding), had improvised their own methods of coping. Field Ambulances were set aside as divisional exhaustion centres and all cases were sent to these units. Watterson welcomed this initiative and moved to encourage divisional psychiatry, without psychiatrists, in all British divisions. He explained that "The advantages of having Divisional Centres were considerable. First divisions were continually switching about between Corps so that the division was the only stable entity. Second, men treated at a divisional centre were still within the family, and intimate contact was still possible between the centre and the RMOs of the division. Third, there was no doubt that treatment at a forward medical unit within the sound of battle was easier than at more rearward centres. Fourth, the number of casualties was such that Corps Centres alone were swamped."[16]

By late July the system was in operation throughout the Second Army. Watterson and his colleagues believed that its most important achievement was to reverse the practice of evacuating the majority of exhaustion cases to the UK. In June, XXX Corps had been able to return less than 15 per cent of its neuropsychiatric casualties to full duty in their unit. This figure rose to almost 45 per cent in July when divisional exhaustion centres were functioning.[17] One of the most dramatic turn-arounds in return unit rates was experienced in the 43rd (Wessex) Division, then part of VIII Corps. A medical officer, with psychiatric experience, who was detailed to establish a divisional exhaustion centre at a casualty clearing station was able to send 70 per cent of his cases back to their units.[18] The 3rd British Division, which had lost 736 men to exhaustion in July, established a divisional centre on 6 August. Of the first ninety-eight cases, seventy-eight were returned to their battalion. The ADMS commented: "This figure, while giving no guarantee against relapses, is most encouraging and it has been decided that in future every case of exhaustion will be admitted to a divisional FDS and retained there until it is clear that there is no possible chance of his being returned to his unit."[19]

British army psychiatry emerged from the battlefields of Normandy with new confidence in the virtues of forward treatment of exhaustion. The introduction of divisional psychiatry was viewed primarily as a method of reversing the practice of mass evacuation of psychiatric casualties. Given the enormous manpower problems facing the British Army, the promise of saving large numbers of exhaustion cases won support from all elements of the army. Regrettably no systematic follow-up studies of exhaustion cases returned to unit at the divisional level were undertaken. One Second Army study of "relapses reaching the hands of Corps Psychiatrists" suggested that only "10% of return to duty had relapsed after 6 to 7 weeks." Although it was recognized that this method "was not reliable" because it only measured those who returned to the same CEU, it served to encourage attempts to return a large percentage of psychiatric casualties to their units.[20]

By the end of the war British psychiatrists were less certain about their level of success in treating exhaustion. The official history, without citing any sources, offers this summary: "In spite of an appreciable relapse rate, it can be stated that over the entire campaign about one third of all exhaustion cases treated eventually remained at full duties. This represents just over 4,400 men saved for further battle at a time when the manpower situation was the most critical."[21] The forward psychiatry system created by the British Army in Normandy fulfilled all the requirements of proximity, immediacy, and expectancy. During the summer and fall of 1944 it may well have succeeded in accomplishing its purpose of a high return to duty rate but this is by no means certain. The rate of neuropsychiatric hospital admissions rose sharply in the last quarter of 1944[22] as did rates for other diseases that may have had psychological components,[23] casting doubt on the success of the policy.[24]

The Canadian Army's views on returning exhaustion casualties to unit were strongly influenced by the Canadian experience in Italy. The commander of the First Canadian Army, Lieutenant-General Crerar, had been shocked by the situation he had encountered in that campaign in 1943. When he left the Mediterranean to take up his appointment for Operation Overlord, Crerar had provided his successor with a summary of his view on "*exhaustion neurosis both real and artificial*," which emphasized disciplinary measures.

On 15 July, in the midst of the exhaustion crisis in Normandy, Crerar sent a copy of this memorandum top his Canadian Corps Commander, Lieutenant-General Simonds who needed no prompting on the matter. When II Canadian Corps was faced with a rising exhaustion rate Simonds was adamant that tighter discipline and exemplary punishment were required.

He put these views on paper in late August when the Canadian divisions were suffering from a severe manpower shortage.

Fighting Strengths

1 I have checked the figures of our deficiencies in unit establishments with the figures for battle casualties and there is a marked discrepancy between the two.

2 Records show that this discrepancy is not attributable to sickness, which is low throughout the Corps. It may be attributable to the following causes, and I consider that this matter must receive the personal attention of all commanders and commanding officers:

a. *Battle Exhaustion*

Medical Officers may be inclined to take a lenient view of so termed "battle exhaustion" cases. It requires the close attention of commanders to see that malingering is not only discouraged, but made a disgraceful offence and disciplinary action taken to counter it. Battle exhaustion may be an acute problem under the most adverse fighting conditions – winter, bad living conditions and bad feeling resulting from small parties of troops having to fend for themselves – the drabness of static warfare with its inevitable drain on morale. It is quite inexcusable under the conditions in which we have been fighting in the last few weeks.

b. I am certain there is some straggling and absenteeism in units for I have seen soldiers in villages far from the area in which their unit is fighting. Though in some cases these may be Rear Echelon personnel, I am satisfied that some are not. Firm disciplinary action is necessary on the part of commanding officers to deal with absenteeism or straggling. This is particularly important now that we are moving through a country where the civil population is present in the towns and villages and through the countryside. It is a great temptation to the soldier who is weary, especially if plied with wine by the ill considered friendliness of local civilians, to take 24 to 48 hours away from duty.

3 I appreciate the problem which faces unit commanders who have a high proportion of reinforcement officers, short of regimental experience and with very little opportunity to get to know their men before they are actively engaged with the enemy. Whilst I understand the difficulties, I will not condone malingering or straggling and I request that you will give your personal attention to this matter and take active steps to see what disciplinary action is taken and examples made wherever offences occur. The reinforcement situation being what it is, every serving soldier must be made to pull his weight whether or not he may feel temporarily disinclined to do so.[25]

Three days later Crerar issued his own directive on the need to tighten discipline:

It is essential to battle discipline and fighting efficiency that the appropriate disciplinary action is taken in all cases of absence, cowardice and desertion. It is quite improper and bad for the general morale of the troops to place a soldier, who is regarded as not being dependable as a result of previous experience, in a rearward echelon and thus keep him out of battle. I emphasize that if improper conduct in action is permitted to go unpunished, or be condoned, morale will be seriously affected. Prompt disciplinary action in such cases is, therefore, essential. The following will guide Commanders in considering these cases:

a. Unauthorized absence for the purpose of avoiding action constitutes desertion chargeable under Sec 12 (1) (a) of the Army Act. In such circumstances a charge of desertion should be laid and not a charge of cowardice. Upon such charge it is necessary to provide (1) that the accused knew with reasonable certainty that he was required for some particular service or duty (e.g. service in the forward area in which active operations are taking place) and (2) that he absented himself and thereby avoided or attempted to avoid such service or duty.

b. Cowardice is an offence under Sec 5 (7) if it consists of misbehaviour before the enemy in such manner as to show cowardice or inducing other soldiers to misbehave in such manner. It must be shown that the accused, from an unsoldierlike regard for his personal safety in the presence of the enemy, failed in respect of some distinct and feasible duty imposed upon him by a specified order or regulation, or by the well-understood custom of the service, or by the requirements of the case, as applicable to the position in which he was placed at the time.

c. There are other Secs in the Army Act which deal with improper conduct in relation to the enemy. In all such cases as well as in cases of desertion or cowardice, commanders may obtain advice from the formation legal officers.

For the offences of desertion and cowardice penal servitude may be awarded. The minimum period of penal servitude is three years and the maximum is life. Experience indicates tht punishments of three years penal servitude have been awarded for the offences of cowardice or desertion in the face of the enemy.[26]

The attitudes reflected in these directives were not shared in the rifle companies at the sharp end of the battle. Nor were most Canadian psychiatrists impressed with the notion that the enforcement of the kind of discipline permissible in the Canadian Army would have a measurable effect on the manpower problem. As far as the psychiatrists could tell the number of malingerers was very small.[27] The figures for *suspected* self-inflicted wounds (95[28] during the Normandy campaign, 232[29] during all of 1944) did not seem alarming. Absence without leave was a minor problem in most regiments. Desertions from the infantry averaged about twenty men a month,[30] an insignificant number in a field force of twenty-four battalions.

This left battle exhaustion as the one area where manpower savings might be made if the correct policies were adopted. But throughout June and early July the 3rd Division had been following the approved doctrines for treating exhaustion, returning 70 per cent of all cases to their unit. And when the 2nd Division was confronted with a large number of such cases the ADMS, Colonel Leech, had quickly established a divisional centre where 79 per cent of those admitted were sent back to their regiment.[31] Yet hundreds of soldiers, almost all of them precious trained infantrymen, were disappearing from their regiments. What had happened?

The answer is not hard to find. Lieutenant-Colonel Richardson, who arrived in Normandy in early August to co-ordinate all aspects of Canadian psychiatry in North-West Europe, had a good overview of the situation. While at Basingstoke he had treated more than three hundred neuropsychiatric cases from the 3rd Division, casualties that Gregory was quite unaware of.[32] Most had been evacuated without having passed through the divisional exhaustion centre, but some were men who had been sent back to their units. Major T.T. Ferguson, who ran the I British Corps exhaustion unit reported that he had evacuated Canadian cases "at their 2nd, 3rd and even 4th attack of exhaustion."[33] Richardson found that between 6 June and 30 August 1,838 Canadian soldiers[34] had been treated for exhaustion at field dressing stations, exhaustion units, and hospitals. At least two-thirds of them had been permanently lost to their original units.[35]

Richardson's findings did not come as a surprise to McNeel, the officer commanding I CEU. McNeel's initial experiences in July, when his facility was operating as a primary treatment centre for hundreds of exhaustion cases from the 2nd and 3rd Divisions, led him to question the accuracy of Gregory's claims.[36] In his preliminary report dated 24 August 1944 McNeel described what he had observed.

The original purpose of the exhaustion unit, he noted, had been to "retain a large proportion of psychiatric casualties in the Corps area, and after a short period of treatment return them to duty." But at the end of just three days of operation "accommodation was full and evacuation had to be commenced." The proposed five-day treatment program was cut to just three days (24 hours continuous sedation, 24 hours rest, 24 hours rehabilitation, with one period of group psychotherapy), but as the numbers grew both two-day and one-day schedules were attempted.[37] McNeel then fell back on 19 Sec "as a sort of rehabilitation and observation unit."[38] Such units were intended to perform useful labour while keeping neuropsychiatric casualties in the theatre of war, they were not intended to rehabilitate men.

McNeel's analysis of patients admitted and discharged, 13 July–15 Aug 44, provides a detailed look at battle exhaustion in Normandy. The number of admissions recorded was 1,206 and only 20 per cent of them had been to a Canadian reinforcement unit for return to combat. McNeel noted that "a good number" were sent there "on trial" without great expectations. No information on those sent in July is available but the August-September figures indicate that most of the exhaustion cases were downgraded for duty in line of communication jobs, not sent to combat units of any kind.[39]

In the conclusion to his report McNeel tried to describe some of the problems encountered in Normandy. He was convinced that the rehabilitation system needed more thought and was quite certain that the exhaustion unit could not accomplish its purpose unless further facilities were provided. A large Corps exhaustion centre with its own administrative, quartermaster, and medical components was required if the army was serious about trying to return large numbers of men to combat. He also wanted the authority to return men directly to their regiment instead of to the divisional reinforcement battalions where exhaustion cases were mixed with fresh reinforcements and men recovered from wounds. Promising exhaustion cases needed prompt reintegration into their own platoon, not posting to the general reinforcement stream.

McNeel did not develop this argument in his preliminary report. The reinforcement system was well established and quite outside the jurisdiction of the RCAMC, let alone the exhaustion unit. But when interviewed for this book he insisted that the reinforcement system was a major obstacle to all attempts to deal with morale. The reinforcement units in Europe, he maintained, were "cesspools" demoralizing both uninitiated replacements and returning casualties. "It seemed to me," he wrote, "that during the period in the RU the man was feeling detached from his comrades, alone and adrift." Many of those "returned to unit" were in fact sent to a battalion "that was quite unfamiliar to them with men who were practically unknown." The problem as far as McNeel could tell was "inherent in the system which required that men being evacuated to base must return through the RU. "For a short period McNeel tried to short circuit this system by sending particularly promising cases directly back to their regiments. "However this practice violated the ordained pattern and had to be discontinued."[40]

McNeel's pessimism about the restoration of exhaustion cases to combat duty was in sharp contrast to the ideas of most American and British psychiatrists. However his colleagues Major Burch and Captain Fraser shared his view, as did Lieutenant-Colonel Richardson. The explanation of these differences is most likely to be found in the history of the three armies. British and American optimism about psychiatric casualties in late July and August was based on experience very different from that of the Canadian Army. For the Americans the breakout from the Normandy bridgehead, 24 to 29 July, and the rapid drive through France in August "solved" the problem of combat exhaustion. From 21 July to 30 August, the Second British Army was engaged in only one major operation, Bluecoat, which while costly for several divisions[41] did not employ the majority of units for long periods. British casualties declined accordingly. Their exhaustion ratio dropped from its July peak and absolute numbers fell dramatically. After 12 August when British units were pursuing the retreating German Army exhaustion almost disappeared.[42]

For the Canadians late July and August was a period of heavy fighting against a dogged enemy. Casualties were actually higher in August than in July and the NP rate rose to new levels during the month.[43] It is important to realize that Canadian battle casualties in 1944 were 20 per cent higher than those in comparable British formations, largely because of the tasks assigned the Canadian Army in the later summer of 1944.[44] No one could be optimistic in the battle conditions encountered on the road to Falaise.

Between 21 July when Operation Goodwood ended and 30 August the Canadians lost around 3,000 men killed and 7,000 wounded.[45] More than 1,500 exhaustion cases were evacuated beyong the regimental aid post for an average NP ratio of 16.[46] The period began with Operation Spring, a costly defeat that was seen as having destroyed the self-confidence of much of the 2nd Division. Later in the summer McNeel was asked to examine the circumstances which had led to the apparent vulnerability of the division. His investigation included visits to the divisional Field Ambulances and dressing stations, as well as conversations with medical officers, battalion commanders, and the men at the sharp end.[47]

By the time he was through McNeel had begun to grasp the complexity of the problem. His report included this important statement:

The sources of error in the compilation of statistics and in the use of such a figure as an Exhaustion ratio are so numerous as to make any conclusion based on statistics alone of very doubtful value. The incidence of Exhaustion in any unit is only a part of the picture of that unit's efficiency and may be outweighed in a positive direction by a generally high standard of performance and in a negative direction by large numbers of AWL, POW and trivial illnesses. I have been told that one regiment which has a relatively high Exhaustion ratio is always reliable and has never withdrawn from an action whereas another regiment with a low exhaustion ratio has usually withdrawn from action whenever the stress became great ... The Exhaustion ratio will also be altered by the wholesale evacuation of trivial sick or wounded. The degree to which this takes place will necessarily vary with the tactical situation but will depend a good deal on the policy within the unit. For these reasons the thoughtful appraisal of the unit's overall performance by responsible officers who know all the factors is of more value than any set of statistics or ratio can hope to be. However the latter may be used as a lead.[48]

As a lead but not much more. Close examination of the history of each battalion produced a complex and contradictory picture. In 4 Brigade two regiments, the Royal Hamilton Light Infantry, (RHLI) and the Essex Scottish, had low exhaustion ratios and relatively low total casualties.[49] The RHLI was recognized as an effective unit with high morale and excellent leadership while the Essex Scottish struggled throughout August to recover from its disastrous initiation into battle at Verrières Ridge. Yet the RHLI had the highest number of men absent without leave. The third unit, the Royal Regiment of Canada, had a consistently high exhaustion ratio with an average level of casualties. The Royals had enjoyed no great triumphs and known no sharp reverses but they had been kept at it throughout the period.

A particularly careful investigation of 5 Brigade was conducted. One of its units, the Black Watch, had the most cases in the division. But this was just one facet of the catastrophe that overtook the regiment on 25 July and as a consequence the exhaustion ratio was quite low. The Régiment de Maisonneuve, with the highest ratio in the division, also had a high rate of absence without leave. Despite all of this the "Maisies" were a successful battalion with high morale and inspirational leadership.[50] Their real problem was the shortage of French Canadian reinforcements and the inadequate training of many of those they did obtain. The Calgary Highlanders had the highest total casualties of any unit in the Corps, largely because neither of their sister regiments had the manpower to undertake the vanguard role. Exhaustion casualties were high in absolute numbers, and thus somewhat notorious, but the ratio was, in fact, lower than in most other regiments. Strangely the Calgaries functioned well despite enormous tension between the co and the company commanders, suggesting that section, platoon, and especially company leadership could be the key to high morale in battle.

A French Canadian battalion of 6 Brigade, the Fusiliers Mont Royal, suffered from the same manpower shortages as the Maisonneuves. It also reported a large number of men AWL and the most deserters, forty-five in the division. Its NP ratio was, however, the lowest in the division and apart from difficulties due to being understrength it was a first class fighting unit. The South Saskatchewan Regiment, devastated in the last stages of Operation Goodwood, appeared to have a low exhaustion ratio. But by the end of August there were hardly any men left from the original battalion. The 1,280 casualties the regiment suffered in three months of battle were in fact concentrated in brief, furious encounters like Verrières Ridge and the Forêt de la Londe.[51] The Queens Own Cameron Highlanders were in a position similar to the Calgaries'. A competent regiment with no single-day disasters, it was regularly in line throughout the period with high casualties and a low NP ratio.

It is not possible to integrate statistics for accidental injuries into this account, though McNeel was surely right when he insisted that they should be made part of the picture. McNeel tells a story that crystallizes his feelings about the complexity of battle exhaustion and the danger of attempting to use exhaustion ratios as anything other than a starting point. He was with Colonel Van Nostrand when a discussion on the use of NP ratios in judging regiments and their commanders arose. McNeel recalls fumbling for a way of expressing his own doubts when Van Nostrand, who was known for his colourful language, brought the debate to a halt with a limerick. He recited:

There was a young man name Paul
Who had an hexagonal ball
The square of its weight
Plus his penis times eight
Was two-thirds of three-fifths of fuck all.[52]

In his official communications Van Nostrand avoided limericks but his message was the same – given the nature of the fighting in Normandy anxiety neuroses on a very large scale were inevitable and predictable. If they were not treated as exhaustion casualties they would show up somewhere else.

McNeel did not undertake a separate investigation of the 4th Canadian Armoured Division, which had joined II Canadian Corps at the end of July, but his War Diary describes the consequence of their entry into combat.[53] When the 3rd Division was withdrawn for a rest 10 Infantry Brigade, which with 4 Armoured Brigade made up the division, was rushed into the line. The Lincoln and Welland Regiment was the first unit to be tested. Their attack on Tilly la Campagne produced heavy casualties and much chaos.[54] Their sister regiment, the Argyll and Sutherland Highlanders, was the next to undertake a probing attack of the German defences with similar results. Battle exhaustion accounted for 10 per cent of the casualties and McNeel persuaded the ADMS to allot a field dressing station for forward treatment.[55]

The armoured brigade did not go into action until 8 August when Operation Totalize, the first attempt to reach Falaise, began. One unit, the British Columbia Regiment, was then virtually annihilated and "three or four tank crews" were evacuated from the field dressing station to the exhaustion unit.[56] For the rest of August it was impossible to keep track of which battalions casualties were from. British soldiers from the 51st Highland Division[57] and Poles from the 1st Polish Armoured[58] joined the steady stream of Canadian patients. These now included large numbers of rear echelon troops caught in two major short bombing incidents. The following extracts from the exhaustion unit War Diary convey impressions of the situation:

11 August 44   Admissions 81 Discharge 28
The influx continues with numbers of British still high. These come from units made famous in North Africa and Sicily and consist chiefly of two types (a) recent recruits, many of whom give histories of inadequacy in civil life and are evidently not fighting men and (b) war weary veterans who have had just enough taste of home in the interval to make them uncertain at the prospect of another long campaign and what they consider to be the increasing odds against their individual surviving of it.
The Poles we have seen are chiefly those who have developed hysterical symptoms in fairly sharp action or inadequates. A number of these were in the German Army in Italy where inadequacy was dealt with by disciplinary measures.

15 August 1944   Admissions 43 Discharges 29
Last night was not the most desirable night for a move. The unit opened here (Busse) at about 1900 hours yesterday and within an hour an influx of patients began which amounted to 140 by 2300 hrs. This evidently followed the accidental bombing of our own formations by the Lancasters which we cheered on yesterday. Some of the patients also report being strafed by Spitfires. The Jerries evidently seized these golden oppor-

tunities to complete the confusion by opening up with 88s. The whole story is a lurid and sorry tale as reported to us by large numbers admitted last night and today. Evidently there was some degree of mass panic in numerous units and a good deal of unauthorized self-evacuation. Last night, after this event, there was the greatest enemy air activity in our area since we opened ... The patients took to the fields and this morning 16 were missing.

McNeel, like most of those who concerned themselves with exhaustion casualties, believed that armoured units had few cases and that exhaustion would only be a problem in the infantry brigade of an armoured division. While it was generally true that there were few such casualties in armoured regiments, this was primarily a function of the low total casualties in these units. A review of Canadian battle exhaustion cases, by arm of service, was prepared for the period 6 June to 30 November 1944. It revealed that .8 per cent of armoured corps battle casualties were due to exhaustion against 10.2 per cent of the infantry. The Royal Canadian Artillery, whose self-propelled anti-tank regiments had been in action as frequently as the tank squadrons, turned out to have a 10.0 per cent rate. The infantry accounted for 74 per cent of all exhaustion cases because 76 per cent of all battle casualties occurred in that arm.[59]

DURING THE MONTH of September the Canadians were able to advance rapidly without being forced into grinding battles of attrition. Exhaustion casualties were rarely seen beyond the division level[60] and there was time to re-assess the psychiatric services. The return to unit rate in August had been no better than in July and there was considerable pressure on Colonel Van Nostrand to do something to stop the manpower drain.

The structure of neuropsychiatric services in the fall of 1944 may be briefly summarized. All three divisions maintained a field dressing station as a forward exhaustion centre during periods of intense contact with the enemy. Only the 3rd Division had a full-time psychiatrist but the responsible medical officers in the 2nd and 4th Divisions used the methods of treatment advocated by Gregory. The CEU was intended to function as the secondary treatment centre dealing with cases that could not be rehabilitated at the divisional level. No. 19 SEC worked in close liaison with the exhaustion unit providing "psychiatric rehabilitation." A reallocation centre provided further examination of psychiatric referrals and transferred patients to appropriate line of communications jobs. Two further SECs functioned as additional holding units. No. 20 was essentially for overflow from the reallocation centre, while No. 21 served as a more permanent home for soldiers downgraded for instability who were unfit for normal rear arm postings. The military purpose of the SECs was to limit the number of evacuations to the United Kingdom and thereby counter army mythology about battle exhaustion as a "ticket to Blighty." No. 1 Neuro-psychiatric Wing, which was attached to the 8th Canadian General Hospital, was intended to deal with more severe cases. If prolonged treatment was indicated patients were evacuated to Basingstoke.[61]

This was the situation when severe fighting began again in early October. The First Canadian Army had been ordered to open the part of Antwerp captured on 5 September. Antwerp was sixty-five miles from the sea and the Germans were holding both the south bank of the Scheldt estuary, the Breskins Pocket, and Walcheren Island on the north side.[62]

The task was urgent since the Allied armies were still dependent on supplies brought in through the Normandy beaches. Unfortunately Generals Montgomery and Eisenhower had decided to gamble on a quick crossing of the Rhine in September. Operation Market Garden, the attempt to use three airborne divisions to accomplish this, failed in its original purpose and created a salient that had to be defended at enormous cost. The small Canadian force was left to get on with the battle for the Antwerp approaches under the most adverse circumstances. Logistical problems, terrain, weather, and well-organized German resistance made October a dreadful month for Canadian infantry regiments.

The 2nd Canadian Division was required to fight its way north from Antwerp to near Bergen-Op-Zoom. It was then to turn west across the Beveland Isthmus in preparation for the assault on Walcheren. The division began the operation short 889 riflemen, approximately one-fifth of its authorized strength.[63] The fighting at the entrance to the Beveland Isthmus involved some of the bloodiest encounters of the war. The Black Watch and the Royal Hamilton Light Infantry in particular suffered a high (50 per cent) casualty rate, but no battalion was spared. The German defence of the area was spearheaded by the 6th Parachute Regiment, a formation that had lost none of the skill it had demonstrated against the Americans in Normandy.

After the 4th Canadian Armoured and 49th (West Riding) Divisions had come to the aid of the 2nd Division, the turn west could be made. Movement towards Walcheren was rapid, though 5 Brigade's failed attempt to rush the narrow causeway to the island provided a costly finale to the month's misery. The human price of this enterprise was enormous: 465 killed, 1965 wounded, 170 missing.[64] Regimental officers felt that the high casualty figures were partly due to the poor quality of the reinforcements who had to be rushed into battle during the month. Many of these were reluctant "converts" from other arms, hastily converted to infantry as a stop-gap measure.[65]

Curiously the official NP ratio for the 2nd Division failed to reflect the bitterness of the fighting or the descriptive evidence of declining morale. According to divisional reports only 98 men were treated for exhaustion and almost all of these were returned to duty.[66] The Corps psychiatrist put the number at 207[67] when he received other records, but even this figure indicated an NP ratio of under 10. It seems clear that the 2nd Division had reacted to the notoriety of its high exhaustion rates by clamping down hard. One regiment that had suffered serious problems in the summer was given an extra medical officer to take care of exhaustion cases at the regimental aid post.[68] Other units simply stressed tighter discipline.

It is impossible to draw any conclusions from these figures. The exhaustion unit was far away in Ghent during October and was quite out of touch with the 2nd Division. Eventually No. 1 Canadian Neuropsychiatric Wing, attached to a general hospital in Antwerp, functioned as an exhaustion centre for the division. The 200 or more cases handled here were not identified and it is pointless to speculate about them.[69] Perhaps the most difficult problem in interpreting the evidence arises out of statistics on the sickness rate, which increased threefold in October with almost 900 men hospitalized for at least short periods.[70]

The situation is made all the more puzzling by the very different pattern of exhaustion casualties in the 3rd Division during the month. On 6 October 7 Brigade had launched an assault crossing of the Leopold Canal. This attack was designed to hold German troops at the canal while 9 Brigade completed an amphibious landing on the northwest corner of the Breskins Pocket. Unfortunately 9 Brigade was delayed and the full weight of the enemy's fire was directed at 7 Brigade. After the success of 9 Brigade landings the division forced its way forward, dyke by dyke, for the next twenty-four days.

The casualty figures were 314 killed, 1532 wounded, and 231 missing.[71] Exhaustion casualties appeared to total 421, an NP ratio of 17.[72] The bulk of these came from 7 and 8 Brigades where the ratio was as high as 25. Evacuations for sickness in the 3rd Division were less than half the number[73] reported in the 2nd Division so it is possible that we are simply dealing with a difference in labelling.

Gregory, the 3rd Division psychiatrist, wrote a detailed report on his division's exhaustion cases in October. Two-thirds of these casualties were admitted to the field dressing station where Gregory worked. It was safely behind the lines, and after moderate sedation the first day, the men were allowed passes into town. The report notes that "the man was in no way treated as a patient. He was informed that the condition was often due to fatigue, from which he would recover quickly and for which the Army granted him 48 hrs at this unit. Following this he was expected to return to duty." Gregory, who had never wavered in his commitment to a high return to unit rate, was nevertheless uncertain about October's casualties, 90 per cent of whom were veterans with at least three months of battle experience. He feared their morale was cracking. He commented: "There was one thing to note among all troops admitted for exhaustion – lack of morale or lack of volition to carry on. The foremost cause of this seemed to be futility. The men claimed there was nothing to which to look forward to – no rest, no leave, no enjoyment, no normal life and no escape. The only way one could get out of battle was death, wounds, self-inflicted wounds and going 'nuts'."[74]

The men seemed convinced that "the Division had no interest in them except to get blood from a stone in order to bring glory to others." Gregory concluded that while two-thirds could be returned to combat they should not be required to go back to their units until the battle of the Scheldt was over. If Gregory really thought he could keep 199 apparently fit men at a divisional reinforcement centre in the midst of a desperate battle he was wrong. They were quickly fed into the general replacement stream and it was not possible to find out what happened to them.

At the CEU, casualties sent back by Gregory, as well as others who were not treated at divisional level, filled the ward. Total admissions for the battle period were 266.[75] Major John Burch, who had replaced McNeel when the latter became Corps psychiatrist, kept patients for less than forty-eight hours because space was limited and there were no rehabilitation facilities. The SEC was soon filled with men, almost all of whom were downgraded as fit for only limited service.[76]

On 20 October, while the battle was still raging, Major Dancey arrived to take charge of the exhaustion unit. Dancey, an experienced psychiatrist from the Montreal General Hospital, had been at Basingstoke since the spring and had followed the course of the campaign closely. His quarterly report for the fall of 1944 developed the views first expressed by Gregory. Dancey wrote: "The type of NP case seen during the past few months has been much different from that so frequently described in the literature and from that admitted during the summer. Although recent reinforcements who break down tend to show gross demoralization characterized by conversion hysteria or anxiety hysteria, we are handling an increasing number of men who have carried on under considerable stress for long periods of time. These individuals, on examination, show a minimum of objective findings ... The principal complaint, which is almost invariably present, consists of a realization that they will never again be able to face front line service."[77] Later Dancey summarized his attempts to determine why men broke. He found the most common themes were the realization that the misery and danger would never end and the growing sense of personal vulnerability. Whereas previously the man had believed that whatever happened to others he would not be hit, "he now begins to feel he is a marked man, that there is a bullet with his name on it."[78] Dancey was describing a kind of "reversed fatalism" which had become common in the army during the Scheldt campaign. Many Canadian soldiers believed they had done more than their share and it was time for someone else, anyone else, to take over.

Some of their bitterness was directed at the government of Prime Minister Mackenzie King, which had resisted sending conscripts into battle until the heavy losses of October forced the issue. But most of the anger was directed at higher command. Few Canadian generals had made any attempt to win the affection of their men and fewer had tried to lead from the front. Division and Corps were vague entities that seemed to have only one message – press on, move more quickly. The brigadier was little more than a conduit for detailed orders. If unit morale was to be sustained it was up to the battalion's commander. But the regiment, now filled with strangers who had arrived by chance from the reinforcement units, could rarely be the focus of loyalty it had once been. A man's vision might extend to his regiment or company but increasingly his platoon or even section was all that mattered.

This attitude was evident in combat where the test of a leader was becoming "will he get us killed?" The operations of all three Canadian divisions in October were marked by caution, reliance on the artillery, and a strong belief in the power of the "Tiffies" to overcome enemy resistance. Veterans of the battles frequently describe the lift they got from watching a Rocket Typhoon attack on an enemy position. The planes, swooping down from the overcast skies, unleashing furious explosive power at a house or dyke-embankment, had an almost supernatural quality for the foot solider. Even when the pilots missed their target, which they frequently did, even when they struck their own troops, which was not uncommon, the infantry wanted air support.[79] Air power promised more that it could deliver, but men can go a long way on hope.

FROM THE END of the battle of Scheldt to the beginning of Operation Veritable in February 1945 no division in the Canadian Army was committed to action. There were endless patrols and company or battalion size battles[80], however, and a steady drain of casualties including more than 400 exhaustion cases.[81] Many of these were veterans of the Normandy campaign, confirming the picture of burn out or "old sergeant syndrome." McNeel described their symptoms as "chronic exhaustion with complete loss of enthusiasm and energy with mild depression and apathy." This phenomenon was apparent in both British and Canadian divisions serving in the First Canadian Army and McNeel noted that it resembled the picture seen earlier in the veterans of the North African campaign, especially the Desert Rats. Such men could not usefully be returned to unit and were reassigned to limited duty.[82]

The Canadian Army's neuropsychiatric service approached the battles of the Rhineland, February-March 1945, with a sense of foreboding. Colonel Van Nostrand thought that psychiatric casualties might reach a "secondary peak that may be higher than the primary peak which occurred last August." We are, he told the DMS, "taking appropriate measures" but "many of the factors producing psychiatric casualties are beyond our control."[83] The appropriate measures included a series of lectures to combat officers delivered by McNeel during the long winter in the Nijmegan salient.

McNeel approached these talks with much trepidation. Forty years afterwards he still recalled his hesitation in addressing combatant officers about the management of fear.[84] His message was simple enough – every soldier might become an exhaustion casualty if subjected to enough stress. The amount of pressure an individual could take depended on his constitution (physical, mental, and temperamental), his character, and his personal morale, which was strongly influenced by the morale of the unit. McNeel urged the officers to pay constant attention to the state of group morale. "Loss of confidence," he insisted, "is the commonest cause and the commonest result of exhaustion."[85] These talks may have helped regimental officers to pay more attention to the prevention of exhaustion casualties, but in a tired army they may equally have led to greater expectation of their occurrence.

Canadian Army policy on the evacuation of exhaustion was ambiguous. McNeel obtained approval for a policy statement on managing exhaustion in forward areas that provided a rationale for large-scale evacuation and reassignment away from combat. Discussions with combatant officers had convinced McNeel that psychiatrists and other medical officers needed to understand the attitude of the average officer, NCO, and soldier towards the problem, and the premise of the policy statement addressed this point rather than manpower or medical questions. No one, he wrote "wants to have to deal with a 'jittery' man in the heat of action. The general opinion seems to be that not only are most of these men useless but they have a demoralizing effect on their comrades and actually jeopardize the lives of others who have to expose themselves unnecessarily to make up for the 'jittery' man's deficiencies." RMOs had yielded to the pressure of their fellow officers and were evacuating most cases as they arose.

At the divisional level there were sharp differences of opinion about returning men to duty. In the 2nd Division, during the last quarter of 1944, one recovery centre had sent 60 per cent back while the other had returned just 10 per cent. A follow-up, which obtained information on 70 per cent of the returnees, supported the view that a high return to unit rate was justified in terms of the army's manpower needs and should be encouraged. The fact that the follow-up period was a time in which no major battles were fought was not discussed.

McNeel concluded the policy statement with this guideline:

In practice the policy, both in holding cases and in returning convalescents to duty, is one of compromise. There is no possibility of distinguishing "genuine" cases. The definitely unwilling man readily develops symptoms which are genuire even though they are the consequence of his lack of moral fibre. While, for the sake of discipline, this man may be dealt with by immediate disciplinary measures, there is little hope of reclaiming him once he has been evacuated through medical channels or has gone through the formalities of a Field General Court Martial. On the other hand the man of neurotic constitution may give a fair performance as long as his morale is bolstered up by a degree of external pressure and encouragement. The policy which we advocate for MOs and other officers is to judge a man by his record. If he has given good service and is now breaking give him the benefit of the doubt and evacuate him. If he is new and jittery encourage him but hold him to his job. If he is merely a useless type compel him to do his duty as long as it is possible to do so. (The exceptions to this rule are officers and NCOs who, because of their responsibility for other men, must be relieved of their duties when instability becomes evident.) The cases which benefit most by treatment are the acutely fatigued, and those that benefit most by discipline are the young, scared and uninitiated reinforcements, as well as the great borderline group which will be swayed by the general trend of morale in the unit.[86]

These views were broadly shared by Canadian neuropsychiatrists at the end of 1944 and each of the three Canadian divisions was thoroughly prepared for exhaustion casualties when intensive fighting began in February.

Operation Veritable, the great Anglo-Canadian effort to destroy the German Army west of the Rhine, was under the control of the First Canadian Army, but the majority of the troops were British. Lieutenant-General Brian Horrocks, commanding XXX Corps, fought the first stage of the battle with veteran British infantry units as well as the 3rd Canadian Division. The DDMS of XXX Corps had ordered each British division to allot a field dressing station to exhaustion and established a Corps exhaustion centre at 35 (British) FDS.[87] British psychiatrists had also worked hard to prepare RMOs for the renewal of the offensive. On the whole the British remained much more hopeful about returning men to combat than the Canadians.

The battle began on 8 February with the first phase lasting not the four days the more optimistic had hoped for, but three weeks. Gregory had been reassigned to work at a convalescent depot so forward treatment in the 3rd Division was handled by the MO of 7 Canadian FDS. The Canadians, operating on the Rhine flank of the battlefield, initially suffered few battle casualties. The flooded terrain and cold, rainy weather, not the enemy, were the main obstacles and the division took a perverse pride in its new nickmane "the water rats."[88] For the 53rd (Welsh) Division the Rhineland was the most difficult battle of the war, with almost 3,000 men lost to wounds, sickness, or battle exhaustion in a thirty-day period. The return to unit rates for the 373 exhaustion cases treated at divisional field dressing stations was 52 per cent but 95 cases bypassed divisional recovery and were evacuated to British or Canadian Corps units. The division's NP ratio of 21 was the highest in the army.[89]

The Canadians entered the field in strength on 16 February when the 2nd Division joined the 3rd Division east of Cleve. In the following weeks Canadian troops fought their way through the Hochwald Forest to Xanten and Wessel in a series of difficult, costly battles. The 4th Division had entered the battle on 24 February. When it was over the 2nd Canadian Division had taken more than 2,000 battle casualties with an NP ratio of 11. The 3rd Division, perhaps because of the exposure to combat over the entire period, had an NP ratio of 20 with just over 1,500 casualties. The 4th Armoured Division reported a ratio of 10 with 1,049 casualties.[90]

Return to unit rates declined dramatically in both armies. The British, who had consistently sought to restore more than half of all exhaustion cases to combat, reported that just 20 per cent could be returned to duty without change of category. Lieutenant-Colonel Watterson in his report to the DMS noted: "There are several reasons why less men are being returned to fighting duty. The campaign has now lasted a year and men are becoming emotionally depleted. Many of the soldiers now breaking down have been either surgical or psychiatric casualties previously, and the prognosis is no much worse."[91] The psychiatrist at XXX Corps, Major J. Wishart, estimated that 50 per cent of all cases seen at Corps level had been wounded previously, but noted that there was a second group of cases "composed of young, immature boys experiencing their first severe action. On the whole this group looked younger than their age, and quite a number had only recently begun to shave."[92] Neither Watterson or Wishart had any suggestions to make. Psychiatric casualties continued to occur throughout the last month of the campaign but the Allies were moving quickly forward and the rate never exceeded 10, a ratio now accepted as normal.[93]

Major Dancey, the psychiatrist at the Canadian exhaustion unit, had observed much the same characteristics in his patients. He reported that an analysis of 227 Canadian and 138 British soldiers admitted in February showed that 20 per cent had been previously wounded and almost as many previously treated for exhaustion. Doctors at the 3rd Division's FDS "estimated their rate of repeaters to be much higher than this figure."[94] McNeel thought the problem of the "war weary and sensitized soldier" was the major challenge currently confronting psychiatry and he believed such men should be quickly evacuated. He concluded that there was little doubt that "the anticipated end of the war has also brought to many a good man an increased caution and sense of danger."[95]

In April 1944 II Canadian Corps was joined by I Corps from Italy. The five divisions and two independent armoured brigades of the First Canadian Army were reunited for the final drive through Holland and Northern Germany. There was no difficulty in merging the psychiatric services. Exhaustion casualties in both Corps were relatively light with the NP ratio well below 10. Once the fighting stopped exhaustion casualties quickly diminished as did the symptoms of those under treatment. (British soldiers, who had long maintained that the initials of the British Liberation Army stood for "Burma Looms Ahead," still expressed concern about the future but the Canadian government had announced that only volunteers would go to the Pacific.) It was over, there was now a brief moment for rejoicing and reflection.

Conclusion

I marched away
to the glorious trumpets of war,
the haunting horns of ambition,
the laughing trombones of youthfulness,
the pounding tubas of discipline.

I limped back home
to the shivering violins of fear,
the moaning violas of pain,
the sombre cellos of self-knowledge,
the stumbling basses of self-doubt.

Only later
did I discover
that I was my own composer
and my own conductor.

Ken Tout, Tanks Advance

The medical officers who prepared the chapter on neuropsychiatry for the official medical history concluded that "in comparison with medicine and surgery, the advances made by psychiatry during the war were not spectacular."[1] Rather, diagnostic and treatment procedures that had been implemented during World War I were rediscovered and incrementally advanced. The main difference between the two war experiences was that "the psychiatrist in the Second War developed a new relationship to administrative authority ... By the end of the campaigns in the Mediterranean and European theatres, the functions of the psychiatrists in the divisions and in the corps had become more clearly defined. They were useful in conserving manpower, in building morale, in developing treatment units, and for disposal of difficult cases."[2]

Wittingly or otherwise the psychiatrists had to identify, categorize, and label the widest range of behaviour. After the war Major McNeel wrote that they had to explain "any behaviour which impairs the efficiency of the group or which reflects an unsatisfactory state of mind likely to impair efficiency." He continued that "in practice almost every type of individual maladjustment comes under his observation. In addition to individual cases which are recognized to be his rightful concern there are many for whom no one else can suggest satisfactory management or disposal who are sent to the psychiatrist as a last resort."[3] World War II practice differed from that in World War I when, as a civilian psychiatrist noted, "there were many other 'crawl out' labels than neuropsychiatric ... flat feet, myalgia, constipation, debility, gastritis, old fractures, etc. Now there is only one 'crawl out' – a neuropsychiatric one and the neuropsychiatric branches of the armed services have had to accept nearly the full load of all such disaffected personnel as would previously have found a way out through flat feet, or something else. With medicine becoming more accurate and specific, it was only the natural that the neuropsychiatric service would be the 'catch-all' for a large proportion of cast-off personnel."[4]

Any army naturally produces a proportion of "cast-off personnel" during training. There were many reasons why some recruits were either unable or unwilling to adapt to routine army life. Individual needs more or less gratified in society were not easily met within a conformist military structure. Transforming civilians into able soldiers is a complex process, dependent for success on an effective training system. Serious questions may be raised about the effectiveness of the Canadian Army's training in Canada and Britain, which produced such large numbers of non-effectives.[5] Unfortunately there was no administrative provision at the time to discharge evidently incapable individuals simply because they were unlikely to become efficient soldiers.[6] Hence medical disposal evolved into an all-embracing alternative. As McNeel noted, psychiatrists became the final arbiters of the fate of many soldiers for whom units wished others to accept responsibility. It was a broad mandate, and while some psychiatrists possibly displayed on occasion "a sometimes too pretentious confidence in [their] judgments and formulations,"[7] most seem to have been well aware of the limitations of their practice. Nonetheless, they were inevitably subject to criticism for ostensibly allowing individuals to flee the rigours of soldiering through a psychiatric escape hatch. It is impossible to weigh the worth of that charge. Some individuals doubtless took advantage of the medical alternative to disciplinary action. However responsibility for unsoldierly behaviour lay essentially with commanders not doctors. General Chisholm only emphasized the obvious when he remarked that, "it is training officers who find these men not usable, not psychiatrists."[8] The United States Army's Inspector-General echoed the same theme. "Actually," he reported, "the majority of these cases are not psychoneurotic conditions because medical officers wish to make patients out of them but because the line officers have been unable to make soldiers out of them."[9]

Distinguishing between command and medical responsibilities became even more difficult once training gave way to combat. Battle added a significant dimension to the soldier-psychiatrist relationship. Psychiatrists had to consider both the individual needs of their patients and the institutional requirements of the army. On the battlefield lay an infinite range of behavioural possibilities between courage and cowardice. Describing various reactions to the terror and fear of battle as normal or aberrant is, of course, more than a semantic exercise. Rational behaviour is not necessarily militarily effective. It was hardly rational for an individual to expose himself willingly to severe mutilation or death in order to achieve some objective of which he probably was only dimly aware. Persuading soldiers to do so is the essence of effective military performance – the product of discipline, leadership, group cohesion, motivation, and morale. Any number of circumstances could tilt the balance that enabled soldiers to maintain self-control. Some soldiers were unable to keep that balance. The question was: were they sick? McNeel described the nuances:

There is a considerable number of men who show a varying degree of conscious exaggeration of symptoms on the basis of a minor disability. There is a still greater number who show no positive evidence of disability but who apparently make little effort to resist our common tendency to develop certain symptoms under stress. They have no sufficiently strong desire to maintain a well integrated personality in the face of unwanted stress or danger. These may become ineffective due to a condition which is "genuine" that is, not malingering. Is it illness?

One has sometimes heard an obviously "high-strung" officer say of a man who has cringed in his slit-trench or went AWL from action, "well if he's neurotic so am I." In both cases the diagnosis was correct but in one case it led to apparent fearlessness in action and in the other to evasion of duty. Which man was ill?[10]

McNeel's implicit distinction between personality and personal characteristics is useful. Despite elaborate efforts, no one identified a particular personality type that made a predictably effective soldier. This was especially the case with infantrymen, who sustained by far the most physical and psychological casualties. There was no psychological breathalyser or litmus test that accurately predicted which individuals might withstand the stress of battle and for how long. After reviewing hundreds of cases Lieutenant-Colonel Richardson concluded that "to have screened all the predisposed who developed battle neurosis would have screened many borderline personalities who carried on effectively. Many of the cases were in men of previously stable personalities."[11] Major Gregory's report on 544 soldiers who had broken down and were judged incapable of returning to battle is instructive: "Two thirds of the total cases

gave no apparent history of neurotic predispositions or previous instability
... only 19 per cent of the total cound have been considered as originally unfit
... 33 were sensitized by long service alone (average of 230 days). Twenty-
three per cent had an added factor of being previously wounded and 18 per
cent have been previously evacuated for exhaustion ... A further finding of
interest was that of 167 cases with long front-line service ... 42 cases or
23 per cent had carried on in spite of the fact that they had histories of previous
nervous disorders or evident traits predisposing to neurotic breakdown.[12]
"Gregory concluded that "even a neurotic can stand a long period of battle
stress when he has good morale, drive and character."[13] Major Moll elaborated: "Each soldier entering a battle carries within himself a varying degree
of predisposition or vulnerability to combat stress, which may or may not
lead to breakdown, depending on numerous factors, not excluding the fortunes
of war ... breakdown in battle may occur both in individuals who are grossly
predisposed to maladjustment and in individuals with minor or no apparent
predisposition. Severe and prolonged stress may precipitate a breakdown in
the most stable individual, and conversely, in some neurotic individuals, internal
conflicts may be relieved in the face of acute external danger and exceptional
courage may arise from fear itself."[14]

Morale and motivation, as well as luck and timing, were largely immeasur-
able factors in sustaining soldiers. After grappling with personnel selection
trials and methods throughout the war, Colonel Griffin reported to a colleague:

If you have an opportunity to talk to psychiatrists who have had experience with
psychiatric casualties, you will almost inevitably get the same reaction, namely: that
some grossly unstable psychoneurotics and some of the most hopelessly inadequate
personalities are able to carry on and do a most excellent job in the face of difficulties,
simply because they were properly motivated. They give various reasons for their
ability to carry on. In some, it is a case of "my father went through it okay, so I
guess I can." In others it seems to be a question of "I couldn't let the boys down."
Others seem to have a sort of intense sense of responsibility which makes it quite
impossible for them to give up and accept illness or at least disability. These men
are compared favourably with many others of apparently better constitution and
personality makeup who collapse quickly and admit with apparent cheerfulness that
"I guess I am just yellow and can't take it."[15]

By the end of the war there was widespread agreement that the soldier's
performance during training rather than any predetermined personality profile
was the best, if still imperfect, guide to his combat potential. Colonel Van
Nostrand summed up the consensus: "We do not believe that any of the
tests, or batteries of tests now employed in testing recruits, accurately measure stability or the ability of the man to carry his anxieties without breakdown. We therefore think that the rejection at the point of intake should

not be too rigid, but that weeding out during training should be more ruthless and reallocation because of proven unfitness should be more widely used."[16]

The psychiatrists were still left to explain why some soldiers broke so much earlier in combat than others. Individual, situational, and organizational factors all played a part in determining an individual's breaking point.[17] Precipitating causes might be direct battle stress or indirect personal distress. Timing was unpredictable. A wounded infantry officer remarked simply that "a man cannot after six months of an infantry battalion in action be the same man as when he started. I have seen men break who six or eight months ago you would say were afraid of nothing. Every man is different."[18] Then if "one man cracks, his fear is contagious," another thought, because he "can ruin the morale of a whole company."[19] When soldiers did break, psychiatrists had a difficult diagnostic problem. Major Moll wrote: "From the immediate clinical picture, so uniform at this stage, it is practically impossible to prognosticate future events, i.e. to determine in what form the neurosis is going to manifest itself. It is only later on, particularly following the evacuation of the exhaustion casualty from the Exhaustion Unit down the line, that the various psychosomatic syndromes will crystallize out of this, as yet, unformulated generalized state of tension."[20] Despite evident difficulties, it was at this initial stage that the psychiatrists gave their most useful service in providing rapid forward treatment. Rest, reassurance, comfort, and temporary safety were invaluable therapeutic tools. Like his colleagues, Moll "strongly urged that the exhaustion casualty be treated as soon as possible in a forward psychiatric unit, to prevent both an incapacitating 'flight into illness,' one of the solutions of the basic conflict between self-preservation and self-respect, and an unnecessary loss of manpower."[21]

Difficult as diagnosis might be, Richardson remarked, "the medical problem of treating and evacuating battle neurosis is simpler than the administrative problem of employing the casualties who remain unfit for further fighting service."[22] To some degree disposal had to aknowledge the patient's needs as well as those of his unit and the army. They did not always correspond. The psychiatrists could return the soldier to his unit, evacuate him, or reallocate him for non-combatant duties in an SEC. While American and, to a lesser degree, British psychiatrists routinely returned higher numbers of exhaustion cases to their units than Canadians did, the actual effects of that policy are impossible to judge. Reliable comparative statistics on recidivism and on the effectiveness of those returned are elusive. Colonel Van Nostrand summarized the Canadian experience. "We know of no method whereby an appreciable number of the persistently unwilling soldiers or constitutionally timid and neurotic ones can be converted into first class fighting troops."[23] Hence doubtful cases were channelled to non-combatant jobs rather than returned to hard-pressed fighting units. It was a humane and reasonable compromise among unpalatable alternatives. The SECs provided a means to employ individuals productively within the limits of their demonstrated capacities while avoiding an exodus from combat theatres. They also, Richardson thought, prevented "demoralization and aggravation of neurotic invalidism in many soldiers."[24]

The SECs became overloaded during the 1944-45 winter as more combat cases were reassigned to them. Others ended there when in the scramble to produce bodies to alleviate the shortage of infantrymen lower category men were sent overseas. Sending ill-trained or low-category men overseas for combat duties accomplished nothing, except perhaps to offer an illusion that something was being done. It simply passed disposal problems forward from Canada to Britain and eventually to forward fighting units. At least this was how overseas psychiatry saw it, as Colonel Van Nostrand pointed out: "We are still getting as reinforcements a fair number of soldiers who give histories of ill-health, and who break down under stress of very short battle experience. The rate of psychoneurotic breakdown in both theatres of war has been higher in reinforcements than in soldiers serving with units to which they had been posted during the training period.

"One soldier who stated that he enlisted in Canada on D-Day, was invalided from France in August with psychiatric disability. A fair number of other casualties admitted to Basingstoke at this time had less than six months in the army."[25]

The reinforcement system was a weak link, and it is as well that the war ended before the threads of the manpower dilemma stretched beyond repair. The psychiatrists could do little to affect its fundamental cause. Wartime psychiatry was just one part of a greater process encompassing command, medical, legal, administrative, and social spheres. The official history remarks that "the psychiatric problem was always in two parts: the symptoms of neurosis and the morale of the man ... In a soldier who failed the test of battle, the neurosis was first treated and then morale was considered. In short, the [psychiatrists were] dealing with two distinct problems long differentiated by the vulgar but accurate terms 'nerves' and 'guts'."[26] Psychiatrists might treat the first; the second derived from many sources, most of which were beyond their control. Individual and collective morale was affected by personal characteristics and social circumstances: manpower policies, enlistment procedures and standards, personnel allocation practices, training, unit performance, and leadership, among others. All affected the eventual outcome, whether or when and in what conditions a soldier became psychologically dysfunctional. Some were in that state before they enlisted, others became so during training, more broke down very early in battle, yet others burned out from over-exposure to accumulated stress. The psychiatrists saw the negative results of a complex system that tried to transform civilians into effective soldiers. Responsibility for systemic faults extended into every command and administrative niche. Colonel Van Nostrand summarized his experience:

I am not convinced that psychiatry will ever solve the vast problem of the psychiatric breakdown of soldiers during war. It is my opinion that the methods now employed in the British, American and Canadian armies will not materially lower the incidence of psychiatric casualties in a fighting force. There are various reasons for these opinions but two of them are fundamental. First, there is direct conflict between the needs of the service and the needs of the individual soldier as assessed by his physician. Secondly the attitudes and behaviour of the successful soldier are contrary to most of his previous teaching. He must adopt a detached attitude toward the mass destruction of human life. Property ceases to have any value except in relation to his comfort and success as a soldier. He must not allow death or mutilation of his comrades to prevent him from reaching his objective, and finally, he must pretend that he is glad to risk or lose his life for the cause.

The basic conflicts will always exist in armies such as ours which are composed largely of civilians who become soldiers, either voluntarily, or by compulsion for a short period. It is right that this should be so.

This is not a plea for sympathy for the inadequate soldier who is unable to stand the stresses of prolonged combat, nor is there any wish that discipline be relaxed or that any of the defections which fall under the heading of cowardice in the face of the enemy should be condoned. It is a plea for the adoption of realistic attitudes toward the reactions of normal men and women to the stresses of war.

We who formulate the medical policy should keep constantly before us certain premises which we believe to be true, but which we have ignored in practice –

1 An army's killing power is not necessarily proportionate to its numerical strength.
2 We fight our wars with human material and not with what we think we would like.
3 Although there are wide variations in the capacities of normal soldiers to withstand stress, every soldier has his breaking point, and if this is reached, he becomes a liability to his unit.[27]

THERE WAS NO PROFESSIONAL STRUCTURE to project the psychiatrists' collective military experience into peacetime society. Psychiatrists were as eager to demobilize as other amateur soldiers, and scattered to pick up the pieces of interrupted careers. Their case records and reports were packed up and deposited in archives where they have remained, largely unconsulted, ever since. A few wrote of their wartime experiences, but their professional futures were uncharted. Of 119 psychiatrists who responded to a questionnaire asking about their post-war plans only eight wanted permanent mental hospital appointments. Others would accept part-time privileges to supplement private practices. Most considered financial problems "as blocking the average psychiatrist from establishing himself in private practice."[28] Lack of funding and facilities for further training were other obstacles. Twenty-one military psychiatrists indicated their interest in advanced training but the four-year program at McGill University's Allan Memorial Institute, for example, could accept just four annually. Medical officers who had taken the six-month psychiatric primer during the war encountered difficulties in obtaining formal recognition of that training. Prospects were not promising.[29]

Nor was it at all clear just how the psychiatrists might best apply the professional insight they had acquired during the war to peacetime society. Military psychiatrists in Canada had quite different experience from those overseas, working mainly in areas of appraisal, allocation, and morale. They "stressed the term 'psychiatry' rather than sail under false colours and claim to be 'neuropsychiatrists'." Colonel Griffin thought that the real need was for a broadly based community mental health system: "While holding to the importance of developing within the medical frame-work and general medicine, psychiatry had an important responsibility to expand the frontiers of medicine so that they include responsibilities for the broad field of social and mental health. It is our belief that medicine must develop insights into the emotional, social and welfare problems which underlay so much physical illness and inefficiency. Furthermore, it must learn not only to give lip service to the concept of 'paying attention to the whole man' but must be prepared to investigate carefully those factors just as now it concerns itself with clinical and laboratory methods of physical examination."[30]

Overseas psychiatrists had been clinicians, diagnosing and treating patients. Neuropsychiatry came naturally to them. Colonel Van Nostrand wrote that "while we frequently changed policy because some of our earlier beliefs and organisation were impracticable ... we have never wavered in our opinion that psychiatry should remain as a branch of general medicine, and that the General Duty Officer and the Medical Specialist should view mental illness in the same way as any other disease."[31] In their view civilian psychiatric practice should remain closely associated with general hospitals.

The elaborate neuropsychiatric service overseas disappeared and Basingstoke was restored to Lord Camrose. Van Nostrand went to his farm north of Toronto and worked as a consultant for Veterans Affairs and other organizations.[32] Richardson returned to Toronto General Hospital committed to keeping the neuropsychiatric tradition alive, but psychiatry became a separate field of medicine in 1967. Richardson abandoned his dual career and became senior neurologist at Toronto General.[33] Arthur Doyle became chief psychiatrist at the Toronto Western Hospital.[34] Travis Dancey, Jack Griffin, Burdett McNeel, Charles Gould, and Albert Moll all had active post-war careers. Ken Hunter remained in the army, becoming its Director General of Medical Services.

The fate of the soldiers who suffered from battle exhaustion is less certain. One follow-up study was undertaken in 1950 when 346 men who had been treated in Dancey's exhaustion unit agreed to meet with a psychiatrist, a psychologist, and a medical social worker.[35] The survey, unfortunately typical of much psychiatric research in that era, had no control group and did not clearly define its objective. Dr Kingsley Ferguson, afterwards a professor of clinical psychology at the Clark Institute, was the young psychologist who participated in the project. In reviewing the long-forgotten report in 1988 he concluded that the results were of little value. The suggestion that 171 men were "adjusting" at the same level as before enlistment, 78 were "adjusting more adequately," and 97 "less adequately"[36] was largely meaningless because terms were not defined and baseline data not identified.[37]

The survey nevertheless lends some support to a view expressed by psychiatrists interviewed for this study, namely that the experience of battle exhaustion by itself was unlikely to have long-term consequences for the individual. The acute "breakdown" that occurred in combat was quickly relieved by removing the soldier from danger. Such individuals might well react similarly under comparable stressful situations but otherwise they were unlikely to be affected. Post-traumatic stress syndrome was not more likely to occur among battle exhaustion cases than among other veterans, possibly because the battle exhaustion casualty had not continued to repress his fears.

The army lost its interest in psychiatry as quickly as it did in most other aspects of its hard-won recent war experience. Within weeks of the German surrender Colonel Van Nostrand informed the DMS in London that there was no provision for psychiatrists to remain with the 25,000 strong Canadian Occupation Force in Europe.[38] There were strong grounds for supposing that there would be continuing incidence of psychiatric disorders following the war. For instance, post-traumatic stress reactions had been reported among Canadian troops who had participated in the assault landings in the Aleutian Islands in 1942.[39] Van Nostrand recommended that two psychiatrists would be needed – one with field units, the other at a base hospital. As well as usual clinical work they would be available to advise commanders on morale and disciplinary cases.[40]

His advice was accepted but demobilization overtook other concerns and there was no place in the small post-war army for psychiatrists. In September 1946 the DGMS told an enquirer from the American Psychiatric Association that military psychiatrists were unnecessary because "the strain of battle no longer exists and it is probable that army life in peacetime is no more hazardous, from the psychiatric point of view, than many civilian occupations."[41] He added, however, that "the importance of careful selection of Army personnel is fully appreciated and will continue in the post-war Army."[42] Army examiners, or personnel selection officers as they became, were the selectors. They screened recruits with a battery of tests and referred doubtful cases to civilian psychiatrists. The system proved less than satisfactory. Personnel officers were "not equipped by training and experience" to assess cases, one staff officer reported in 1948, while "civilian psychiatrists have a civilian approach to emotional fitness and this does not always conform with the military approach."[43] He concluded that the "economical use of manpower in war required the professional assistance of psychiatry."[44] Personnel and administrative staffs agreed, and the DGMS recommended that "this is a field of medicine that will contribute greatly to the utilization, allotment, and production results of manpower."[45] Major F.C.R. Chalke, a serving medical officer, became special advisor in psychiatry soon after. He advised on personnel selection and allocation, research, operational treatment and handling, and mental hygiene.

Chalke's appointment was connected with concern about behavioural and morale problems in the peacetime army. The onset of the Korean War two years later raised more immediate questions of manpower policy, personnel screening, and battlefield performance. When it decided to send troops to Korea in the summer of 1950 the government chose not to commit its only regular force infantry brigade. Instead the brigade was used as a training cadre to prepare a hastily recruited special force. The intention was to recruit veterans, reservists, and other volunteers, and a flood of recruits immediately swamped limited facilities. Political expediency dictated that deliberate recruiting procedures be jettisoned in order to accept anyone who wished to join up. Individuals were simply enrolled and sent off for training. It was an unfortunate decision. "The situation was one that generated legend," the restrained official historian has written. "... among the anomalies of this unique method of recruiting, the enlistment of a man with an articifial leg and one who was 72 years old stand out as highlights. There is at least one recorded case of a civilian who on impulse got on board a troop train in Ottawa with a newly enlisted friend and was found weeks later in Calgary, drilling with the PPCLI."[46] Within six months a quarter of the 10,000 men enrolled had been discharged or were awaiting discharge as non-effectives. Soon after the first infantry battalion reached Korea men were returned "suffering from chronic bronchitis, flat feet, atrophy of the leg muscles, cardiac palpitation, hypertension." They were in addition to another 150 men – 20 per cent of the unit's fighting strength – sent back for disciplinary, attitudinal, and psychiatric problems.[47]

While more extreme, the recruiting experience was similar to those of 1914 and 1939. Still, it was remarkable to see the army's manpower policy simultaneously afflicted with amnesia and *déjà vu*.[48] When the immediate chaos had subsided Chalke undertook a study of recruit-screening experience in order to advise on manpower planning. His initial appreciation presented two options based on the assumption that 10 per cent of a mobilized army of 500,000 would "present special problems of training, discipline, placement or disposal because of limited intelligence, inadequate stability, faulty habits, lack of maturity, or poor motivation. These individuals manifest themselves as poorly motivated or inefficient soldiers, recurrent delinquents or frank psychiatric patients." One option was to eliminate as many doubtfuls as possible through rigorous psychological screening at intake. The other was to enlist "all but the totally unfit," and employ doubtful recruits within the range of their demonstrated capacities. The first alternative was administratively simpler, promised more efficient training, and required fewer custodians of delinquents. At least this might be the case if screening was reliable, effective, and predictive. Chalke doubted that such tests were available. He explained: "If intensive screening is practised at the recruit level there is considerable loss of suitable recruits. The assessment of potential fitness is made by Personnel Officer and/or medical officer with the aid of the psychiatrist specialist and the man is rejected on either medical or administrative grounds. Unfortunately at the present time any accurate studies indicate that *at best* 50 per cent of the unfit will be detected at the recruiting depot, and *that an equal number of men, who would become effective, will be rejected as well, because of previous histories suggestive of unsuitability.* Optimally then, the most thorough screening would reduce the number of ineffectives finding their way into the army from 50,000 to 25,000, but at the same time would prevent enlistment of at least another 25,000 men *who would be effective.*"[49]

Chalke was no doubt aware at this time of post-war studies, especially in the United States, that were questioning the efficacy of World War II screening procedures. Nonetheless, faced with the recent Korean recruiting debacle, as well as the need to man a vastly expanded cold-war army, personnel administrators could not resist the lure of selection techniques and expanded the use of psychological testing. The new DGMS, Brigadier Hunter, was unimpressed with the claims of the behavioural scientists. Sharing Chalke's scepticism, he advised the Vice Adjutant-General that:

There is increasing attention being paid to the detection of recruits who are unlikely to succeed as soldiers because of defects of character or lack of motivation. Recruits are being rejected on these grounds at recruiting stations and personnel depots, in some cases on the advice of personnel officers or psychiatrists. Also the MMPI was recently introduced to aid in this detection.

DGMS is of the opinion that this represents a revival of the psychiatric screening methods which were utilized during WW II for practically the same purposes. Informed professional opinion in this country, the US and UK is that this approach is fraught with inaccuracy and that criteria upon which to base judgments are not well established.

It is strongly advised that the validity of judgments as to fitness in the area of character and motivation, be subjected to controlled study.[50]

Chalke was interested in conducting controlled studies but first he wanted to find out what had been learned from World War II experience. His published result, *Psychiatric Screening of Recruits*, is comprehensive, instructive, and neglected.[51] It not only thoughtfully reviewed the available research literature on military psychological testing but also placed it in the broader context of manning and manpower policy. Chalke described the almost unani-

mous scepticism of wartime psychiatrists about the value of predicting effective military behaviour on the basis of *a priori* screens and tests. The predictive problem was the huge gap between the personality traits that were
presumed to produce a good combat soldier and those that he actually displayed.
It may seem anachronistic in an era that employs psychologists to screen hockey
players and those in a variety of other occupations, but accurately predicting
an effective infrantryman remains as difficult as ever. Chalke noted that "some
psychiatrists reported that 'obsessive-compulsives' made the best soldiers and
others stated that they could not adjust. A similar conflict occurred concerning
'mild anti-social psychopaths'." He concluded cautiously that "as long as he
is dealing with a serious disability the evidence is more often right than wrong.
Operating within an imposed ceiling of 4 per cent of the population and with
definition of 'reasonable service' the psychiatrist when trained could make
a valuable contribution to manning according to this policy." Beyond that
was a predictive no-man's land.

The difficulty in making best use of the psychiatrist's talents in identifying
the grossly inadequate lay in the wide policy oscillations between no winnow-
ing out at all and overly rigorous screening based on dubious premises, as
Chalke described:

The experience of the past few years has been that in spite of the psychiatrists disavowal
of sufficient justification for screening, manning authorities insist on selection on
grounds of character and motivation. The methods used at times appear to a scientist
as naïve and uncontrolled. Moreover the techniques are mostly of the "all or none"
variety. In periods of increased manpower all attempts at selection in the sphere of
emotional suitability are stopped and large numbers of handicapped are enlisted. Concern over this situation results in sweeping reimposition of what are believed to be
"high"standards. The psychiatrist has few facts upon which to base advice in this
situation. In fact he finds himself, after a decade and a half of experience, faced with
a host of what now being to appear as perennial questions.

a. Who are the individuals "obviously" disqualified by disabling disease of a psychiatric nature?
b. Is it possible to indicate at the initial examination the optimum type of employment for those with non-disqualifying limitations?
c. Can factors available at the recruit examination be weighted to provide a scale of
   probability which permits flexibility in meeting manpower requirements?
d. Does a more specific definition of the emotional requirements of the job increase
   the accuracy of psychiatric predictions?
e. What is the degree of agreement between psychiatrists' predictions?
f. To what degree is psychiatric training and experience a factor in the ability to predict
   in the area of emotional stability?

Manning policies during World War II, or in the 1950s when Chalke wrote, or a generation later, were beyond the purview of the psychiatrists. They were "not formulated on the basis of what a psychiatrist can do, but in terms of practical, political and economic necessity."[52] Those necessities remain in constant flux, and it is exceedingly doubtful that Chalke's questions will ever be satisfactorily answered. In the meantime soldiers' conversations like the following will echo in new battlefields.

"Ferking fool's game, war. Not so bad shooting Jerries. It's when the buggers shoot back ...

"Fool's game, sitting 'ere, mate. Waiting to get your goolies shot off."

"Why don't we just get up and go, instead of sitting here like swallows in the sunset? ...

"Still say we should all get up and go home. They could only shoot us. And we'll get flaming shot, sitting here."

"They don't shoot people in this war. Not for deserting."

"Shot thousands in the last war. For cowardice. Shot 50,000 in one battle. That's what they gave the little lieutenants revolvers for. Not for shooting Fritz. For shooting cowards up the arse."

"Couldn't have shot 50,000 at once. You're a bleeding idiot" ...

"I'd rather be a bleeding idiot taking the chance of being shot for deserting than a bleeding hero being shot for certain by Jerry over that hedge."

"You're safe if you go bonkers. If you go pissie-cologically sick. They can't shoot you then."

"Well why don't we all go bonkers? All start braying like jackasses? All start tickling our armpits and legpits like gorillas? All sit 'ere and stare and drool with our mouths open and refuse to eat?"

"That's mutiny. That is a shootable offence. If you all go pissie-cologically sick it's mutiny. You can only go one by one. Every man to pissie-college by himself."

The imbecile conversation meanders on, but so near to the borders of stark truth that I wonder if the slightest push, or just one more bomb, will send us all hurtling down the mental precipice on whose lip we teeter.[53]

Appendixes

APPENDIX I

The PUHLEMS system of medical classification was introduced in 1943. It was designed to categorize individuals according to their perceived physical, mental, and emotional capabilities. Variations of the system were adopted by the British and American Armies. Following is the guide for recruiters, medical officers, and personnel selection officers in assessing the M (mental) and S (stability) factors. Copy in NA RG 24, Vol. 12, 630.

Mental Capacity (M)

1 One of the most important and at the same time difficult parts of the examination of the recruits is the appraisal of mental status. In spite of the reiteration of the importance of psychiatric standards, there have been more soldiers discharged from the Army because of mental and nervous disabilities than for any other single reason. Each medical examiner must be constantly on the alert for signs of mental or nervous disorder, even though he be engaged in the examination of an entirely different system. Any suspicious sign or symptom should be recorded for the attention of the psychiatrist.

2 High among such disabilities is insufficient intelligence, by which is meant a level of learning ability insufficient for complete military training. For the appraisal of intelligence, test results (Revised Examination M) are usually available and are found to be very helpful.

3 *Diagnostic Criteria* – Insufficient Intelligence. Diagnosis should be based on poor educational and occupational achievements, lack of general knowledge concerning his native environment and poor performance on psychological tests. The results of Revised Examination M may be supplemented by other clinical tests as necessary. The estimation of intelligence, however, remains a clinical judgment and should not be based on test results alone. All factors must be considered. Illiteracy per se is not a cause for rejection. In

recording the diagnosis on MFM2, care should be taken not to use such terms as "imbecile or "moron." A better expression is "intelligence insufficient for military training."

4 *Feigned Mental Deficiency*. This is frequently encountered among illiterates. On careful interview, discrepancies will almost always be found in the educational and occupational history. Non-language psychological tests frequently reveal characteristic responses (e.g., failing on ridiculously easy items and passing harder ones, etc.). Examination by psychiatric specialist is indicated in suspected cases.

5 *Mental Capacity* – Summary of Grading.

MI   Intelligence sufficient for full combatant duty and training, including appropriate tradesman or specialist training.

M2   Intelligence sufficient for non-tradesman or non-specialist combatant duties or trades requiring experience rather than ability. (Assignment of grades MI and M2 will be based upon the recommendation of the Army Examiner).

M4   Specific defect in intelligence or learning ability so that full training cannot be absorbed. Has sufficient intelligence, however to be useful at simple routine duties, simple labour, etc. (M4 will be used for both new recruits and serving soldiers.) Assignment of grades M4 and M5 will be based upon the recommendations of the Army Psychiatrist with the exception that insofar as M4 represents a downward revision of grading, based upon mere failure at a higher level of function, the Army Examiner's recommendation to the medical board will be sufficient. Whenever psychiatric referral is involved and in all cases of rejection or discharge, responsibility for the recommendation of M grading rests with the Psychiatrist.

M5   Unsuitable for service anywhere in any capacity because of insufficient intelligence.

Note   It is stressed that these gradings are definitely not made on the basis of the M test results alone. Careful clinical appraisal of the man's intelligence is absolutely necessary (see para. 3).

Stability (s)

1 The difficulties and problems raised by the acceptance of men who are mentally unfit are legion. Such men have a bad effect on training efficiency and disturb morale and discipline generally. It must be recognized once and for all that the army is not a corrective institution and will never "make a man" out of a mental defective, a neurotic or a psychopath. Such men are much more effectively employed in primary industry where, in the security of their homes and families, they can lead a fairly productive although sheltered existence and in this way contribute to the national war effort. As soldiers, they are failures and usually terminate their service with a long listing of vague illnesses or delinquencies, or both. A conservative attitude should be adopted by the medical board, therefore, especially in connection with the appraisal of recruits. Fairly definite information is usually available as to intelligence and learning ability, but emotional and nervous stability is more difficult to assess. Where there is doubt concerning the latter, error should be made on the side of rejection rather, than acceptance.

2 Examiners should be on the watch for the following types of personality disorders, most of which can be easily spotted during the physical examination:

(a) Inability to understand and execute simple commands quickly and correctly
(b) Unusual stupidity and awkwardness
(c) Resentful, suspicious, sullen or surly attitude
(d) Unusual anxiety and tension
(e) Silly inappropriate laughter
(f) Excessive shyness and seclusiveness
(g) Appearance of sadness – usually with sluggishness
(h) Over-boisterousness
(i) Abnormal autonomic responses, especially excessive blushing, perspiration, fainting, pallor, cold extremities, rapid pulse, tremor

3 The diagnosis of mental disorders depends for the most part on an adequate history. This of course may be difficult to evaluate since it comes from the recruit himself. It should be supplemented, where necessary, by information from the individual's physician, police records, hospital record, employment records, etc. A social worker is provided in the establishment of reception centres in order to help the medical board obtain adequate social histories of this type. In addition to the history, the diagnosis is based on the examiner's appraisal of the recruit's general behaviour in the examination environment and his responses in conversation and questioning.

4 The psychiatric examination should be conducted in private, preferably in a quiet room. The most successful approach is one of straightforward, professional enquiry, coupled with a genuine respect for the individual's personality and with due consideration for his feelings. A friendly objective attitude is required, and brusqueness and haste should be avoided. An adequate examination can never be completed in less than fifteen minutes.

5 Questioning should begin with points obviously relevant to the situation. It is always sound to begin with questions relating to general health, the existence of complaints, pains and aches, etc. This can lead easily and naturally to a canvass of the conditions under which the recruit or soldier has been working and his occupational history. Attitudes toward his boss and his relationships generally with friends and family can then be assessed. From this point the questioning can proceed without embarrassment to school and family history and other significant items.

6 *Standard of Stability*. The criterion of acceptance in the army must be stability sufficient to allow the recruit to adjust satisfactorily to training and employment likely to be required of him.

7 By stability is meant the temperamental and emotional aspects of his personality. The soldier should have reasonable poise and nervous stability as indicated by usual physiological indices, e.g., heart rate, perspiration, tremor, temperature of extremities, etc.

Signs of emotional instability, sullenness, anxiety, shyness, excessive laughter or tears, sadness or over-boisterousness must be regarded seriously as limiting factors in army life. Similarly, evidence indicating inability to get along with family, friends, the various authorities in school, occupation and society indicates temperamental instability. Defects of speech (stuttering and stammering) are often indicative of instability. The man's speech must be readily understood, although a mild degree of defect is allowed if he is otherwise physically, intellectually and emotionally fit.

8 *Psychoneurosis (anxiety states, hysteria, obsessive compulsive states, hypochrondriasis, etc.).* Diagnosis would be based on a history of vague complaints which have interfered with progress in civil occupational life. Family history of chronic physical or mental illness or instability in parent, brothers or sisters is important, as is the history of a home broken during the individual's childhood. The presence of many symptoms without evidence of organic pathology is suggestive, to wit: palpitation, sweating, dizziness, fainting spells, headaches, paralysis or paraesthesia. Psychoneurotics are often emotionally immature, unstable, dependent, suggestible and hypochondriacal. They often have specific fears, (e.g., of dark, certain food, crowds, etc.) and certain types display obsessive and compulsive behaviour, (e.g., inflexible rituals concerning food, sleeping, dressing and recurring obsessional thoughts). In cases where the neurosis is mild and not totally disabling, and of such a nature that a successful adjustment to army life could be made if the man were retained for service in Canada only, grade 4 may be assigned.

9 *Psychopathic Personality.* Diagnosis cannot often be made without full information about the social and occupational background. The chief characteristic of this disorder is inability of the individual to profit by experience. Men with this disorder are unable to meet the usual adult social standards of truthfulness, decency, responsibility and consideration for their fellow associates. They are emotionally unstable and absolutely not to be depended upon. They are impulsive, show poor judgment and in the Army they are continually at odds with those who are trying to train and discipline them. They often present a favourable impression superficially and may have good intelligence. Their past history of incorrigibility, restlessness, frequent changes of job, will indicate the real defect. Among this group are many homosexuals, chronic delinquents, chronic alcoholics and drug addicts. All such men should be regarded as medically unfit for service anywhere in any capacity.

10 *Psychosis. (insanity, frank mental illness)* The most commonly occurring psychoses of the military age group are Dementia Praecox (schizophrenia) and Manic Depressive Psychosis. The diagnosis of Dementia Praecox is based usually on odd, eccentric or bizarre behaviour coupled with unusual seclusiveness, evidence of strange ideas, attitudes and suspicions. Frequently the individual has peculiar attitudes towards his own body and body functions, and the feeling that he is different from others, set apart for a special mission, etc. Often there is evidence of disturbed emotional behaviour such as silly, inappropriate laughter

or unusual apathy or indifference. There may be evidence of delusions and hallucinations. Manic Depressive Psychosis may be suspected in men showing marked emotional depression and melancholia with psycho-motor retardation; or the reverse, euphoric boisterousness with restlessness and over-talkativeness. There may or may not be a history of treatment in a mental hospital.

The diagnosis of a psychosis or any type of a clearly marked pre-psychotic state (schizoid, paranoid, or cyclothymic personality types) or a history of treatment in a mental hospital will exclude or discharge the man from military service.

11 *Malingering*. True malingering is defined as the conscious and deliberate attempt by the individual to feign a physical or mental disease for the definite purpose of attaining a particular end which, in the army, is usually rejection or discharge. It is frequently suspected in those individuals who are more or less unwittingly exaggerating (cf. "skrimshanking"). It is also often confused with clear cut psychoneurotic reactions.

12 The commonest types of true malingering are simulated defects in mentality, visions, hearing and enuresis (bed-wetting).

13 It is always a difficult problem to decide whether a malingerer is worth keeping in the army in view of the trouble and expense he causes. The danger of a rejection or discharge, too easily obtained, is that the malingering will spread and become epidemic. Generally speaking, if the malingerer does not have an unfavourable past record and if he is otherwise acceptable, he should not be rejected. Most of the recruits who attempt to malinger are trying it for the first time and are easily discovered. When confronted with the situation and given time to reconsider, most of them decide to co-operate. Where evidences of psychopathic tendencies are discovered, the recruit should be rejected, and the serving soldier should be discharged.

14 *Simulated Defects of Vision*. Various tests using prisms and coloured lens as well as the opthalmoscope have been designed to test the malingerer. One of the most difficult conditions to judge in this regard is the claim to night blindness. The opthalmologist should examine all such cases.

15 *Simulated Defects of Hearing*. Many simple tests can be used for determining malingering here. One of the best is the use of the binaural stethoscope. This is fully described in the section on hearing.

16 *Enuresis*. This may be real or simulated and is frequently encountered in mild epidemics in barracks and training centres. In either case, it is very difficult to deal with. Careful history and where possible documentary evidence indicating the presence of the disability in civilian life may be necessary to exclude malingering. True enuresis is cause for discharge. Malingerers should be placed in a cot without a mattress until they are cured.

17 *Stability – Summary of Grading.*

s1   Emotionally stable. No signs of psychoneurosis or any serious divergence from the normal in autonomic nervous system function or stability.

s2   Same as s1.

s3   Some history of emotional instability in early life with good adult adjustment. Usable overseas for all but full combatant duty.

s4   Has evidence of emotional instability but not sufficient to preclude successful adjustment to the army if retained for service in Canada. (Grade 4 in both M and S warrants discharge of a serving soldier).

s5   Unsuitable for service anywhere in any capacity because of instability.

APPENDIX 2

Many soldiers proved unable or unwilling to become effective soldiers during the army's lengthy waiting period in Britain. Following is the text of a lecture given by Major C.E.G. Gould describing his experiences with 1,000 of these men in a psychiatric out-patient's clinic in 1942-43. Copy in NA, RG24, vol. 2089.

Observations on 1,000 referred neuropsychiatric cases
C.E.G. Gould, Major, RCAMC

In discussing these neuropsychiatric cases briefly this afternoon, I don't propose to attempt a detailed review or analysis of them, but rather to touch upon some of the salient points of more general interest insofar as they affect all of us.

The neuropsychiatric clinic at this hospital functions as a purely Out-patient Dept, even patients referred from within the hospital being dealt with as if they were out-patients. As it is a one-man clinic, it deals with not over 8 or 9 patients per day, so that the average across the 8 month period which these 1,000 cases cover, is 6 per day, and the average time per case something around 1 1/3 hours.

It is apparent therefore, that neither the work-up nor the treatment can be as extensive as is possible at #1 Neurological Hospital, the purpose being to have the Regional Neuro-psychiatrists set up as segregation points or filters to weed out and deal with neuropsychiatric cases that can be better handled without hospitalization, and to refer in to #1 Neurological Hospital only those cases that require further diagnostic investigation or more extensive treatment.

However, the X-ray and laboratory facilities at this hospital are available, and routine blood Wassermanns are taken on all neuropsychiatric patients. The only other procedures of note are the Intelligence Tests and spinal punctures. The IT used almost routinely is the Raven Matrix, which requires but little supervision, and the spinal punctures are done in the OPD, using a fairly fine needle, and the patient returns to his unit after lying down for 1 1/2 hours. This group of 1,000 cases represents all the cases seen at the Regional Neuropsychiatric Clinic located at No. 8 Canadian General Hospital between August 1942 and April 1943. The case incidence, in summary form, is as follows:

Psychoneurosis	600
Psychoneurosis (with Mental Deficiency)	56
Psychoneurosis (with Psychopathic Personality)	13
Psychopathic Personality	94
Mental Deficiency	72
Psychosis	29
Epilepsy	16
Neurosyphilis	15
Neuritis (all types)	9
Herniated Intervertebrae Disc	8
Reactive Depression (unspecified)	6
Migraine	6
Concussion (Post-traumatic Syndrome)	2
Drug Addiction	2
Myasthenia Gravis	1
Narcolepsy	1
Congenital Syphilis	1
Post-encephalitic Parkinsonism	1
Hypoglycemia	1
NAD (Neuropsychiatric)	67
TOTAL	1,000

First comes the group of psychoneurotics, totalling 669 cases. This particular group represents all the various types of neurosis – acute and chronic, hysteria, obsessive-compulsive and neurasthenic, and have all been dealt with, so far as I am concerned, as out-patients – even those that have been referred from within this hospital. I say "so far as I am concerned" because some of them have been sent on to #1 Neurological Hospital for further treatment.

The history taking on all these cases has been pretty well standardized, the Past, Family and Personal Histories – particularly the Personal History – constituting the bulk of the entire history. The present complaints are dealt with briefly only, in an attempt to demonstrate that they are not the "History of the Present Illness," but merely a cross-section, as existing at the present time, of a longitudinal chain of events that in most cases has existed throughout the entire life of the patient.

In other words, along psychobiological lines, to sketch a biography of the patient as a human being, and show as logically as possible by his life history, that his present reactions whether they be dyspepsia, headaches, back pain, dizziness, or what have you, are a more or less natural reaction, for him, to his present environment.

Many of these cases have been sent in already diagnosed, but in a negative way, i.e., the diagnosis has been arrived at by elimination. All the necessary work to rule out peptic ulcer, heart disease, or disease of the bones or joints, has already been done by the specialists concerned, and with all this necessary information already at hand, all that remains for me is to write out a past and personal history of a type that will put the diagnosis on a positive footing. In addition to these cases, there are some that are already worked up completely, and are referred simply for suggestions as to therapy and disposal – so I don't put forward these 669 cases as 669 diagnostic efforts of my own.

Now while the histories on these cases don't bring to light anything that isn't already well known, I would like to run over briefly some of the points in them, which, by their almost never-failing consistency, have come to be regarded as the criteria of the psychoneurotic state. These are:

1 A history of neurosis in the family, almost always in one or the other parent, and frequently in one or more siblings.

2 A shy sensitive childhood, with the frequent appearance, in pathological degree, of one, or two, or sometimes all three, of the cardinal triad of nightmares, sleepwalking, and bed wetting.

3 Usually a fairly average school history, sometimes above the average, occasionally giving evidence of unusual extroversion – the leader of the gang, or the life of the party type – or more commonly of unusual introversion, with some seclusiveness, a tendency to play individualized sport rather than team games, and very commonly leaving school in the middle of a year before the final exams.

4 The work history frequently shows inadequate reactions, either by frequent shift from job to job, or by work on a plane below the individual's qualifications, i.e., the boy who takes a business course and following this does odd jobs and labour work. The inadequacy of these reactions must of necessity be a surmise, as the individual almost always has a plausible rationalization of them.

5 The marital history frequently gives evidence of inadequate reactions.

Now a point worth noting is that with this history there is quite commonly little or no evidence of the previous existence of the symptoms of which the soldier now complains, after he has been in the army anywhere from a few months to 3 1/2 years, and so commonly the dates of onset are either upon or shortly after enlistment, or upon or shortly after coming overseas. In the light of the past history, the reasons for this become a little more obvious. Prior to enlistment, from childhood up, he was accustomed to take evasive action, and became at an early age adept at soliciting sympathy. And from the moment of enlistment evasive action became nearly impossible – he was held as in a vise – and sympathy, particularly from the Sgt Major, was not forthcoming – and I am speaking now of the psychoneurotic who has signs as well as symptoms. Now where exactly the relationship lies between the psychic factors as aggravants, and the biologic factors as consequences – where this inter-relationship takes place, and what is involved in the transit from psychic to biologic, I don't know. In fact, I try not to think about it too much, because the more I do, I find I know less and less about more and more, and am not attracted by the possible end point of knowing nothing about everything.

Now that is a very rough sketch of the fundamentals in these psychoneurotic histories. But it does not take into account the gradation that lies between the psychological and biological components. If we take at one end these which could be called purely "psychological" and at the other end the case which could be called purely "biological," we have at one extreme the man who seeks to evade service, in a serious way, as the result of reactions going on in his higher thinking centers only and if of average intelligence and insight, is therefore wilful and anti-social, and is consequently a malingerer. At the other extreme we have the purely biological, i.e., the man who is seeking to evade full service only because he finds himself unable to do it, being beset by many distressing symptoms, the cause of which he is totally unaware, and which are obviously the result of some form of pronounced autonomic imbalance.

As in most things, the extremes are rare, and the great majority of these cases fall somewhere in the middle of the group, tapering off at each end.

To make a long story short, in any given case, once the evidence is at hand, the problem, for purposes of treatment and disposition, boils down to two essential factors:

1 The evaluation of the man's mental processes – his motivations, either conscious or subconscious, what appears to be causing them, whether or not they can be influenced, and if so, by what, and in what direction. The evaluation of these factors, without the aid of a crystal ball, is sometimes a bit difficult.
2 Relatively more easy is the evaluation of the man's disability as the result of his symptoms and findings – symptoms such as difficulty sleeping, irritability, lack of pep and energy, loss of interest, memory difficulties, etc., and the findings of labile pulse, B.P. and respiratory rates, leading to quick fatigue, the clammy moist hands and feet, mottled or cyanotic when dependant, the tremor of the outstretched fingers, the fingernails bitten short, to say nothing of the more localized troubles such as dyspepsia, headache, bowel spasm, etc.

To simplify the situation for myself, particularly as regards treatment and disposition, I try by rule of thumb to categorize a case predominantly into one of three neuro-anatomical levels: (1) Cortical, i.e., the level of consciousness; (2) Thalamic, i.e., the level of the undifferentiated emotions, and those symptoms referred to as expressing generalized tension; (3) Brain stem, i.e., the level of control of visceral activity and those symptoms referred to as expressing localized tension.

Roughly speaking most cases, when thought of in these terms, can be placed, although never neatly and completely, in one of these three categories, and that brings us to the question of treatment and disposition.

1 With regard to the first group, where the lesion might be said to be mainly cortical – I see very few cases that could be termed purely cortical, but a fair number in which the lesion could be termed predominantly cortical. With these cases the treatment and disposition is more or less routine. After examination the man is told that his symptoms have been taken into account, and they are harmless. Very little attempt is made to analyse them for him, or to go into the differences between functional and organic disease. The final recommendation on his report is to the effect that the man is a disciplinary rather than a medical problem, and any failure to perform his duties in the future, due to his present troubles, should be treated with disciplinary measures. This final para-

graph is read aloud to the man, and he is returned to duty with the warning that his Colonel is likely to be his next doctor.

The reason for adopting this somewhat arbitrary method in dealing with these selected cases, is the success that I have seen with this method, judiciously administered, by some of my RMO friends – of whom I still have a few even after being on this job 8 months. In one unit I know of, every man who comes on sick parade – apart from incidental cuts and blisters – must come with his kit, prepared to go to hospital direct from the RAP, and false alarms are frowned upon. Some might say that there are a lot of unanswered problems in this unit, that psychiatric disorders are seething beneath the surface. That this is not true, I believe, is evidenced by the fact that the morale of the unit is good, and the Medical Officer is not troubled by men sent in by the NCOs because they dropped out of a route march, or got short of breath on PT. So I feel that there is a definite place for a summary disposal of selected cases, dangerous if used too widely, no doubt, but dangerous also if not used enough.

2 The second group is where the lesion can be termed predominantly mid-brain or thalamic – sleep disturbances, irritability, difficulty concentrating, anorexia, introspectiveness – the symptoms of generalized nervous tension. These cases are the group where the real salvage work can be done. They might be represented as being in a mid-position, with a leg on each side of the fence, and in my opinion are very much worth while spending some time on, as they don't stay in that state for very long. If not rehabilitated within a reasonable time, they reach a state of hopelessness, and require revision of their category.

Due to the time factor, the psychotherapy given these men, as out-patients, has perforce to be short, and is therefore far from ideal. In the first place, I think it is important that the man should be conceded all his symptoms, lock, stock, and barrel. In doing this, I usually add that I would have conceded a lot of other symptoms as well if he had mentioned them. I think this is important in the preservation of his self respect, which in my opinion is just as important with a soldier as it is in civilian life, where it is very important. This total concession is quickly followed by the information to the man that misinterpretation and even exaggeration, of his symptoms are invariably part of the picture, and a part for which, as long as he has no insight, he is not held responsible. Then follows an explanation between disease and functional states, using an example such as a cold hand, with its colour changes, numbness, and motor loss, as a type example of a functional state. Then an explanation of the parallelism between temperature, as the aggravating factor in the case of the hand, and the patient's psychological difficulties (as gleaned from the history) as the aggravating factor in his symptoms, which are pointed out to him as being essentially no different from those of the hand. No mention is made, again for the sake of the patient's self-respect, of the constitutional factor involved in his case, and he is informed that his prognosis can be as good as that of the cold hand, and depends on two factors; his insight into the nature of his troubles (which at this point he will usually admit he has); and the amount of positive effort he makes to adapt to his environment. It is explained to him that his lack of success in the past has been largely due to his lack of insight, but now that he has that, his outlook is better, but no promises of cure are made, and the onus of responsibility to carry on lies with him, now that he knows that he does not have serious disease, and knows that what he does have is a functional state and has some understanding of the significance of that. When possible a few concrete suggestions are thrown in, designed to help him escape from introversion.

If the soldier refuses to accept this explanation, he is returned for a second interview, a second recheck is made to rule out the possibility of an underlying psychosis, a mental deficiency overlooked at the first examination, or the possibility of him being a psychopath, and if this recheck yields negative results, he is given a second psychotherapeutic talk, and if he still refuses to cooperate, he is placed in Group 1, that is, it is assumed his lesion is more cortical than at first suspected, he is told this in language he can understand, and returned as a disciplinary problem.

However, this latter contingency in this group of cases is not very common, and the results in this group are encouraging insofar as follow-up is possible. The necessity for speaking only in language that the patient can thoroughly understand is imperative, and I see no harm in conceding him his symptoms, provided it is followed by strong reassurance, and he is then led, by logical steps, to take the responsibility for his future squarely on his own shoulders.

These cases are almost never recommended for category revision when first seen. The less hopeful ones are seen again after one month (although the patient is never told he is coming back in a month when he leaves) and a proportion of these then require revision, particularly in cases where the precipitating cause is severe and genuine domestic difficulty. But by and large, cases in this group are usually very much worth while the time spent on them.

3 The third group is the brain stem group – in which one can visualize if not the source, at least the relay, of such disturbances as disorders in cardiac rate and respiratory rate, B.P. lability, gastric disturbances, and many other symptoms and signs which are generally classed as expressing localized tension.

In this group as a whole bad family histories are common, the patients themselves might be termed constitutionally neurotic, and are frequently physically inferior. Along with the evidences of visceral autonomic disturbances are frequently those of peripheral disturbance, with sweaty hands and feet, mottled or cyanotic when dependant, and a tremor of the outstretched fingers. The prognosis in these cases is consistently poor. In my opinion they should be recategorized promptly, and the two reasons why I do not as a rule spend much time on psychotherapy with these cases are firstly that I have no hopes of ever altering their constitution, and secondly that many of them are conscientious enough, and only too willing to carry on when placed in a category that enables them to evade legitimately those duties they had found very difficult.

Before leaving the neurotic group as a whole, I would like to say a word about the all-too-common practice of examining a man for a specific complaint, often taking X-rays as well, and then, when no organic pathology is found, telling the man, in effect, that his examination and X-rays are negative, and leaving the matter at that. The necessity for more action than this lies in the fact that the man will also state that his symptom is what is preventing him from doing his training or other regular duties, and that is one statement that can be taken from him as an absolute statement of fact, and quite often amounts to a triumph of underestimation on his part. So the paradox of an ineffective soldier with no organic basis for his ineffectiveness exists, and he will remain ineffective unless further steps are taken to survey him as a whole, and to attempt to see his troubles objectively as they appear to him, and not through our eyes, with our insight, and at our level of social consciousness.

There are two further types of patient that present problems of peculiar interest. The first are those who give a history of amnesia. The five or six cases of this in this series have all been of a very mild order, and gave a history of having lost their memory for a given period while AWL, and apart from this alleged blank period, their memory was otherwise intact. These cases have been dealt with routinely on the basis of whatever manifestations of neurosis they had, and no attention paid to their amnesia, except to be warned that they would be held fully responsible for the one that had occurred, and any more that might occur in the future, and as far as I know there have been no recurrences to date. While I believe this type of summary disposal to be justified in this type of case, it does not apply to cases of more deep-seated hysteria, but there are none of these in this series.

The other group of peculiar interest is the enuretics. Until recently enuresis in soldiers has, to me at any rate, always loomed as a formidable problem, but in the last few months, this problem has practically vanished, and in a most mysterious fashion. Altogether I have referred 9 cases to Major Campbell, and apparently all 9 have been cured, and altogether I believe Major Campbell has treated about 40 cases across a period of 6 months. Many cases referred to as enuresis will not stand up to a careful check on the suspect's bedding ... and further cases dissipate before the regime of a lower bunk in a corner near the door, and a spell on night shift. The cases that remain are those who have had enuresis off and on most of their life, and are more often than not reasonably stable individuals.

It is this type of case that Major Campbell has cured with almost unfailing regularity. He has done it with the use of a cystoscope, and I'll admit that I started, like Goldsmith's fool, to scoff, but remained to pray. And since quite recently, he has had equally good results with a mental defective with enuresis, it seems fair to adopt the Jesuit axiom that the end justifies the means. At first the patients were hospitalized for this treatment, which consists of cystoscopic dilatations of the internal sphincter at weekly intervals, but more recently he has been doing them as out-patients, with equally good results, and I believe that the number of treatments varies between one and six.

The next group I would like to say a few words about are the psychopaths. There are 94 of these in this series, and as a group, they are interesting and distinctive. Most of them are surprisingly cooperative and reasonably honest in the giving of a history, which makes diagnosis easy and practically automatic, but an appreciable percentage are either evasive, or very plausible in giving a fictitious history or one that suffers from errors of omission. These cases are the ones that lead to missing the diagnosis, and a miss on this diagnosis is usually a bad miss, and I have learned this to my sorrow more than once. There is one lever, however, which is almost always successful in prying open the lurid record of the past and that is possession of the man's crime sheet. If this is gone over with him in some detail, it rarely fails to bring forth the history of his civilian difficulties, and in the antisocial type of psychopath there is characteristically a record that starts with a dissolute or a broken home, visits to juvenile court, reform schools, and from there a more or less continuous record of temperamental instability, evidencing impulsiveness and gross defects in judgment, and usually punctuated by civilian crimes of one sort or another in adulthood, and very commonly a long army crime record.

Psychotherapy in these cases is about as rational as trying to sell a block of ice to an Eskimo, and once they are diagnosed, they become a problem in disposition. Some of these men are both intelligent and aggressive, and whether or not they can be used for fighting remains to be seen, and it can be surmised with considerable certainty, that there are a goodly number of aggressive psychopaths still in the ranks of field units, whose commanding officers are putting up with their misdemeanours, as far as possible, in the apparently reasonable hope that when the fighting starts they will be of value in action. Of the 94 cases in this series, however, the reasonably intelligent and aggressive types, in whom one could visualize the possibility of using them as fighting troops, were in the minority, and the majority of them were complicated by either psychoneurosis or mental deficiency.

The mental defectives in this series, a group of 72, varying from Mental Dullness to Moron, also constitute little more, once the diagnosis is made, than a problem in disposition. The mental defectives are liable to be overlooked when they have developed symptoms of psychoneurosis, due to their inability to cope with their environment in the army, of such a degree as to mask over the underlying mental defect. While the crime sheet is often the key to a hitherto unrecognized psychopath, by the same token a report from the man's section officer or NCO is often the key that suggests a diagnosis of mental deficiency. It is sometimes amazing to see how long some of these cases got by in the army, and the common reason for their referral is not that the man has been reported as being mentally dull, but because of symptoms of a psychoneurotic order, of which he himself has complained. Some of these cases adjust reasonably well at fatigue duties in a lower category.

The Personnel Selection organization is integrated as closely as possible with neuropsychiatry. It covers a wide range in the Army, but the sector of it that is related to a neuropsychiatric out-patient clinic has to do with the disposal of particular groups of patients. The patients who are disposed of almost routinely by Personnel Selection are the mental defectives, and a relatively small number of psychoneurotics. With the recent inception of a Special Company designed for psychoneurotics who are considered to be rehabilitatable, it is possible that more psychoneurotics will be transferred to this company, but so far I have conscientiously avoided referring the great majority of the psychoneurotics to Personnel Selection, even in some cases where it seemed, ostensibly, that work maladjustment was a factor in the man's symptoms. The reason that Personnel Selection does not represent a panacea for these cases is that the cause of the trouble is more commonly the man's own instability rather than the incompatibility of the job, and referring such a man to a Personnel Selection Officer is to saddle the officer with a problem that is unlikely to improve regardless of what he does.

The problem of employment in quite a large number of the psychoneurotics in this series has settled itself by a process of gravitation across a period of months or years, the man having finally gravitated to a job of B-2 or C category work. He is happy to be there, and his CO is happy to see him there, and the only trouble is that his category has not yet caught up with him, still being A. It is sometimes a great temptation to attempt to stir a man up to a greater degree of activity, especially when there appears to be an obvious degree of wilful intent in his ineffectiveness, but the few cases in which I have suggested that the category be left at A, and an attempt made to get the man to function in Category A, were distinct failures. It is my impression that once a man has been allowed to relapse into a job such as hut orderly for any appreciable length of time, it is an extremely difficult job to get him back up the ladder again, even though his functional complaints are relatively mild ones. Possibly a rehabilitation unit, with an extra-special brand of discipline and PT may offer a solution to this particular source of wastage.

There have been one or two interesting alterations in general trends that have been noticeable in the last 8 months. One has to do with a definite change in the attitude of men toward return to Canada. About 4 or 5 months ago there was a change in policy that involved the setting up of facilities to employ unstable neurotics in England rather than return them to Canada.

This policy was noised abroad as amounting to a "closed door policy" which it was not, in actual fact, although much more nearly so than the pre-existing policy. The effect this had on the average run of neuropsychiatric out-patients was noticeable and in a remarkably short time, indicating that it must have spread, possibly with an element of exaggeration, with the speed that rumours sometimes do in the Army, or, to be more strictly correct in this particular case, the reinforcement area, as CRU [Canadian Reinforcement Unit] troops constitute at least 90 per cent of this series.

The change noticed was, that prior to this policy change it was relatively common to have to deal with a man whose obsession to be returned to Canada was so strong as to amount almost to a primary disease, and he often enough received the information that he was not a candidate for Canada with nothing but scepticism and resentment. Following this policy change, this type of case has largely disappeared, and it is several months now since I have had any of what could be termed violent arguments trying to convince a man that he was not a candidate for Canada. No doubt the desire still exists in just as many men as it did formerly, but in contrast to burning fiercely it could be said to be smouldering quietly in a somewhat latent form, and causing far less actual trouble.

This may or may not be a factor in morale, but beyond this conjecture I don't feel qualified to say anything about the question of morale, in fact I feel definitely disqualified, as the bulk of my experience has been with psychoneurotics in the holding unit area, whose morale is obviously low, and for intrinsic rather than extrinsic reasons. Consequently any impressions I might form from this material would be bound to be distorted in relation to the average.

This brings to an end these somewhat random observations, and in conclusion I would like to apologize for the too-frequent use of the personal pronoun, and to thank you for your attention.

APPENDIX 3

Following is a comprehensive clinical report on neuropsychiatric cases admitted to No. 14 Canadian General Hospital at Caserta, Italy, between January and May 1944. Copy in DHIST, 147.71E 13009 (D3).

Canadian Neuropsychiatric Base
attd. 14th Cdn General Hospital
RCAMC, CA (O) CMF

DMS
CMHQ (Attention Consultant in Neuropsychiatry)

Re: Report on Neuropsychiatry (Base) in Italy

1 During the four months period (approx) from 15 Jan. 44 to 16 May 44, 1,104 cases have been admitted to the Canadian Neuropsychiatric Base as Inpatients, and 451 cases seen in consultation as Out Patients. The Neuro. Base commenced to function as such on 15 Jan. 44, and the following report is made up from material that has passed through the base up to and including 16 May 44, on which date there were 77 In patients, so that statistical data is based on 1104-77 = 1027 cases.

2 Diagnosis and disposition are as follows:

Diagnosis				Total	Duty	Reboard	Evac. by HS
Psychopathic Pers. (Inad.)				464	82	382	
,,	,,	,,	Bord. Intell.	46		46	
,,	,,	,,	Reactive Depression	1			1
,,	,,	,,	Chronic Alcoholism	2		2	
,,	,,		(Anti-social)	11	5	6	
,,	,,		(Abn. Sex)	2	1	1	
Mental Deficiency Moron				13		13	

Diagnosis		Recommended Disposition		
	Total	Duty	Reboard	Evac. by HS
Mental Deficiency Borderline	30	1	29	
Chronic Alcoholism	2		2	
Psychoneurosis Anxiety State	329	135	194	
" Hysteria	16	8	8	
" Anxiety State with Bord. Intell.	4		4	
" Hysteria w/ Schizoid Personality	1	1		
Psychosis Schizophrenia	32			32
" Paranoid State	1			1
" Unspecified	6			6
" Manic-depressive	3			3
Reactive Depression	7	2	5	
Prepsychotic Pers. Schizoid	11		11	
" " Cyclothymic	2		2	
Migraine	2	1	1	
" with psychoneurosis	1		1	
Post-traumatic syndrome	3	2	1	
Physical Inferiority	5	1	3	1 (N/S)
Epilepsy	4		3	1
Probable Epilepsy	2	2		
Peripheral nerve lesions and diseases	8	4	1	3
Amyotrophic Lateral Sclerosis	1			1
Disseminated Sclerosis	1			1
Vaso-vagal attacks	1	1		
NAD(N)	13	13		
NYD(N)	3			3
	1,027	259	715	53

3 Analysis of 700 Cases

Of the above 1,027 cases, the first 700 consecutive cases were analysed in reference to the following:

a Percentage of cases that had been in action

c Age Group

d Period of service

e Unit distribution

f Analysis of the essential factor resulting in evacuation

a 685 or 97.8% had been in action.

b Rank – Officers – 20 cases

WO	– 10	"
NCO	–109	"
Pte	–561	"
	700	

c Age Groups

15 to 19	22 cases
20 to 24	252
25 to 29	186
30 to 34	128
35 to 39	70
40 to 44	37
45 to 49	5
	700

d Period of Service

0 to 1 year	28 cases
1 to 2 years	157
2 to 3 years	125
3 to 4 years	141
4 to 5 years	232
Unspecified	17
	700

e Unit Distribution.

R 22^{e}R	54
WNSR	53
H&PER	47
48 H of C	44
C & YR	40
RCR	38
PPCLI	32
SH of C	30
EDMON. R	18
SLI	25
CBH	23
IRISH R	15
PERTH R	13
WEST. R	7
4 PLDG	11
3RD RECCE	2
11 CTR	10
12 CTR	8
14 CTR	5

IST FD REGT	6
2 FD REGT	14
3 FD REGT	7
2ND LAA REGT	11
5 LAA REGT	3
I LAA REGT	5
I A/T REGT	10
4 A/T REGT	2
7 A/T REGT	2
8 FD REGT	4
I MED REGT	4
2 MED REGT	1
5 MED REGT	1
17 FD REGT	2
II FD REGT	1
POSTAL CORPS	1
PROVOST CORPS	6
2ND ARM. REGT	3
2ND ECHELON	1
MISCELLANEOUS	15
I SSF	8
IST CDN ARM. CAR REGT	4
CBRG	6
IST FD COY RCE	6
2ND FD COY RCE	1
3RD FD COY RCE	1
4TH FD COY RCE	5
9TH FD COY RCE	1
IOTH FD COY RCE	1
13TH FD COY RCE	1
12TH FD COY RCE	1
IST FD PARK COY	1
2ND FD PARK COY	1
RAILWAY CORPS	1
I CIB W/S RCOC	3
3 " " "	3
MISCELLANEOUS RCOC	18
RCASC	35
RCCS	12
RCAMC	17
CDC	1
	700

f Analysis of the essential factor resulting in evacuation

An attempt is made to assess some of the essential factors resulting in evacuation of neuropsychiatric cases from battle area, to base area. Two distinct types of cases present themselves as suitable for statistical segregation. The first of these is the case who, under varying degrees of battle stress, is evacuated because he has become shaky, confused, weeping, unable to leave his slit trench, or, in a paroxysm of hysteria, may run around aimlessly in the open. The adjective frequently used by the man's line officer or by the forward psychiatrist in describing this type of case is "demoralized", and since this adjective is an apt one – at least from a pragmatic standpoint – these cases are grouped under the heading Demoralized. The second type of case distinct enough to warrant statistical segregation is the case evacuated by reason of, and usually for investigation of, a specific somatic complaint, such as dyspepsia, headache, precordial pain, low back pain, shortness of breath, joint pain, etc. When these symptoms are recognised as being psychosomatic, these cases constitute a portion of the total neuropsychiatric casualties.

The 700 consecutive cases [categorized] were therefore analyzed using the following criteria:

i) The Demoralized Group to contain only those cases of gross breakdown of a demoralization type under battle stress, and in whom other factors such as frank mental defect or psychosis did not exist. If these, or other frankly relevant factors did exist, they were not placed in this group, but in the third group.

ii) The Psychosomatic Group to contain only those cases evacuated by reason of psychosomatic complaints. If evidence of gross demoralization existed or other frankly relevant factors, they were placed in the third group.

iii) The third group, termed The Rest, contained all other cases not fitting clearly into either of the first two groups.

Of the total 700 consecutive cases, 357 (51%) were seen by the forward psychiatrist.

Group segregation was as follows:

i) Demoralized   243 cases
ii) Psychosomatic   217 cases
iii) The Rest   240 cases

(i) *Demoralized (243)*

(a) Seen by forward psychiatrist 224 (92%)
(b) Diagnosis
   Psychopathic personality (inad.)   176
   Psychoneurosis   <u>67</u>
                                       243

(c) Disposition

Reboarded 240

RTU 3 (1.2%)

243

(ii) *Psychosomatic*

(a) Seen by forward psychiatrist 30 (13.7%)

(b) Diagnosis

Psychopathic personality (inad.) 88

Psychoneurosis 129

217

(c) Disposition

Reboarded 108

RTU 109 (50%)

217

(iii) *The Rest (240)*

(a) Seen by forward psychiatrist 103 (43%)

(b) Diagnosis

Mental defect 71

Psychosis & pre psychosis 45

Physical Disability 23

Overage 15

Neurologic 14

Alcoholism 13

Psychopathic personality (inad.) 36

Psychoneurosis 23

240

Comment

(a) It is noted that the above method of classification resolves the total neuropsychiatric casualties into three roughly numerically equal groups.

It is also noted that of the total 700 cases, 357 (51%) were seen by the forward neuropsychiatrist. Since all cases evacuated by the forward neuropsychiatrist passed through the neuropsychiatric base (att. 14 Cdn. General Hospital) it can be inferred that about one half of cases passed through the neuropsychiatric base were not held to be neuropsychiatric cases in the forward area.

(b) Of the 243 cases in the first group 92% (all but 19 cases) came through the forward neuropsychiatrist, all were labelled by him for downgrading, and this was done at base in all but 1.2%. The salvage rate in this group has been, therefore, almost nil. These cases are regarded by combat officers as "bona fida psychiatric" cases, and in the minds of most combat officers constitute the entire psychiatric problem. Combat officers are most anxious to get these cases out of their unit as quickly as possible and by whatsoever method (especially when the case is one on which they have already made one or more attempts at rehabilitation in the unit). It is the opinion of the writer that the salvage rate at base of 1.2% (and that only a "possible" rate) for full combat duty is a fair one. The salvage in this type of case lies in the unit, and in forward neuropsychiatric installation. In those cases passed through the forward neuro-psychiatric filter back to the base, the salvage rate is practically nil, as the above figures show.

(c) Of the 217 cases in the second group, it is noted that only 13.7% were passed through the forward neuropsychiatrist, the remaining 86.3% being labelled NP, at a point some-where on L of C, or at base.

In contrast to the first group, the salvage rate in the psychosomatic group is rela-tively high (50%), and could in the opinion of the writer be made higher were it possible to overcome certain administrative difficulties.

Also in contrast to the cases in the first group, these cases do not present to their combat officers the urgent problem in evacuation that the cases in the first group do. This group contains the "exaggerators" and the "lead swingers" of both mild and severe degree. In some cases the unit has gladly used the man's psychosomatic complaint as an excuse for evacuating him via medical channels and thereby increas-ing the efficiency of the unit. In other cases the man's unit officer is willing, even anxious, to carry the man in the unit provided he (the officer) can be assured that there is "nothing wrong" (organically) with the man.

(d) Of the 240 cases in the third group 103 (43%) passed through the forward neuro-psychiatrist. A survey of the diagnosis suggests that (with the exception of 36 inadequate psychopaths and 23 psychoneurotics) the disposition follows the diagnosis somewhat routinely. It is evident that in this group salvage for return to full combat duty is an almost negligible consideration. The majority of cases in this group entail either the evacuation from the theatre or re-allocation in a lower category.

4 Consideration of factors involved in salvage for full combat duty of neuropsychiatric cases in a theatre of war

The following premises are ... in the opinion of the writer, statements of fact:

(a) That it is the policy of the RCAMC, to give to the Canadian troops the best possible type of medical practice. Therefore any new method, or alteration of existing methods, that might involve haphazard medical practice, or guesswork, would not be feasible.

(b) That the key man in the medical organisation is the unit or Regimental Medical Officer.

(c) That the exercise of discipline is the best prophylaxis against neuropsychiatric casualties, recognising that it will affect some types of neuropsychiatric cases, such as psychosis, but little, if at all, while it will affect others, such as psychosomatic cases, very greatly.

(d) That in a Corps, only 50 to 60% of the troops have their own unit MO, the remainder, mainly ancillary services, obtaining their medical services on a "casual" basis, from the nearest available medical installation.

(e) Considerable psychological damage is done when a man is evacuated from his unit for psychiatric reasons that are not grave, and this damage is proportionately increased the further back toward base he is evacuated.

From the evidence contained in para 3 section (f) it seems reasonable to conclude that while there is little hope, or necessity, of altering the existing state of affairs, from a standpoint of salvage, as far as the first and third groups (Demoralized and the Rest respectively) are concerned, there is adequate scope, and a definite need, for alteration in present conditions as far as the second group (Psychosomatic) is concerned. Since this group is almost one third of total cases at the neuropsychiatric base, it constitutes a worthwhile field of endeavour. In addition to this group of psychosomatic cases that have passed as In-patients through the Neuropsychiatric Base, there is a considerable number of borderline, many even frankly, psychosomatic cases that pass through the Medical Division, and ENT, Orthopedic and other specialists, of the General Hospitals at base. A proportion of these cases (exact percentage unknown) are neither referred to a neuropsychiatrist nor listed as psychiatric casualties – which in truth they are – but they should, for practical purposes, be given the same consideration as the psychosomatic cases that have passed through a neuropsychiatric base.

It is the present purpose, therefore, to accept the psychosomatic group only, as presenting a practical and substantial field in which to attempt reduction of psychiatric casualties, and to examine possible methods whereby the handling of this group of cases could be improved. At first glance it would appear as if the logical place for effecting a change would be at the level of the RMO. It would seem a simple matter to instruct the RMO, in a theatre of war to practise a more comprehensive type of clinical medicine, and to rely less on specialist opinion and X-rays than he did in England, and in the Mediterranean theatre to date. This first impression is further strengthened when one sees the high proportion (87%) of psychosomatic cases that the RMO evacuated through medical channels, and the small proportion (13%) that he referred to the neuropsychiatrist. In this respect one recalls the three and one half year period in England during which consultative services in all the specialties were readily available to the RMO, and during this period the onus lay on the RMO to avail himself to the fullest degree of these consultative services, in fact he was open to censure should he fail to do so. This state of affairs was based, it is presumed, on the principle that the Canadian soldier was to be given the highest possible standard of medical attention. If, therefore one feels that the RMO is referring, in a theatre of war, a large number of cases for specialist opinion – which entails in many cases their evacuation to base – the principle involved in this is beyond the province of the writer, and the situation is therefore taken, for the purpose of this discussion, to be a non-changeable state of affairs.

A further factor influencing this question is the fact that the specialist services at present set up in the Medical Corps are quite well known to the soldier. This automatically places a heavier diagnostic and therapeutic responsibility on the shoulders of the RMO, leaves him a minimal margin for error, and in the event of such occurring, would almost automatically saddle him with the opprobrium and loss of confidence of the men of his unit, whether justified or not.

To instruct the RMO to deal within the unit, with more psychosomatic cases than he has dealt with heretofore, is therefore not feasible.

Of practical value, however, is the making available of adequate consultative services within the divisional area. A neuropsychiatric consultative service has been available within the divisional area since 1 Cdn Div. came to the Mediterranean, and more recently other specialists, as well as medical and surgical, have been available on a consultative basis within the divisional area. However, the neuropsychiatric service has not been utilized by the RMO with respect to the type of case with which we are now concerned (psychosomatic). Only 13% of psychosomatics seen at base were referred to the neuropsychiatrist in the forward area. In this respect, then, there is room for improvement. An Instruction to the RMO to refer to the area neuropsychiatrist, on a consultative basis, cases in which there were nil organic findings, would increase the work of the neuropsychiatrist but decrease the flow of psychosomatics to base. Seen on this basis they would not be sos their unit or listed as psychiatric casualties unless evacuated. It is the opinion of the writer based on the cases seen at base that an appreciable number of these cases could be diagnosed and returned to duty by a neuropsychiatrist on the basis of a single consultative visit, and without the man being sos his unit. In considering the above it must be remembered that the psychosomatic case as a general rule does not become a casualty in the heat of battle, but rather in the lull or rest period, and this factor greatly facilitates a procedure such as the one suggested above.

There remain for consideration those cases which the forward neuropsychiatrist feels require further investigation at base, and he therefore returns the man to his unit with the recommendation that his unit evacuate him to base. Regardless of what investigation is required, whether ENT Orthopedic, et al, it is strongly recommended that the case be evacuated as an NP case labelled for the neuropsychiatric base. There the required investigation can be carried out expeditiously, and, barring disposal on non-psychiatric grounds, the case can be quickly considered for return to duty. It is the opinion of the writer that the two essential factors in the handling of these cases, are firstly, the free use of specialist opinions, in addition to the neuropsychiatric opinion, and secondly, speed in disposal.

For those cases recommended for return to duty from the base – 50% of the total in this series (psychosomatic) and it could be higher – there remain the problem firstly of getting them back to the forward area, and secondly of preventing a further evacuation for the same complaint in respect of which they were evacuated and investigated the first time. Return to the forward area in some cases goes into reverse at the RU where his base neuropsychiatric report having been sent to 2nd Echelon (and consequently strictly not available), the man is sent to the neuropsychiatric base from which he had just come, for a further neuropsychiatric opinion.

Considerably more important than this, however, is the prevention of re-evacuation. The essential factor in this is the forwarding of the neuropsychiatric report to the man's unit when he goes forward. That this would entail some administrative difficulty is understood, but it is the opinion of the writer that the overcoming of this difficulty would be more than amply repaid in that it would constitute a material step forward in dealing with one of the most important problems in neuropsychiatry in a theatre of war.

For your information, please.

(Signed) (C.E.G. Gould) Major. RCAMC.

17 May 1944   Neuropsychiatrist

8 June 1944.

In considering the above excellent report by Major Gould, the reader should bear in mind that the admissions to a base Neuropsychiatric Centre do not represent a cross section of the total neuropsychiatric casualties in the theatre of war. Since many of the less serious cases treated in forward area or L of C are returned to duty without evacuation, the admissions to the Base Neuropsychiatric Centre show a high proportion of soldiers with constitutional personality defect. Patients suffering the various psychoses are all collected at the Base Neuropsychiatric Centre prior to evacuation from the theatre of war, as are most patients suffering from organic nervous disease.

A recent report from Major A.M. Doyle covering neuropsychiatry in forward area will shortly be circulated.

(F.H. van Nostrand) Colonel. RCAMC.

FHvanN/YA   Consultant Neuropsychiatrist
Canadian Military Headquarters

APPENDIX 4

The following table shows the disposal of all neuropsychiatric cases seen by Forward Psychiatric Units from 10 July 1943 to 3 February 1945. Taken from A.M. Doyle, "The History and Development of Canadian Neuropsychiatric Services in the CMF," NA, RG 24, vol. 12,630.

Canadian Army – Italy.

10 July 43–1 April 44	*1,234 cases*	%	*1 April 44–9 Feb. 45*	*2,128 cases*	%	*Total*
Returned to full duty	394	31.9	Returned to full duty	439	20.6	833
Evacuated for reboard and reallocation	767	62.6	Evacuated for reboard and reallocation	556	26.1	1,323
Posted to secs	–	–	Posted to secs	959	45.1	959
Evacuated to General Hospital	44	4.6	Evacuated to General Hospital	174	8.2	218
Unknown	29	1.9		–	–	29
Totals	1,234			2,128		3,362

Relationship of Neuropsychiatric Casualties to Battle Casualties
(Battle Casualties = killed, wounded, and died of wounds).

Total New Cases examined at #1 Cdn Base NP Centre	1,658
Total New Cases examined at #2 Cdn Exhaustion Unit	3,362
Total Neuropsychiatric Casualties in CMF	5,020*
Total Battle Casualties	25,090

$$\text{NP Ratio} = \frac{5{,}020 \times 100}{5{,}020 + 25{,}090} = 16.7$$

* The total new psychiatric cases as reported above is a conservative figure, and does not include any of the cases at the Reallocation Centre. The true NP Ratio is probably closer to 20%.

#2 Canadian Exhaustion Unit
Case Analysis by Diagnosis (Canadian Army – Italy)

Diagnosis	*10 July 1943 – 20 June 1944*	*20 June 1944 – 20 Sep. 1944*	*1 Oct. 1944 – 31 Dec. 1944*	*31 Dec. 1944 – 9 Feb. 1945*	*Total*
Psychoneuroses	618	281	192	85	1,176
Mental Defectives	99	16	9	1	125
Psychopathic Personality (Inadequate Type)	754	133	(113 (Mixed) 360 (247	(31 (Mixed) 83 (52	1,330
Psychopathic Personality (Anti-social Type)	9	10	4		23
Epilepsy	12	2	4	1	19
Reactive Depression	5	2	3		10
Manic Depressive	4	0			4
Schizophrenia	24	7	9	1	41
Exhaustion	20	11			31
No Diagnosis	70	55	83	48	256
Medical	83	8			91
Others	131	50	29	15	235
Totals	1,829	575	703	234	3,341

Source: A.M. Doyle, 'The History and Development of Canadian Neuropsychiatric Service in the CMF,' NA, RG 24, vol. 12,630.

APPENDIX 5

Infantry soldiers suffered the most physical and psychiatric damage because of the nature of their war. The immense variety of their individual destinies defies generalization. Following is a report of the experience of one infantryman who eventually presented himself to Major A.E. Moll at No. 2 Canadian Exhaustion Unit in Italy. Copy in NA, RG 24, vol. 12,630.

(Major Moll): He is 30 years old, a L/Cpl in an Infantry Regt. His past history shows no evidence of instability or neurotic traits. Had a normal childhood in a pleasant home environment. Well adjusted within himself and to the outside world. Healthy and physically robust, a born "leader." He went to school up to age 13 and reached grade 7, then worked with his father in a truck concern up to enlistment. Always regularly employed, Stable. Enlisted in Aug. 41, arrived in the CMF in May 44. Fought in all actions including the Hitler and Gothic lines, latter part of the Lamone (River). On 13 Dec., he was evacuated from his unit following GSW (gunshot wound) of the right arm and minor wounds in the lumbar region. After discharge from the Hospital, he was sent to the Convalescent Depot and from there evacuated to the #2 Cdn. Exhaustion Unit as he was complaining of inability to fully extend his right arm and of paraesthesia of hand. Examination showed some involvement of the ulnar nerve following scar tissue but all his symptoms could not be explained entirely on an organic basis. Furthermore he was quite tense and presented marked psychosomatic manifestations of anxiety. His recent battle experience had proven too much for him and his motivation towards return to the front line had been considerably affected by his having been wounded. He was asked to describe in writing his battle experiences, his emotions and reactions to shell fire; his behaviour in the front line during the days preceding his wound. This is what he wrote:

The Company Commander gave the order to move up to the Lamone River at 1130; the barrage was to go in at 1150 so B Coy and C Coy was on the bank on time. We sat there on the bank waiting, then all at once, we heard the guns start and the shelling started. The first few went over the bank then it broke loose, and one landed right behind my sec(tion) about 50 yards, but it had hit right in a section of C Coy and killed 6 outright, but we didn't know that at the time. Then the shells were lighting all around us, so I yelled to my section to follow me. I didn't know where we were going so long as I got them away from the bank, but we ran about 100 yards and came to a little ditch, and it was impossible to get any further so I gave the order to stay in the ditch which they did.

The barrage lasted 12 minutes by my watch, and I made a reccy or took a look, so to speak, and I could see the house so I said is everyone ready and they were so I said the house is right there, about 50 yards on our left, and when we start we will keep going, and bring all weapons.

I started and all the men followed and when we got to the outbuilding I discovered I had more than my section, and I said we are making a dash for the house. I knew where the door was, so I showed them all, and at that time Jerry was sending back some shells but they were going on over our heads, so I started and just as the last man in my section came through the door, 2 shells landed right in the yard, and the 3 that had come with me was still in the yard. I heard one of them yell for help but I didn't know how it was at the time but I ran out and one of the boys was coming on his hands and knees so I got him up and gave him a hand to the house. Then I ran out and I had to pick the other one up and carry him. Those two were L/Cpl L. and Pte B., one from 12 Platoon, B Coy, the other from support attached to B Coy. By the time I got out to the other chap he was all on fire, and the acting CSM (Company Sergeant-Major), Sgt S. was there trying to get the web off him, for the fire was coming from the 77 Grenade he was carrying in his pocket, so I ran over and gave him a hand. I said boy am I glad to see you, and he replied how are you feeling. I said not bad, but I really didn't know how I felt.

I wanted to get him inside but he said he was dead so when we got the web off the chap, we threw it in the mud. The CSM said to me I guess its you and I for it, Mitch, there is a lot of wounded out here, lets go. So we run around the house and there was a chap there with his guts all hanging out. He was from Coy (Company) H.Q., Mac, a runner. He wanted us to get him in the house but we couldn't move him as he was, so I ran in to find a stretcher bearer and I saw one in the corner and asked him to come and bring a stretcher but he said I'm hit Mitch. I asked him if it was bad and he said lets go, so I said get your stretcher. He said its right there so I brought it and he started to work on the lad but only being a stretcher bearer for a short time he didn't know just what to do but he was doing the best he could so the lad just relaxed. The CSM said I guess he's gone, and the lad tensed right up again and shouted no I'm not, I'm O.K., get me to the house but that was too much for me and I took right out and I wasn't just sure which way I was going either.

I had only taken a few steps and I heard some more shells come and I shouted a warning to the rest to take cover so they put the lad on the stretcher and made for the house. The shells lit close but done no damage but I heard another cry over by some hay stacks and I run over and there was another wounded man. I didn't ask any questions, I just picked him up and made for the house and laid him on the table. That was Pte H. He was dead in about 5 minutes and so was Mac.

The CSM asked for someone to go with him up to the river to see if there was anymore up there that needed help. There was seven up there but were all dead. We lit some matches to see if there was anyone there we knew, and the first one I saw was a good friend of mine and the family and his newly married wife's family, lying there all in little pieces, so I said I can't stand anymore, I will have to go some place S., so he said that's all anyway and we come back to the house and the wounded had all gone.

The next thing was to make out a guard for the rest of the night because the order had come through that we wouldn't be going over that night, so I walked around and done guard the rest of the night.

At six in the morning, we got the order we were going over the river and a thousand yards inland, so when we were ready to take off I didn't feel too bad. We went across and started for our objective, but we only got about half-way when we met the enemy. We lost one man there and had to withdraw to the houses at the river bank. We were just there about 20 minutes and Jerry started to shell the house so then we got the order to come back across the river which we did. Just as we got back Jerry started to shell the road which he knew we would take and we had 6 more men wounded, 2 of which were killed. It was the rear platoon and the rest took out for the house which we had left in the morning, and as we only had 2 stretchers left I took Pte M. on my back to the house. I am a small man but I didn't have any trouble making it and I guess most of my strength came from the excitement.

That evening we were moved out and back across highway 10, and took over a house from the 5th Div(ision) which we stayed in for 3 days. It was very good there, not much shelling. It came time for us to take our turn to go back up to the houses along the river to do guard and run patrols. The patrols were to go up the river about a mile to contact the RCR (Royal Canadian Regiment).

On the night I was to take the patrol, on the 11th about 2.30 in the morning, Jerry started mortaring the bank on our side, and I lost 2 men in the patrol. There was only 4 of us altogether, so I went on to the RCR and sent the other man back for help, so we got them out without anything worse happening.

At 12 o'clock we got the order that the C & Y Regt (Carleton and York) had made their crossing and we were going through them, so we started and got on our first objective just at dark. At 12 o'clock that night, we got another order that we were going to cross the second river and we would have to wade it, so we did and we got on our objective and stayed there till the morning of the 13th. We were then told that the C & Y Regt. had gone across the river but it was a dry one and they had very little trouble so at 1 o'clock we started out and D Coy came back to take over our house and came under mortar and 88 shell fire and lost 6 men, 2 killed. There was no one to take the wounded back so our Coy 2 i/c (Second-in-Command) of ours asked for volunteers to go and get the wounded but there were only 2 men in the platoon of Don Coy which would go, so I went with him and we got the men in the house.

We then started out to go through the C & Y Regt, and we got through them O.K. Jerry let us right in once he seen what our plan was. We were about 25 yards from our objective when a patrol of Jerries came between us and the house so the order came back from the front of the Coy to lay low and not have any trouble till we got dug in. We did and while we were there a fighting patrol came up behind us and opened fire on me and my section. I never seen them till they started to shoot. Finally he found his mark and two slugs hit me and I thought I was finished so I jumped up and started firing back and one of the cpls (Corporals) in another section threw a hand grenade which killed 3 of them and I had killed one with my mad try. The other 2 started to crawl away and I could see men take after them so I did. Someone took after me and turned me the other way.

I came right back to my section and someone said get away Mitch you're hit, so I didn't know which way to go. I guess I was shouting or something. Anyway, one of the boys was crying there in the ditch and I thought he was hit but he wasn't. He wanted to come out with me but I guess I wouldn't let him.

Then the section started to move off so I took off and the next thing I remember was being challenged and I couldn't think of the pass-word but I do remember saying don't shoot for I have plenty of holes in me now. Then I heard another fellow coming and more guns started to go and someone said get in that ditch, here comes Jerry so I fell in the ditch. By this time Jerry had seen me and they were all shooting at me but didn't hit me but our boys of C Coy had drove them off.

Then a Sgt came out and gave me a hand back to the house where one of the Coy's were, and they dressed my back there. I wanted to go back but they wouldn't let me and they said there was a counter-attack coming. Just then I heard on the 19 (wireless) set that my Coy. was cut off and would have to give up if they didn't get help right away.

I don't remember much from then on, I do remember a Sgt handling me a little rough but I guess I must have had it coming for I had a pistol and I wanted to shoot 2 Jerry wounded there in the shed. Then a jeep came in with ammo and I wanted to go out with that but they said it wasn't very safe, it just had a 50-50 chance of getting through but I got in it and they made the 2 Jerrys get in too and we started out. I guess I had a few words on the way out with the csm in the jeep about the Jerrys but when I got to the ADS (Advanced Dressing Station) or whatever it was, they gave me a needle or something and I felt a little better. I was still talking about my Coy but I got back to the 4 ccs (Casualty Clearing Station) right away and was put to sleep. When I woke up I had been talking a lot but they wouldn't tell me what about.

But I'm out of it and I don't want to ever go back because I just never could be responsible in a tight place again and I know it."

(Major Moll:) It is a platitude of war that even a sound individual may develop symptoms of "exhaustion" if exposed to intense and prolonged emotional stress.

Here is a young man, a solid citizen in civilian life, a good soldier, in action for 8 months, tempered and proven in battle, who yet concludes "I'm out of it and I don't want to ever go back because I just never could be responsible in a tight place and I know it."

Can anybody doubt his "intestinal fortitude"?

Chances are that this man would have been able to endure the stress of battle conditions for a further period of time had he not been wounded. Conversely it is also possible that he might have been reaching the breaking point even prior to his wound.

Notes

INTRODUCTION

1 Earle Birney, *Turvey* (Toronto, 1976), 207.

2 See for example Z. Solomon and Rami Benbenishtz, "The Role of Proximity, Immediacy and Expectancy in Frontline Treatment of Combat Stress Reaction Among Israelis in the Lebanon War," *AJP* (1986).

3 W.R. Feasby, *Clinical Subjects*, vol. 2, *Official History of the Canadian Medical Services 1939-45* (Ottawa: Queen's Printer, 1956).

4 *Canadian Who's Who 1938-39* (Toronto, 1939), 276.

5 R. Pos, *History of Psychiatry at Toronto General Hospital*, typescript, n.d., Griffin-Greenland Archives, Toronto, 53.

6 Ibid., 60.

7 The best contemporary description is in W. Sargant and Eliot Slater, *Physical Methods in Psychiatry* (London, 1944), chapter 1.

8 See, for example, *Annual Report Verdun Protestant Hospital* (1937), 36. Osler Library, McGill University. Dr Travis Dancey was placed in charge of the insulin-coma ward after attending courses in New York.

9 F.C. Redlich, "Metrazol Shock Treatment," *AJP* 96 (1939).

10 Albert Deutsch, "The History of Mental Hygiene," in J.K. Hall, ed., *One Hundred Years of American Psychiatry* (New York, 1944), 365.

11 See J.D.M. Griffin, "Mental Hygiene in Canada," *CPHJ* (1941).

12 Freud died on 20 September 1939. Most obituaries were published in the November issues of monthly journals, and the winter or occasionally spring issues of quarterlies.

13 Karl Menninger, "Sigmund Freud," *Bulletin of Menninger Clinic* (Nov. 1939): 161.

14 C.B. Farrar, "Sigmund Freud," *University of Toronto Medical Journal* (January 1940).

15 Abraham Myerson, "The Attitude of Neurologists, Psychiatrists and Psychologists Towards Psychoanalysis," *AJP* (1940).

16 Travis Dancey, *Memoir*, (1982). The memoir was written for Terry Copp in response to a request for an interview. (It will be deposited in the Osler Library, McGill University, together with other material by and about Dr Dancey.)

17 The literature on Dr Ewan Cameron includes Anne Collins, *In the Sleep Room* (Toronto, 1988). See also *Opinion of George Cooper, Q.C., Regarding Canadian Government Funding of the Allan Memorial Institute in the 1950s and 1960s* (Ottawa, 1986).

18 Dr Jack Griffin, interview with Terry Copp, Toronto, 25 Oct. 1982.

19 Minutes of meeting, Committee on Cases of Anxiety Neurosis CASF, 3 Feb. 1941, Russel Papers, vol. 4.

20 Ibid.

21 W. Sargant and E. Slater, "The Acute War Neuroses," *The Lancet* (6 July 1940).

22 H.S.M. Carver, *Personnel Selection in the Canadian Army*, typescript (Ottawa, 1945), chapter 1. In possession of the authors.

23 Ibid., 69. Infantry M test scores were lower than those for the specialized corps.

CHAPTER ONE

1 Quoted in C.P. Stacey, *Six Years of War* (Ottawa: Queen's Printer, 1955), 54.

2 W.R. Feasby, *Organization and Campaigns*, vol. 1, *Official History of the Canadian Medical Services*, 1939-45 (Ottawa: Queen's Printer, 1956), 8.

3 Ibid., 34.

4 Ibid., 51.

5 W.R. Feasby, *Clinical Subjects*, vol. 2, *Official History of the Canadian Medical Services* 1939-45 (Ottawa, 1956): 100.

6 Dr Jack Griffin, interview with Terry Copp, Toronto, 25 Oct. 1982.

7 Feasby, vol. 2, *Clinical Subjects*, 56.

8 *General Instructions for the Medical Examination of Recruits for the CASF and NPAM* (Ottawa: King's Printer, 1940).

9 Report of Selection of Personnel and Mental Disease in the Canadian Army Overseas 18 July 1941, National Archives of Canada (NA), Record Group (RG) 24, vol. 12,620, File 31.

10 J.P.S. Cathcart, "The Neuro-Psychiatric Branch of the Department of Soldiers' Civil Re-Establishment," *The Ontario Journal of Neuro-Psychiatry* 8 (1928): 46.

11 Thomas W. Salmon and N. Fenton, "Neuropsychiatry in the American Expeditionary Force," in M.W. Ireland, ed., *The Medical Department of the*

United States Army in the World War, vol. 10 (Washington, 1929), part 2.

12 War Office (United Kingdom) *Report of the War Office Committee of Enquiry into Shell Shock* (London: HMSO, 1922).

13 Memo from J.P.S. Cathcart to Deputy Minister, Dept. of Pensions and National Health, 4 Oct. 1939, NA, RG 24, vol. 19, 466.

14 Feasby, *Organization and Campaigns*.

15 Details from F.L. McNaughton, "Colin Russel, A Pioneer of Canadian Neurology," *Canadian Medical Association Journal (CMAJ)* 77 (1957): 719-23.

16 Lewis Jefferson, *Something Hidden: A Biography of Wilder Penfield* (Toronto, 1981) 114-7.

17 Ibid., 163.

18 Colin K. Russel, "The Nature of War Neuroses," *CMAJ* 41 (1939): 550.

19 Ibid., 533.

20 C. Russel, "A Study of Certain Psychogenetic Conditions Among Soldiers," CMAJ 7 (1917): 711.

21 Russel, "The Nature of War Neuroses," 544.

22 Memorandum, Russel to DGMS, 8 Dec. 1939, Russel Papers, Osler Library, McGill University, vol. 3. Samuel McLaughlin, the Canadian automobile pioneer, was then president of General Motors, Canada.

23 Memorandum, Russel to DGMS, 31 Oct. 1939, Russel Papers, vol. 3.

24 E.H. Botterell, "Kenneth George McKenzie, MD, FRSC 1923-63," *Surgical Neurology* 17, no. 2 (1982): 81-9, and E.H. Botterell, interview with Terry Copp, 30 Oct. 1986.

25 Quoted in memorandum, Russel to DGMS, 8 Dec 1939, Russel Papers, vol. 3.

26 A small mobile group, No. 1 Mobile Neurosurgical Unit, was introduced into the field in late 1944 under the command of one of McKenzie's colleagues, Bill Keith. It was similar in function to the head unit established in the British Army by Hugh Cairns, not to Russel's 1939 proposal.

27 The meeting ended with "Drs Penfield and Cone both expressing themselves strongly in favour of the Combined Neurological and Neurosurgical Unit."

28 See A.J. Glass, ed., *Overseas Theatres*, vol. 2, *Neuropsychiatry in World War II* (Washington, 1973), chapter 1.

29 Dr Clifford Richardson, interview with Terry Copp, December 1982.

30 Feasby, *Organization and Campaigns*, 98.

31 Ibid., 99.

32 Botterell, interview.

33 Memorandum, Russel, n.d., Russel Papers.

34 Ralston Papers, vol. 54, File "No. 1 Neurological Hospital, Jan. 1941."

35 R.M. Luton to Senior Officer, CMHQ, 21 Dec. 1940, NA, RG 24, vol. 12,583.

36 F.H. Van Nostrand to Luton, 1 May 1942, NA, RG 24, vol. 12,604.

37 There are a number of versions of this story. I have made no attempt to track down the original. It is perhaps worth recording that 45 per cent

of the neurosurgical cases admitted to Basingstoke were accident victims. H. Elliott, "Head Wounds Canadian Army, Word War II" *Treatment Services Bulletin* (Aug. 1949): 10.

38 Feasby, *Clinical Subjects*, 60.

39 Russel Papers, vol. 4, Russel to DMS, CMHQ, 11 Jan. 1942.

40 F.L. McNaughton, "Colin Russel, A Pioneer," 722.

41 F. Somers, *A History of Psychiatry at the Toronto General Hospital*, typescript, n.d., Griffin-Greenland Archives, Toronto, 31-2.

42 The quotations in this paragraph are from H.H. Hyland and J.C. Richardson, "Psychoneurosis in the Canadian Army Overseas," *CMAJ* 47 (1942): 432-43.

43 Richardson and Botterell, interviews.

44 Botterell, interview.

45 J.M. Hitsman, *The Problem of Personnel Selection in the Canadian Army Overseas 1939-46*, report no. 64, Historical Section CMHQ, (1946), typescript, DHIST, Dept. of National Defence, 28, 4.

46 Minutes of Meeting, Committee on Cases of Anxiety Neurosis, CASF, 3 Feb. 1941, Russel Papers, vol. 4.

47 Ibid.

48 Ibid.

49 Hyland and Richardson, "Psychoneurosis," 20-1. All quotations in the paragraph are from this account of treatment at Basingstoke.

50 Minutes, Committee on Cases of Anxiety Neurosis, 3 Feb. 1941.

51 Ibid.

52 Obituary, Dr Frederick Van Nostrand *CMAJ* 113 (1975): 432; and Dr Peter Van Nostrand, interview with Terry Copp, Oct. 85. Dr Van Nostrand had been recommended to Russel as a neuropsychiatrist when No. 1 Neurological Unit was formed, but Russel had selected doctors with stronger academic credentials. Dr G.F. Boyer to Russel, 25 Nov. 1939, Russel Papers, vol. 7.

53 Dr Peter Van Nostrand, interview with Terry Copp, Oct. 1985. Two of "Van's" oldest friends, Dr Bill Keith and Dr Bill White were present during this interview. Both tried to explain Van Nostrand's practical common-sense approach with numerous examples.

54 Van Nostrand repeatedly expressed these views in reports and memoranda throughout the war.

55 Minutes, Committee on Functional Nervous Disease, 31 Oct. 1941, NA, RG 24, vol. 12,620.

56 Ibid.

57 *The Lancet*, editorial (26 April 1940): 530.

58 Ibid., letter of 20 July 1940, 82.

59 G. Debenham, Denis Hill, William Sargant, Elliot Slater, "Treatment of War Neuroses," *The Lancet* (25 Jan. 1941): 107.

60 Ibid., editorial (7 Sept. 1940): 299.

61 J.R. Rees, "Three Years of Military Psychiatry," *BMJ* (2 Jan. 1943): 4278. Rees writes, "The Royal Navy and Royal Air Force have priority of choice and the Civilian Defence Services have claimed a great many men. The Army comes last in the list ... [and] has therefore to deal with very considerable numbers of dull, neurotic and unstable men."

62 R.H. Ahrenfeldt, *Psychiatry in the British Army in the Second World War* (London: Routledge and Kegan Paul, 1958), 149. Northfield Military Hospital, Birmingham, opened in April 1942 with a 200-bed hospital wing and a 600-bed training wing. The hospital was entirely devoted to the rehabilitation of psychoneurotics who it was hoped would be able to return to "high grade military duties." The program was not a success.

63 For a summary of the post-1942 experience at Basingstoke see "Report on Neuropsychiatric Division of b.n. & p.s. Hospital 6 June 44 to 18 July 45," NA, RG 24, vol. 12,631.

64 Between the wars the RAMC employed a total of four "specialists in mental disease," two in England, two in India. Their basic function was the treatment and disposal of soldiers suffering from psychoses. See Alienist, "Some Recollections of Army Psychiatry," *JRAMC* 84, no. 2 (Feb. 1945): 47.

65 W. Sargant and E. Slater, "Acute War Neuroses," *The Lancet* (6 July 1940): 6097. All quotations in the following paragraph are from this article.

66 W. Sargant, *The Unquiet Mind* (London, 1967), 114. Sargant recalled this initial experience with acute cases in terms of some interest. He wrote: I shall never forget the arrival of these Dunkirk soldiers in their 'tin hats' and filthy uniforms, some of them wounded, many in states of total and abject neurotic collapse, slouching along, mixed up with Belgian and French civilians who had scrambled aboard the boats at the last minute. What the papers termed a great British achievement seemed to us at the time nothing better than a defeated and defeatist route. Men swarmed into the hospital, some raging mutinously against their officers for having deserted them in a panic, others swearing that they would never fight again. So complete a loss of morale in some was scaring to witness. Most of them were half-trained Territorials who had joined their regiments only to get a free summer holiday or because patriotic employers had ordered them to join."

67 G. Debenham and others, "Treatment of War Neuroses," *The Lancet* (25 Jan. 1941).

68 Sargant, *The Unquiet Mind*, 117.

69 Ibid., 118.

70 Debenham, "War Neuroses," 108.

71 Ibid. See also Sargant's account of the accidental discovery of insulin sub-coma in *The Unquiet Mind*, 119-21.

72 Richardson, interview. See also W. Sargant, "Physical Treatments of Acute Psychiatric States in War," paper read at a visit of American and Canadian Military Psychiatrists, published in *War Medicine*, 4 (1943): 377.

73 Botterell remembers Hanson going off on these expeditions. The United States Army's official history speaks of raids on the Normandy coast, Dieppe, the Sicilian Landings and the front line activity in Tunisia which won him the nickname of the "Phantom". A.J. Glass, ed., *Overseas Theatres*, vol. 2, *Neuropsychiatry in World Word II* (Washington 1973), chapter 1.

74 Ibid., chapter 2.

75 Richardson, interview.

CHAPTER TWO

1 R.H. Ahrenfeldt, *Psychiatry in the British Army in the Second World War* (London: Routledge and Kegan Paul, 1958) 36.

2 C.S. Myers, *Shell Shock in France* 1914-18 (Cambridge, 1940) cited in Ahrenfeldt, *Psychiatry in the British Army*, 14. The quotation continues "and on lack of proper discipline and esprit de corps" but these questions were not within the province of personnel selection.

3 P.E. Vernon and J.B. Parry, *Personnel Selection in the British Forces* (London, 1949), a history of British Army personnel selection.

4 J.M. Hitsman, *The Problem of Selection and Reallocation of Personnel in the Canadian Army Overseas*, Report No. 164, Historial Section CMHQ (London, 1946), 2.

5 For a summary of Bott's career see Myers, "Edward Alexander Bott."

6 See H.S.M. Carver, *Personnel Selection in the Canadian Army*, typescript (Ottawa, 1945), chapter 1, for an account of the development of the M test. For a brief but easily understandable summary of the progress of intelligence testing at the outbreak of the war see Robert Thompson, *The Pelican History of Psychology* (London 1968), chapter 18, "The Development of Tests 1918-40." For a modern review of the issues see S.H. Irvine and S.E. Newstead, eds, *Intelligence and Cognition: Contemporary Frames of Reference*, NATO ASI Series (Dordrecht, 1987). Stephen Jay Gould's *The Mismeasure of Man* (New York 1981) influenced the author's approach to the subject.

7 N. Pasture, "The Army Intelligence Test and Walter Lippman," *Journal of the History of the Behavioural Sciences* (1978).

8 Ibid.

9 J.R. Rees, "Three Years of Military Psychiatry," *BMJ* (2 Jan 1943): 3. The senior British Army psychiatrist in England, Rees seems to have believed that a quarter of the population was dull, feeble-minded, or had a low capacity to learn. Dr J.D. Griffin offered a similar estimate – Griffin interview.

10 See M.J. Wright and C.R. Myers, eds, *History of Academic Psychology in Canada* (Toronto, 1982) for background information on the Canadian Psychological Association.

11 Russel to DMS, 23 June 1941, Russel Papers, vol. 7.

12 J.A. Linton to DMS, 23 June 1941, NA, RG 24, vol. 15,650.

13 "Report on the Selection of Personnel and Mental Disease in the Canadian Army Overseas," author unknown, 18 July 1941, NA, RG 24, vol. 12,620.

14 Ibid.

15 Linton to GOC II Cdn. Corps, 31 Oct. 1941, NA, RG 24, vol. 12,630.

16 Ahrenfeldt, *Psychiatry in the British Army*, 84.

17 Ibid., 86.

18 Hitsman, *Problem of Selection*, 5.

19 Ibid., 6,7.

20 Obituaries, *Psychiatry* 34 (Aug. 1971): 330. Carver, *Personnel Selection*, 36-7.

21 G.B. Chisholm, *A Platoon Leader's Responsibility for the Morale of His Men* (Ottawa: Department of National Defence, 1941), 2.

22 H.F.G. Letson became Adjutant-General effective 2 Feb. 1942. Lieutenant-General Kenneth Stuart became Chief of the General Staff, 24 Dec. 1941.

23 "Memorandum of Meeting of Selection of Personnel, Ottawa 4-8-51," NA, RG 24, vol. 13,302, folder 1.

24 Carver, *Personnel Selection*, 41. James Willis Howard had a "wide knowledge of both practical and theoretical psychological methods acquired through his study of psychology (PhD Cornell 1936) and experience in educational work in Belleville, Ontario."

25 Hitsman, *Problem of Selection*, 6.

26 The fullest discussion of the surveying of the overseas army is in Carver, *Personnel Selection*, chapter 5.

27 Russel to DMS, 25 April 1942, Russel Papers, vol. 7.

28 Van Nostrand to DMS, 7 July 1942, NA, RG 24, vol. 12,604.

29 Ibid.

30 War Diary DMS, 20 Sept. 1942, NA, RG 24, vol. 12,604.

31 DMS Circular Letter 61/42, 24 Aug. 1942, NA, RG 24, vol. 12,604.

32 Ibid.

33 Figures calculated from H.H. Hyland and J.C. Richardson, "Psychoneurosis in the Canadian Army Overseas," *CMAJ* 47 (1942): 6. No figures of psychiatric illness per 1,000 of the army population are available and if they were such figures would be highly suspect since the system in place was *intended* to prevent "treatment" of psychoneurosis except in extreme cases.

34 Hyland and Richardson, "Psychoneurosis," 1.

35 War Diary, DMS 20 Sept. 1942 NA, RG 24, vol. 12,604.

36 Van Nostrand to DMS 7 July 1942.

37 DMS Circular Letter 61/42.

38 DMS Circular Letter 57/42, 11 Aug. 1942, NA, RG 24, vol. 12,604.

39 DGMS Circular Letter 162, 6 May 1942, NA, RG 24, vol. 13,302.

40 "Memorandum of Meeting on Selection of Personnel," (Ottawa, 4 August 1941).

41 Brock Chisholm became DGMS on 7 September 1942 and Bill Line was promoted to colonel and became Director of Personnel Services at the same time.

42 During the course of research for this book Terry Copp met with Dr Griffin on a number of occasions and conducted three separate interviews. Dr Griffin's comments on psychological testing in World War II suggest that while he recognized the limitations of the M test he believed the test, together with the "psychiatric" interview, was better than no screening. On one occasion he stated that the predictions of the army examiner conducting the psychiatric interview were "better than tossing a coin" and thus saved the army from dealing with some unsuitable personalities including many who were so poorly motivated that they were unlikely to make good soldiers.

43 W. Line (for G.B. Chisholm) to all AEs and AAEs, 6 January 1942, NA, RG 24, vol. 13,302. This was the only document marked *Secret* in the Personnel Directorate files used.

44 Ibid.

45 *Report*, 15 May 1942, NA, RG 24 vol. 13,302.

46 "Notes on Trip," HQ Military District 6, NA, RG 24, vol. 13,302.

47 Griffin, interview.

48 The Canadian National Committee for Mental Hygiene, *A Survey of the Ontario Hospitals*, typescript, February 1937. The copy consulted was found in the Russel Papers, vol. 4.

49 J.D.M. Griffin et al., "Psychiatry in the Canadian Army," *AJP* (1943): 140.

50 This is indicated both by the documentary evidence and the recollections of the psychiatrists interviewed.

51 J.D.M. Griffin et al., "Psychoneurotics Discharged From the Canadian Army," *CMAJ* (1945).

52 Ibid.

53 W.C. Menninger, *Psychiatry in a Troubled World* (New York: Macmillan, 1948) 589. US rates went from 8.8 (per thousand annual mean strength) in 1942 to 22.3 in 1943 and 13.9 in 1944. The rate gradually crept back up in 1945. Ibid., 594.

54 E.L.M. Burns, *Manpower in the Canadian Army* 1939-45 (Toronto: Clarke Irwin, 1956), 120.

55 Ibid., 129.

56 Ibid., 120. Burns gave the rate of psychiatric rejections for 1944 as 25 per cent, whereas S.C. Meakins in "The Pulhems System of Medical Grading" *CMAJ*, 49 no. 5, (1943): 349, gives a figure of 45 per cent. Between July 1943 and March 1944 14.9 per cent of volunteers and 32 per cent of conscripts were rejected on psychiatric grounds. Signal, Defensor to CanMil, 25 Aug 44, NA, RG 24, vol. 12,631.

57 DMS Circular Letter No. 210, 12 February 1943, NA, RG 24, vol. 13,303.

58 Memo Chisholm to All Psychiatrists, 5 Oct. 1943, NA, RG 24, vol. 13,303.

59 Griffin, interview.

60 Major G. Scott, "An Experiment in Conditioning the Unstable Soldier to Army Life," n.d., NA, RG 24, vol. 12,630.

61 F.H. Van Nostrand, "Three Years of Neuropsychiatry in the Canadian Army Overseas" *CMAJ* 49 (October 1943): 295.

62 G.S. Burton, "The Pioneers of the Canadian Army Overseas," unpublished paper, NA, RG 24, vol. 12,631.

63 Ibid.

64 Ibid.

65 A. McNaughton, Circular Letter, June 1943, NA, RG 24, vol. 13,303.

66 J.V. Coleman, "Prognostic Criteria in Soldiers with Psychiatric Problems," professional papers, USMHI. Capt. H.J.C. L'Etang, "A Criticism of Military Psychiatry in the Second World War," *JRAMC* 97 (1951): 192-7, 236-44, 316-27.

67 The details of the short unhappy life of #10 Training Co. may be traced in its War Diary, NA, RG 24, vol. 16,851. Originally the unit was to be composed of prepsychotics but no such fine distinction was drawn in practice.

68 Burton, "The Pioneers."

69 Van Nostrand, "Three Years."

70 Burton, "The Pioneers."

71 AAG(SP) to Van Nostrand, 12 May 1944, NA, RG 24, vol. 12,583.

72 A. McNaughton, Circular Letter, June 1943. In an earlier draft of this chapter the author described McNaughton's proposal as idiotic. All readers of the draft, including the co-author Bill McAndrew, insisted that this word must go. Idiotic still seems appropriate to me (Copp). General Andrew McNaughton, in my view, spent far too much of the army's time on personnel selection and other administrative activities that were not directed at combat training.

73 There is an inherent tension between individualistic and collective values in an organic military unit like a battalion or a platoon. One psychiatrist in the field wrote: "Experience and skill in group activities and games is commonly low in men that come to this centre ... One of the lessons that democratic powers have found hard to learn is the necessity for group experience as pre-combat training. It requires an adaptable personality to change from the competitive, individualistic, civilian existence to the close, co-operative, self-sacrificing life at the front. Some men take longer to learn this lesson than others. Some men break down in combat before they learn the lesson. It is possible they may have sufficient personality resources to modify their point of view so that they can get along better at the front." Captain G.O. Watts, "Psychotherapy in a Psychiatric Convalescent Depot," NA, RG 24, vol. 12,631. For recent comment on the importance of unit cohesion see the papers in S. Sarkesian, ed., *Combat Effectiveness* (Beverly Hills:

Sage Publications, 1979); G. Belenky, ed., *Contemporary Studies in Combat Psychiatry* (New York: Greenwood Press, 1987); and A. Millett and W. Murray, eds, *Military Effectiveness* (Columbus Ohio: Ohio University Press, 1988).

74 Crerar to McNaughton, 25 September 1943, NA, RG 24, vol. 10,771.

75 Carver, *Personnel Selection*, 49.

76 Major B.H. McNeel, "Report of Survey of Soldiers Under Sentence at the Canadian Detention Barracks, November 1943 to April 1944," NA, RG 24, vol. 12,630.

77 Richardson, interview; Dr Travis Dancey, interview with Terry Copp, Montreal, July 1983; Dr Burdett McNeel, interview with Terry Copp, November 1982.

78 J.C. Richardson, "Neuropsychiatry with the Canadian Army in Western Europe," typescript, n.d., provided by Dr Richardson. Copy in NA, RG 24, vol. 12,630.

79 Minutes of NP meeting, 26 Feb. 1943, NA, RG 24, vol. 12,631.

80 "The Army Psychiatric Service Middle East Force 1940-43" In F. Crew, ed., *History of the Second World War: United Kingdom Medical Services – Army Medical Series Campaigns*, vol. 2, 467. See G.W.B. James, "Psychiatric Lessons from Active Service," *The Lancet* (22 Dec. 1943): 801, for an overview of James's eclectic approach to military psychiatry.

CHAPTER THREE

1 Richardson to oc Basingstoke, 10 June 1943, NA, RG 24, vol. 12,631. Richardson wrote: "The present situation is not a new one, nor are any of the views expressed here of recent origin. For about two years I have been repeatedly worrying the previous oc and yourself with such grievances and requests."

2 Allan Walters, interview with Terry Copp, 13 Jan. 1983. Walters was not a Freudian but he "had never been resistant to Freud or psychoanalysis."

3 Van Nostrand to Luton (DMS), 1 May 1942, NA, RG 24, vol. 12,604.

4 Obituary A.M. Doyle, *CMAJ* 112 (8 March 1975) and Griffin, interview.

5 See A.M. Doyle, "Practical Aspects of Community Mental Health," *CJMH* (1938): 80.

6 "Minutes, meeting of Basingstoke psychiatrists," 12 April 1943, NA, RG 24, vol. 12, 631.

7 A.M. Doyle, "Plan for the Efficient Triage of Acute Neuropsychiatric Casualties," NA, RG 24, vol. 12,631.

8 Ibid.

9 A.M. Doyle, "The History and Development of Canadian Neuropsychiatric Service in the CMF," unpublished typescript, n.d., NA, RG 24, vol. 12,630. A much less detailed version of this paper was published in *CMAJ* (January 1944).

10 Doyle, "Plan for Triage."

11 Ibid.

12 Ibid.

13 R.H. Ahrenfeldt, *Psychiatry in the British Army in the Second World War* (London: Routledge and Kegan Paul, 1958) 185.

14 Admissions for injuries, enemy action, accounted for less than a twentieth of the hospital case load in the Mediterranean theatre, in contrast to North-West Europe where, in 1944, approximately half of the 225 per 1,000 admissions were due to enemy action. In 1942 there were 670 admissions to hospital per 1,000 men on strength in the Middle East but only 40.35 per 1,000 were due to enemy action. Injuries not from enemy action accounted for 51.42 cases per thousand. Mental diseases including psychoses and psychoneuroses were responsible for 20.03 admissions per 1,000 troops. From an overall medical or manpower point of view, dysentery, infectious hepatitis, malaria, sandfly fever, and venereal disease (39.7 per 1,000) were more important problems than battle casualties, never mind battle-induced neuroses. See W.F. Mellor, *Casualties and Medical Statistics* (London: HMSO, 1972), chapter 2, Middle East Forces, table 55, 282.

15 F. Crew, ed., *History of the Second War: United Kingdom Medical Services – Army Medical Services*, vol. 1 *Campaigns* (London 1957), 464.

16 Ibid., 466.

17 Crew, *Campaigns*, table J, 491.

18 Ibid., 512.

19 E.L. Cooper and A.J.M. Sinclair, "War Neuroses in Tobruk," *MJA* 2, no. 5 (1 August 1942): 73.

20 Ibid., 76.

21 H.B. Love, "Neurotic Casualties in the Field," *MJA* 2, no. 6: 137. Dr Love pays tribute to Dr James, the British consultant in psychiatry, who visited the Australians in Tobruk.

22 Ibid.

23 A.J.M. Sinclair, "Psychiatric Aspects of the Present War," *MJA* 23:501.

24 The Australian 9th Division suffered 2,089 battle casualties (wounded) 1 Sept. 1942 to 30 Dec. 1942. Most casualties occurred in the El Alamein battle 23 Oct.–7 Nov. The psychiatrist working at the Divisional Rest Station classified just 152 men as NYD (N) but large numbers were treated for sicknesses and physical exhaustion. Overall a 50 per cent return to unit rate was achieved. War Diary, ADMS, 9 Australian Division, WO 222 1606.

25 Crew, *Campaigns*, 447.

26 T.D.M. Stout, *War Surgery and Medicine* (Wellington: War History Branch, Dept. Internal Affairs, 1954), chapter 19; and M.H. Aiken, "Psychoneuroses in the Second New Zealand Expeditionary Force," *New Zealand Medical Journal* 40 (1941): 345.

27 Ahrenfeldt, *Psychiatry in the British Army*, 184.

28 A.J. Glass ed., *Overseas Theatres*, vol. 2, *Neuropsychiatry in World War II* (Washington: Office of the Surgeon General, 1973) 5.

29 Ibid., 6.

30 R. Grinker and J.P. Speigel, *Men Under Stress* (New York: McGraw Hill, 1945).

31 R.R. Grinker with J.P. Spiegel, *War Neuroses in North Africa: The Tunisian Campaign* (Jan.–May 1943) (New York: Josiah Macey Jr Foundation, 1943) and Melvin Sabshin, "Twenty-five Years After *Men Under Stress*" in D. Offer, ed., *Modern Psychiatry and Clinical Research* (New York, 1972).

32 Glass, *Overseas Theatres*, 9.

33 Ibid.

34 Ibid., 15-19.

35 A.M. Doyle, "Summary of Neuropsychiatric Activities in the Sicilian and Italian Theatres with the Canadian Forces," War Diary, No. 1 Canadian Corps Neuropsychiatric Centre, May 1944, appendix 1, NA, RG 24, vol. 15,951.

36 G.W.L. Nicholson, *The Canadians in Italy, 1943-1945* (Ottawa: Queen's Printer, 1956), 50-84. The best overall campaign study of Sicily is Carlo D'Este, *Bitter Victory: The Battle for Sicily, 1943* (London: Collins, 1988).

37 W.R. Feasby, *Organization and Campaigns*, vol. 1, *Official History of the Canadian Medical Services, 1939-45* (Ottawa: Queen's Printer, 1956), 123-53.

38 A.M. Doyle, "Report, 10 July – 10 November 1943," NA, RG 24, vol. 15,951.

39 A.M. Doyle, "Report of the Canadian Medical Rest Station in the Sicilian Campaign," *JCMS* (January 1944): 104.

40 "Operations of British, Indian, and Dominion Forces in Italy, 3 September 1943 to May 1945," Part 5, Administrative Monographs, no. 13, Medical Papers, part I – "The Battle Against Malaria" (British Historical Section, Central Mediterranean, 31 March 1946).

41 Anti-malarial planning was badly disrupted by difficulties in liaising with distant British headquarters in the Middle East. Security considerations hampered the dissemination of medical intelligence, and supplies of mepacrine tablets were disrupted. There were almost 1,200 cases of actual or suspected malaria in the 1st Division, most following active operations, and after some acrimonious debate the decision was made to provide blanket quinine treatment of ten grains for three successive days to the entire division. See Feasby, *Organization and Campaigns*, 124-30, 146-8.

42 Doyle, "Report, 10 July – 10 November 43."

43 A.M. Doyle, "Report of the Neuropsychiatrist on the Sicilian Campaign," *JCMS* (January 1944): 106.

44 Doyle, "History and Development CMF."

45 Ahrenfeldt, *Psychiatry in the British Army*, 185-6; S.A. MacKeith, "Lasting Lessons of Overseas Military Psychiatry," *JRAMC* (July 1946): 542-50.

46 Glass, *Overseas Theatres*, 15-21.

47 Ibid., 26. The outstanding American commander in Italy, Lucian K. Truscott, had his Judge Advocate in the 3rd Division interview every psychiatric casualty to detect those suspected of malingering. Ibid., 27. Truscott's horizons broadened with his elevation in rank from divisional to Fifth Army commander, when he told a group of psychiatrists: "The whole business of psychoneurosis is a command responsibility and extends to all echelons of command." He added that those responsibilities began with himself as Army Commander. Ibid., 96. Truscott's *Command Missions* (New York: Dutton, 1954) is one of the best memoirs of the Italian campaign.

48 Doyle, "History and Development CMF."

49 Doyle, "Report, 10 July 43–10 November 43."

50 Doyle, "History and Development CMF."

51 D. Hunter, "The Work of a Corps Psychiatrist in the Italian Campaign," *JRAMC* 86 (1946): 127.

52 C. Comfort, *Artist at War* (Toronto: Ryerson Press, 1956); G.W.L. Nicholson, *The Canadians in Italy* (Toronto: Ryerson Press, 1956), 304-39.

53 Nicholson, *Canadians in Italy*, 338. See also Farley Mowat, *And No Birds Sang* (Toronto: McClelland and Stewart, 1979).

54 Nicholson, *Canadians in Italy*.

55 Major-General B.M. Hoffmeister, interview with Bill McAndrew.

56 Nicholson, *Canadians in Italy*, 308.

57 Quoted in DHIST CMHQ Report No. 165.

58 Doyle, "History and Development CMF."

59 Ibid.

60 Ibid.

61 Ibid.

62 A.M. Doyle, "Summary," NA, RG 24, vol. 15,951.

63 A.M. Doyle, "Address to 1 Cdn Div Medical Society, 6 April 1944," NA, RG 24, vol. 10,924.

64 Doyle, "History and Development CMF."

65 Doyle, "Address."

66 The psychiatric literature on the situational causation of battle exhaustion is extensive. See the annotated papers in N.D.C. Lewis and B. Engle, *Wartime Psychiatry: A Compendium of the International Literature* (New York: Oxford University Press, 1954).

67 A.M. Doyle to DDMS, I Canadian Corps, 8 February 1944, NA, RG 24, vol. 10,924.

68 Roger J. Spiller, "S.L.A. Marshall and the Ratio of Fire," *RUSI Journal* (Winter 1988): 63-71.

69 "Manpower Problems of the Canadian Army in the Second World War," DHIST, AHQ Report no. 63, 155.

70 C.E.G. Gould, "Observations on 1,000 Referred Neuropsychiatric Cases," n.d., NA, RG 24, vol. 2,089.

71 Personal communication.

72 Gould to Van Nostrand, 15 December 1943, NA, RG 24, vol. 12,631. See also Gould, "Report on Neuropsychiatry (Base) in Italy," 17 May 1944, DHIST: 147.71G 13009 (D3).

73 Gould to Van Nostrand, 15 February 1944, NA, RG 24, vol. 12,630.

74 Ibid.

CHAPTER FOUR

1 Major-General C. Vokes to GOC V Corps, 3 January 1944, DHIST, CMHQ Report 165, appendix.

2 For the most comprehensive recent history of the Italian campaign see D. Graham and S. Bidwell, *Tug of War: the Battle for Italy* (New York: St Martin's Press, 1986).

3 G.W.L. Nicholson, *The Canadians in Italy* (Ottawa: Queen's Printer, 1957), 362-79.

4 Quoted in G.R. Stevens, *A City Goes to War* (Brampton: Charters Publications, 1964), 284.

5 G.R. Stevens, *The Royal Canadian Regiment, II*, 1933-1966 (London: London Printing, 1967), 123-9.

6 Ibid., 130.

7 Stevens, *A City Goes to War*, 285.

8 Vokes to commanders, 21 February 1944; copy in NA, MG 30 E 157, Crerar Papers, vol. 3.

9 Stevens, *Royal Canadian Regiment*, 130. For powerful historical evocations of soldiers in battle see John Keegan, *The Face of Battle* (New York: Vintage, 1977); D. Winter, *Death's Men: Soldiers of the Great War* (London: Penguin, 1979); G. F. Linderman, *Embattled Courage: The Experience of Combat in the American Civil War* (New York: Free Press, 1987); John Ellis, *The Sharp End of War* (London: David and Charles, 1980).

10 War Diary, DDMS, I Corps, NA, RG 24, vol. 15,651. Officially diagnosed self-inflicted wounds rates for 1944 (per 1,000 strength) were British 0.21, Canadian 2.40, New Zealand 0.10. W.F. Mellor, *Casualties and Medical Statistics* (London: HMSO, 1972). Accidental injuries accounted for (per 1,000 strength) British 39.06, Canadian 64.80, New Zealand 107.47. It would be interesting to determine why such widely varying rates were reported and why New Zealanders were so accident prone.

11 War Diary, Field Punishment Camp, February-April 1944, NA, RG 24, vol. 16,516. The film *The Hill* offers an unexcelled portrayal of the finely turned tension of military detention.

12 Nicholson, *Canadians in Italy*, 340-62; Lieutenant-General E.L.M. Burns, *General Mud* (Toronto: Clarke Irwin, 1970), 120-37.

13 See the version in K. Beattie, *Dileas: History of the 48th Highlanders of Canada 1929-1956* (Toronto: 48th Highlanders, 1957).

14 Major-General C. Vokes, *Vokes: My Story* (Ottawa: Gallery Books, 1985), 152-3.

15 Major-General F. Richardson, in A. Babington, *For the Sake of Example: Capital Courts-Martial, 1914-1920* (London: Leo Cooper, 1983), 218.

16 Burns, *General Mud*, 133.

17 E.L.M. Burns, *Manpower in the Canadian Army, 1939-1945* (Toronto: Clarke Irwin, 1956), 106.

18 See Babington, *For the Sake of Example*; also Desmond Morton, "The Supreme Penalty; Canadian Deaths by Firing Squad in the First World War," *Queen's Quarterly* (Autumn 1972): 345-52.

19 Brigadier E.A. McCusker to Major-General R.M. Luton (DMS) CMHQ, 22 April 1944, War Diary, DDMS, I Canadian Corps, April 1944, NA, RG 24, vol. 15,651.

20 Ibid., January 1944.

21 A.M. Doyle, "The History and Development of Canadian Neuropsychiatric Service in the CMF," unpublished typescript, n.d., NA, RG 24, vol. 12,630.

22 Ibid.

23 War Diary, No. 2 Canadian Exhaustion Unit, June 1944, NA, RG 24, vol. 15,951.

24 Crerar to Lieutenant-General G.G. Simonds, 15 July 1944 (quoting from a letter Crerar had written earlier to General Burns on turning over command of the Corps). NA, MG 30 E157, Crerar Papers, vol. 3.

25 Ibid.

26 Ibid.

27 Doyle, "Report 10 July – 10 November 1943," NA, RG 24, vol. 15,951.

28 J.R. Rees, *The Shaping of Psychiatry by War* (New York: Norton, 1945), 27. He continued: "To some of the tougher soldiers who declaim about the supposed kind-heartedness of psychiatrists, one is tempted to say, I thoroughly approve of shooting provided you shoot the right man. The fire-eater who regards all nerves as 'fiddle-sticks' and anxiety as malingering normally lives at the base, and in practically every case that I have met is recognizable without much difficulty as a man carrying a considerable load of personal anxiety, and shame about it."

29 Personal communication.

30 5 CAD Medical Society, minutes of meeting, 11 May 1944. War Diary, ADMS, 5 CAD, May 1944, appendix 6, NA, RG 24, vol. 15,664. The death penalty as deterrent is discussed in R.H. Ahrenfeldt, *Psychiatry in the British Army in the Second World War* (London: Routledge and Kegan Paul, 1958) 271-5.

31 Burns, *Manpower*, 107, 110.

32 Ibid.

33 Doyle, "History and Development CMF."

34 Burns, *Manpower*, 108.

35 Doyle, "History and Development CMF;" Medical Administrative Instructions, War Diary, DDMS, I Canadian Corps, May 1944, NA, RG 24 vol. 15,651; 8th Army, "Casualties – Reporting of," 12 February 1944, PRO WO 177/326, 111366.

36 Burns, "Notes for Talk to Brigadiers on Necessity for Economy of Manpower," 11 May 1944, War Diary, General Burns, May 1944, NA, RG 24, vol. 17,507.

37 Ibid.

38 Ibid.

39 A.M. Doyle to ADMS, 1st Division, "Stress Reactions in Officers," 19 December 1943, NA, RG 24, vol. 10,924.

40 Memorandum, "Battle Weary Officers," 28 November 1944, DHIST 147.98009 (D4).

41 Norman Craig, *The Broken Plume* (London: Imperial War Museum, 1982), 75.

42 Personal communication.

43 D. Pearce, *Journal of a War* (Toronto: Macmillan, 1965), 165.

44 W. Smith, *What Time the Tempest* (Toronto: Ryerson, 1953), 278. The lack of reference to clergymen in the documents on handling psychiatric casualties is as striking as the lack of reference to Freud.

45 Ibid.

46 Ibid.

47 Ibid.

48 Burns, "Notes for Talk."

49 Ibid.

50 War Diary, I Canadian Corps, Neuropsychiatric Centre, May 1944, NA, RG 24, vol. 15,951.

51 Doyle, "History and Development CMF."

52 Ibid.

53 Nicholson, *Canadians in Italy*, 387-417. For a very good recent account of the operations see John Ellis, *Cassino: the Hollow Victory* (New York: McGraw Hill, 1984).

54 Other than Nicholson's official operational history, and unit accounts in regimental histories, very little has been written on the Canadian experience in the Liri Valley. McAndrew has compiled a collection of primary source data for battlefield studies of the operations on which this partial account is based. There is a I Canadian Corps file in NA, RG 24, vol. 10,779, and others in vols 10,781, 10,788, 10,881, and 10,992. Coordinating infantry movement with artillery and tank fire support was a continuing problem. See

McAndrew, "Fire or Movement? Canadian Tactical Doctrine, Sicily – 1943," *Military Affairs* (July 1987): 140-5.

55 War Diary, PPCLI, 23 May 1944, NA, RG 24, vol. 15, 156-7.

56 Nicholson, *Canadians in Italy*, 423.

57 Ibid., 452.

58 W.R. Feasby, *Organization and Campaigns*, vol. 1, *Official History of the Canadian Medical Services* 1939-45 (Ottawa: Queen's Printer, 1956), 179-191.

59 Ibid., 188.

60 A.M. Doyle, "Report of I Cdn Corps Neuropsychiatrist, period 1 April – 20 June 1944, including battles of Gustav and Adolph Hitler Lines," copy in War Diary, ADMS 5th Canadian Armoured Division, NA, RG 24, vol. 15,664.

61 Doyle, "The History and Development CMF."

62 The American journalist-historian S.L.A. Marshall concluded from after-action research interviews with battle participants that comparatively few soldiers (15-25 per cent) actually fired their weapons in combat. This raised questions about what they did do during a firefight. Marshall's views in *Men Against Fire* (New York: William Morrow, 1947) and subsequent books have been uncritically accepted until recently. Questions are now being asked of the veracity of his methodology and the thoroughness of his research. See Roger Spiller, "S.L.A. Marshall and the Ratio of Fire," *RUSI Journal*, (Winter 1988): 63-71; and Frederic Smoler, "The Secret of the Soldiers Who Didn't Shoot," *American Heritage* (March 1989): 37-45. See also the discussions in Roger Spiller, ed., *S.L.A. Marshall at Leavenworth* (Fort Leavenworth, 1980).

63 ADMS, 5 CAD, "Quarterly Report of Medical Activities of 5 CAD, April-June 1944," NA, RG 24, vol. 15,664. For comment on British battle absenteeism see Williamson Murray, "The British Armed Forces, 1939-1945," in A. Millett and W. Murray, eds, *Military Effectiveness, III: The Second World War* (Boston: Allen and Unwin, 1988), 100.

64 Personal communication.

65 We are grateful to many veterans for sharing their hard-won insights about the role of commanding officers and other aspects of unit cohesion and morale.

66 Quoted in Shaun Brown, *The Loyal Edmonton Regiment* (MA thesis, Wilfrid Laurier University, 1985), 171.

67 S.A. MacKeith, "Lasting Lessons of Overseas Military Psychiatry," *Journal of Mental Science* (July 1946): 542-50.

68 General J.V. Allard, *Memoirs* (Vancouver: UBC Press, 1988), 76-7.

69 We are grateful to Major Harry Pope, R22ᵉR for the insight into success and failure as variables. Doyle, "Report of I Cdn Corps Neuropsychiatrist."

70 Doyle, "History and Development CMF."

71 Ibid.

72 Captain K.A. Hunter, "Psychiatric Casualties," NA, RG 24, vol. 19,466.

73 Ibid.

74 Ibid.

75 Ibid.

76 Hunter, "Observations by ADMS 5 Canadian Armoured Division" (on Doyle's report), n.d. (but from the context it was prepared in mid-August 1944), NA, RG 24, vol. 15,664.

77 Ibid.

78 Ibid.

79 Doyle, "History and Development CMF," and D. Hunter, "The Work of a Corps Psychiatrist in the Italian Campaign," *JRAMC* (1946): 127-30. See also F. Crew, *The Army Medical Services, Campaigns*, vol. 3 (London: HMSO, 1959), 241-3.

80 A.M. Doyle to DDMS I Canadian Corps, 19 March 1944, copy as appendix to "History and Development CMF." Doyle was encouraged to learn that Canadian neuropsychiatric incidence compared favourably with that in Allied armies, writing: "There is no doubt that neuropsychiatric casualties constitute one of the most important military considerations, but it has been ascertained that there is no need for odious comparison of our troops with others; on the other hand there is reason for every confidence in them as fighting men."

81 MacKeith, "Lasting Lessons of Overseas Military Psychiatry."

82 A.J. Glass, ed, *Overseas Theatres* vol. 2, *Neuropsychiatry in World War II* (Washington: Office of the Surgeon General, 1973) 25-109.

83 5 CAD, "Quarterly Report," NA, RG 24, vol. 15,664.

84 The material in this paragraph is from the War Diaries of Nos. 16, 17 and 18 Special Employment Companies, NA, RG 24, vol. 15,326. See Major Gerald D. Resch, "Combat Stress Reaction Casualty Management: Canadian Personnel Conservation Experience in a Theatre of War," paper prepared for the Sixth Users' Workshop on Combat Stress, San Antonio, Texas, 30 November – 4 December 1987.

CHAPTER FIVE

1 The authors are grateful to Colonel Strome Galloway for this apt jingle.

2 See W.J. McAndrew, "Eighth Army at the Gothic Line: Commanders and Plans," *RUSI Journal* (March 1986). For another view see R. Ryder, *Oliver Leese* (London: Hamish Hamilton, 1987).

3 Quoted and cited in DHIST, AHQ *Report No. 63*, part 2, 349.

4 Major E.D. Wittkower and Captain J. Cowan (RAMC), "Some Psychological Aspects of Sexual Promiscuity: Summary of an Investigation," copy in DHIST 147.98009 (D4).

5 I Canadian Corps Administrative Instruction no. 49, NA, RG 24, vol. 12,559.

6 Ibid.

7 "Operations of British, Indian and Dominion Forces in Italy, 3 September 1943 to 2 May 1945," Part 5, Administrative Monographs, no. 13, *Medical Papers*, part 2, "The Battle Against Venereal Disease," (British Historical Section, Central Mediterranean, 1 March 1946).

8 Ibid.

9 W.F. Mellor, ed., *Official Medical History of the Second World War: Casualties and Medical Statistics* (London: HMSO, 1972) 232ff. Canadians were especially susceptible to infectious hepatitis and influenza, the rate for the latter being 10.8 per thousand compared to an overall rate of 2.2. African troops had the highest incidence of psychiatric disorders followed by Canadians and others. Indians had the lowest recorded incidence.

10 See the recent official British account: W. Jackson and T.P. Gleave, *The Mediterranean and the Middle East*, vol. 6, part 2, June to October 1944 (London: HMSO, 1987).

11 W.J. McAndrew, "Eighth Army at the Gothic Line: the Dogfight," *RUSI Journal* 131 (June 1986).

12 G.W.L. Nicholson, *The Canadians in Italy* 1943-45 (Ottawa: Queen's Printer, 1956), 562, 640.

13 A.E. Moll, "Neuropsychiatry: Summary of 280 patients examined at Nos. 4 and 5 CCS, 12 June – 30 November 1942," and follow-up memorandum, NA, RG 24, vol. 2089.

14 Ibid.

15 A.E. Moll, "Psychosomatic Disease Due to Battle Stress," in Eric D. Wittkower and R.A. Cleghorn, eds, *Recent Developments in Psychosomatic Medicine* (Montreal: J.B. Lippincott, 1953), 436-54.

16 Ibid., and case reports of No. 2 CEU, NA, RG 24, vol. 12,631.

17 A.E. Moll, "Report on Psychiatry in the Field, No. 2 Canadian Exhaustion Unit," n.d., NA, RG 24, vol. 12,559.

18 Ibid.

19 Ibid.

20 A.E. Moll, "Army Psychiatry with CMF," 24 September 1944, War Diary, No. 2 Canadian Exhaustion Unit, NA, RG 24, vol. 15,951.

21 Ibid.

22 Ibid.

23 Ibid.

24 Nicholson, *Canadians in Italy*, 565-605. For a valuable detailed account of the Rimini operations see Amedeo Montemaggi, *La Linea Gotica* (Roma: Edizion Civitas, 1985).

25 Major-General Hubert Essame, quoted in Carlo D'Este, *Decision in Normandy* (London: Collins, 1983), 285. See Field-Marshall Lord Wavell, "In Praise of Infantry," in Wavell, *The Good Soldier* (London: Macmillan, 1948), 70-94.

26 Van Nostrand, "Report by Consultant Neuropsychiatrist CA (0): Liaison

Visit Italian Theatre: 16 November – 16 December 1944," NA, RG 24, vol. 12,631.

27 Foulkes to Crerar, 7 December 1944, Crerar Papers, vol. 7.

28 Historical Officer's Note, n.d., DHIST 145.2P7011 (D3).

29 C. Sydney Frost, *Once a Patricia* (St Catharines: Vanwell, 1988), 306.

30 Ibid.

31 There are a large number of questionnaires in NA, RG 24, vol. 10, 450. Command problems were not confined to Canadian units and formations. It must be remembered that the Canadian Army, like those of Britain and the United States, was a hastily mobilized, amateur one. Unfortunately commanders had to learn on the job and some never learned. On British difficulties see Gregory Blaxland, *Alexander's Generals* (London: Kimber, 1979). On American problems see the candid and very instructive comments in Romie Brownlee and William Mullen III, *Changing an Army: an Oral History of General William E. DePuy, USA Retired* (Washington: US Center of Military History, 1988). A Canadian chaplain wrote of his time in hospital in Italy: "After every action there is a review of what happened. There were such reviews in the ward of officers, lieutenants to majors, who had had to carry out the orders from above. They were candid affairs. Colonels and above were not in these wards. If they had been they would have heard much to increase their wisdom. I suggest that in the next war these discussions be tape recorded and played over to brigadiers, generals and their staffs." W. Smith, *What Time the Tempest* (Toronto: Ryerson, 1953), 295.

32 G. Kitching, *Mud and Green Fields* (Vancouver: Battleline Books, 1986), 236-7. For rueful observations on the uninspiring personalities of senior Canadian commanders see C.P. Stacey, "Canadian Leaders of The Second World War," *The Canadian Historical Review* (March 1985): 64-72.

33 S. Galloway, *Bravely Into Battle* (Toronto: Stoddart, 1988), 229. See also his *Some Died at Ortona* (London: The RCR, 1983); and *With the Irish Against Rommel* (Vancouver: Battleline Books, 1984).

34 Ibid.

35 The most comprehensive overview is in A. Kellett, *Combat Motivation* (Boston: Klower-Nijhoff, 1982).

36 Captain G.O. Watts, "Psychotherapy in a Psychiatric Convalescent Depot," NA, RG 24, vol. 12,631.

37 Moll, "Psychosomatic Disease Due to Battle Stress."

38 Frost, *Once a Patricia*, 308. The legendary American journalist, Ernie Pyle, wrote earlier that year: "A lot of people have morale confused with the desire to fight. I don't know of one soldier out of ten thousand who wants to fight ... The old-timers are sick to death of battle, and the new replacements are scared to death of it. And yet the Company goes on into battle and it is a proud Company." David Nichols, ed., *Ernie's War: The Best of Ernie Pyle: World War II Dispatches* (New York, 1986), 207-8.

39 On the conscription crisis see J.L. Granatstein, *Broken Promises* (Toronto: Oxford Press, 1977); and C.P. Stacey, *Arms, Men and Governments* (Ottawa: Information Canada, 1970), 397-484. Both are more concerned with policy considerations than with battlefield effects.

40 E.L.M. Burns, *Manpower in the Canadian Army, 1939-45* (Toronto: Clarke Irwin, 1956); J.M. Hitsman, "Manpower Problems of the Canadian Army in the Second War," DHIST, AHQ Report No. 63.

41 Hitsman, "Manpower Problems," 353-4. Canadian personnel administrators accepted rates of wastage through casualties based on British experience in North Africa. These were inappropriate for the nature of fighting in other theatres of war.

42 Ibid. A personal account of an NCO in the Lanark and Renfrew Scottish regiment, which was formed primarily from reluctant anti-aircraft gunners, is in Fred Cederberg, *The Long Road Home* (Toronto: General Publishing, 1984).

43 Stuart to Burns, 22 September 1944, NA, RG 24, vol. 10,825. Fifty of the 496 Corps tradesmen became unavailable due to hospitalization or other reasons soon after arriving in Italy in early October. Of the rest – "their previous training in infantry subjects was almost non-existent." Two hundred and twenty-one were sent forward in early December, the others being retained for further training. Neither they nor those men on the next draft were told that they were to become combat replacements until they arrived in Italy. This second group were infantrymen but had not served as such for several years in England. The report on them commented that "Presumably these men had, at some time, undergone infantry basic training. As they had subsequently been employed at trades, however, nearly all traces of their training had disappeared before their arrival in this theatre. Consequently, it was necessary to start their training here at the bottom." War Diary, No. 1 Canadian Base Reinforcement Depot, October-December 1944, NA, RG 24, vol. 16,715. Within the theatre 33 men from other Corps volunteered to remuster as infantrymen in October 1944. Another 563 were transferred compulsorily in the same month. "Liaison Letters," No. 2 Echelon, NA, RG 24, vol. 10,410.

44 Quoted in "Psychiatric Casualties in Battle," *The Lancet* (15 April 1955).

45 No. 1 Canadian Base Reinforcement Battalion, War Diary, April 1944, appendix 28, NA, RG 24, vol. 16,715.

46 Quoted in Brown, *Loyal Edmonton Regiment*, 146.

47 Brigadier E.G. Weeks, "General Observations on the Visit to Italy of Col the Hon. J.L. Ralston – Minister of National Defence," n.d., DHIST 110. (DI), Kim Beattie, *Dileas: History of the 48th Highlanders of Canada, 1929-1956* (Toronto: 48th Highlanders, 1957), 671-2. 'Colonel Ralston asked for their names and the records of half the men were examined. All had been in the army for at least one year. Apparently this was accepted as evidence that

they were adequately trained as combat infantrymen. It was a dubious assumption held by those well behind the front, not fighting commanders. There was only a tenuous connection between time in service and the quality of training as the above discussion suggests. However Ralston and his government had reason to be confused because they were receiving conflicting information from field commanders and personnel administrators.' See Stacey, *Arms, Men and Governments*, 441–60.

48 Beattie, *Dileas*, 671.

49 Smith, *What Time the Tempest*, 270-1. On 30 January 1945 the Deputy Chairman of the National Selective Service Mobilization Board in Toronto wrote in a letter to the Deputy Minister of Labour that "it may be a coincidence but I regret to report that several law students who graduated from Osgoode Hall last year were turned down on account of Mental Instability and only one of those who was turned down on this ground had any other disability. When these cases were called to my attention the situation seemed so remarkable that it looked to me almost as though the thing had been planned by those who were examined ... Curiously enough we find that many prominent athletes suffer from the same disability. On the Maple Leaf Hockey Team there are perhaps four or five otherwise physically fit young men who have been turned down on the ground of Mental Instability. One very prominent football player who had graduated from Western University a year or so ago has also been turned down on the ground of Mental Instability and a certain well known golfer who also plays hockey in the winter was turned down for similar reasons." Quoted in DHIST, AHQ Report no. 63, 311-12. Unequal sacrifice for the war effort was not uncommon, but morale was bound to suffer when this inequality was so clearly demonstrated.

50 Van Nostrand, "Report of Liaison Visit, 16 November–16 December 1944," NA, RG 24, vol. 12,631.

51 Foulkes to Burns, March 1945, NA, RG 24, vol. 10,825.

52 Ibid.

53 War Diary, DDMS I Canadian Corps, December 1944, NA, RG 24, vol. 15,651.

54 A.E. Moll, "Neuropsychiatry in the Field, No. 2 Canadian Exhaustion Unit, CA CMF, Period 1 October – 31 December 1944," copy in DHIST 147.98009 (D4). Moll, "Quarterly Report, 1 January – 31 March 1945," NA, RG 24, vol. 12,631.

55 K. Hunter, "Quarterly Report on Medical Activities of 5 CAD, October-December 1944," War Diary, ADMS 5 CAD, NA, RG 24, vol. 15,664.

56 Moll, "Neuropsychiatry in Field."

57 Van Nostrand, "Report of Liaison Visit."

58 Doyle, "Report of Adviser in Neuropsychiatry, Canadian Section, 1 Echelon, AFHQ, for period December 1944," NA, RG 24, vol. 12,631.

59 Ibid. While the number of battle casualties in the 1st Division declined towards the end of December the NP ratio rose sharply. In the last week

of the month the ratio of psychiatric casualties (47) to wounded (74) was a remarkable 63 per cent. The rate for December, as well as for the last quarter of the year, was 23 per cent. War Diary, ADMS, I CID, NA, RG 24, vol. 15,658. At the end of December there were also 437 men from the 1st Division's infantry battalions in military detention. NA, RG 24, vol. 10,410.

60 Van Nostrand, "Preliminary Report of Liaison Tour of Duty in the Mediterranean Theatre of War – 14 November 1943-15 January 1944," copy in NA, RG 24, vol. 12,631.

61 Lord Moran, *Anatomy of Courage*, 3rd ed. (New York: Avery Publications, 1987), xvi.

62 Personal communication.

63 Personal communication.

64 Personal communication.

65 "Psychiatric Standards: Opinions from Overseas," 9 December 1944, copy obtained from Dr Jack Griffin.

66 Quoted in Brown, *Loyal Edmonton Regiment*, 165.

67 Galloway, *Bravely Into Battle*, 321.

68 G.O. Watts, "Psychotherapy in a Psychiatric Convalescent Depot," NA, RG 24, vol. 12,631.

69 "Record of Trials by Court Martial During Period 1 September 1939 to 30 September 1946," compiled by the office of the Judge Advocate General, copy in authors' possession. Some of the courts martial were to try more usual offences: civil crimes, theft, etc. Crime and desertion spawned a thriving underground economy in Italy. By late 1944 more than 1,000 Allied military vehicles had been sold to civilians. See Major S.R. Elliot, *Scarlet to Green: A History of Intelligence in the Canadian Army*, 1903-1963 (Ottawa, 1981), 243. Because of the complexity of the Italian military landscape in 1944-45, with a civil war being fought within the greater war, thousands of hill dwellers – escaped prisoners, allied and axis deserters, partisans, and fugitive Italians – roamed the interior mountains. For a touching perspective of the human costs see Iris Origo, *War in Val D'Orcia: A Diary* 1943-1944 (London: Jonathon Cape, 1947). A delighful memoir is Eric Newby, *Love and War in the Apennines* (Newton Abbot: Readers Union, 1972).

70 "Historical Officer's Note," n.d., DHIST, 145.2P7011 (D3).

71 Frost, *Once a Patricia*, 352. See also Roger Spiller, "Ison's Run: Human Dimensions of Warfare in the 20th Century," *Military Review* (May 1988); and "The Tenth Imperative," *Military Review* (April 1989).

72 Frost, *Once a Patricia*, 352.

73 Crerar to Commander II Canadian Corps, 2 September 1944, Crerar Papers, vol. 4. This was standard policy in Italy as well.

74 "Operations of British, Indian and Dominion Forces, Part 5, "The Problem of Desertion," (British Historical Section, Central Mediterranean, 31 March 1946).

75 The material in this paragraph is taken from Doyle, "Report of Survey of Canadian Soldiers Under Sentence in the CMF," n.d., NA, RG 24, vol. 12,631.

76 "Operations of British, Indian, Dominion Forces, Part 5." See also Gregory Blaxland, *Alexander's Generals* (London: William Kimber, 1979).

77 A.E. Glass, ed., *Overseas Theatres*, vol. 2, *Neuropsychiatry in World War II* (Washington: Office of the Surgeon General, 1973) 85.

78 Morse P. Manson and Harry M. Grayson, "Why 2,276 American Soldiers in the Mediterranean Theater of Operations Were Absent Without Leave, Deserted, or Misbehaved Before the Enemy," *AJP* (July 1946). See also the remarks on disciplinary problems in Eric Sevareid, *Not So Wild a Dream* (New York: Atheneum, 1976), especially 361-7.

CHAPTER SIX

1 Major-General E. Phillips, Address to 21 Army Group psychiatrists Jan. 13, 1945. "Minutes of a Conference ... held at 32 (BR) General Hospital on 12 and 13 January 1945," NA, RG 24, vol. 12,631.

2 Dr Clifford Richardson, interview with Terry Copp, December 1982.

3 RMOs were told to complete Form AFB 193 (revised) and to accompany each patient unless the exhaustion casualty occurred in a quiet time when form AFW 3118 was to be used. The assumptions about forward diagnosis and careful segregation of exhaustion patients at the battalion level did not survive the reality of combat. Most exhaustion cases arrived without any documentation.

4 "Handling of Psychiatric Battle Casualties," 19 May 1944, draft version of appendix B to Standing Orders, 21 Army Group, NA, RG 24, vol. 15,646.

5 Ibid.

6 Ibid., 175. Ahrenfeldt writes "for the first time in British military history the possibility of psychiatric casualties in large numbers had been envisaged and at least some provision made to meet it."

7 School of Military Neuropsychiatry, 312 Station Hospital (NP) United States Army, *Combat Exhaustion*, NA, RG 24, vol. 10,066.

8 Van Nostrand to DMS, 6 April 1944, NA, RG 24, vol. 12,630.

9 Ibid.

10 Dr Robert Gregory, a native of Saint John, New Brunswick, received his MD at McGill in 1931. He worked for the New Brunswick Provincial Hospital prior to enlistment in 1939. He joined the neuropsychiatric branch in the expansion of 1941. He is remembered as a colourful character who wore a leather aviator's jacket and was frequently seen with a rifle over his shoulder. Obituary, *CMAJ* (Dec. 1976), and Richardson, McNeel, Burch, interviews.

11 "Psychiatrist Report," HQ 3 Cdn. Inf. Div., 18 March 1944, War Diary appendices ADMS 3 Cdn. Inf. Div., NA, RG 24, vol. 15,611.

12 Ibid., 17 May 1944.

13 Ibid.

14 Ibid., 8 April 1944.

15 Ibid., 17 May 1944.

16 Ibid.

17 A.J. Glass, ed., *Overseas Theatres*, vol. 2, *Neuropsychiatry in World War II* (Washington: Office of the Surgeon General, 1973), 279. First United States Army reported no psychiatric casualties on D-Day; 4 on D-Day+1; 47 on D-Day+4; Ibid., 280. British and Canadian figures were similar.

18 See R.R. Grinker and J.P. Speigel, *War Neuroses in North Africa: The Tunisian Campaign (Jan.–May 1943)* (New York: Josiah Macey Jr Foundation, 1943), 29ff for an elaboration of this view.

19 War Diary, ADMS 3 Cdn. Inf. Div., June 1944, NA, RG 24, vol. 15,661.

20 C.P. Stacey, *The Victory Campaign* (Ottawa: Queen's Printer, 1960), 132.

21 Ibid., 136.

22 Robert Gregory, "Divisional Neuropsychiatric Report 27 June 1944," appendix, War Diary, ADMS, 3 Cdn. Div., June 1944.

23 "Weekly Report by Psychiatrist Second Army for week ending June 24th," War Diary, DDMS Second (Br.) Army, PRO WO 177/321. British (and American) exhaustion casualties were evacuated directly to the UK in the first days of the Normandy battle. I and XXX British Corps opened their exhaustion centres on D+8. The Second British Army designated two field dressing stations as exhaustion centres on D+11, 17 June. F. Crew, *The Army Medical Services, Campaigns*, 3 (London: HMSO, 1959) 206.

24 Ibid., US casualties were higher than the British-Canadian figures as a result of offensive operations to capture Cherbourg, but the battle exhaustion casualties were similar, about 11 per cent of all non-fatal casualties. Glass, *Overseas Theatres*, 293.

25 "Weekly Report by Psychiatrist attached to Second Army for week ending Sat. 24 June 1944," PRO WO 177/321.

26 Ibid.

27 Ibid.

28 Gregory, "Report, 27 June 1944."

29 It is impossible to report an accurate figure for all exhaustion cases in June or any other month. Many psychiatric cases were evacuated through normal medical channels and were not diagnosed until their arrival in England. For example, Basingstoke received 209 cases in June, most of them from Normandy, while Dr Gregory was claiming that the 3rd Canadian Division had received only 200 cases. "Report on NP Division of B.N. & P.S. Hospital 6 June 1944 to 18 July 1945," NA, RG 24, vol. 12,631; and Gregory, "Report, 27 June 1944, War Diary, ADMS 3 Div. British exhaustion figures are equally problematical but there must have been "thousands" of evacuations, judging from reports such as "Exhaustion Figures for the Week

Ending July 1, 1944", War Diary, DDMS XXX Corps, WO 177/356: Total Admitted – 524; Total Evacuated – 433; Returned to Unit – 49; Remaining – 85.

30 Medical Diaries, DMS 21 Army Group, appendix D, 4 July 1944, WO 177/316.

31 War Diary, DDMS XXX Corps, July, 1944.

32 Monthly Report, "Psychiatrist attached to Second Army June 1944," PRO WO 177/321.

33 Ibid., July.

34 Ibid.

35 Glass, *Overseas Theatres*, 292.

36 Major T.T. Ferguson, the specialist in psychological medicine assigned to I British Corps, thought that personnel selection was the key factor in battle exhaustion. He believed 51 (Highland), an "unselected" division, had a higher exhaustion ratio than 3 (Br.) Div. or 6 (Br.) Airborne Division for this reason. In fact 3 (Br.) Div., a highly selected division with "high morale" appears to have had the highest ratio. "Psychiatric Report I Corps," 22 Nov. 1944, NA, RG 24, vol. 12,630. Battle exhaustion ratios from War Diaries, ADMS 51 (H) Div. and 3 Br. Div., PRO WO 177/405 and 177/377.

37 See for example "Summary of the month of June," War Diary, 5/7 Gordon Highlanders, PRO WO 171/1301.

38 The division NP ratio was 20 for June, at least 30 in the Epsom battle, War Diary, ADMS 49 (WR) Div. PRO 177/399. The 49th (WR) Division was transferred to the First Canadian Army and an enquiry into battle exhaustion casualties was ordered. The division's reputation in the British Army was also unfairly blemished by the collapse of one of its battalions. See Carlo d'Este, *Decision in Normandy* (London: Collins, 1983), 282. The 49th (WR) Division was in no worse shape than other divisions by mid-July.

39 F.M. Richardson, the author of *Fighting Spirit: Psychological Factors in War* (London: Leo Cooper, 1978) chaired the investigation of NP casualties in 49 (WR) Division. It has not been possible to locate the lengthy report he wrote, but Richardson's claim that there was a low incidence of exhaustion in units of one brigade that had been subjected to "propaganda" on battle exhaustion would be interesting to investigate. See F.M. Richardson, "Competitive Health Preservation in the Army," *JRAMC* (May 1948): 208.

40 "Report by Psychiatrist Attached to Second Army for month of July 1944," WO 177/321.

41 Quote is from *Sunday Pictorial*, 2 July 1944, cited in War Diary, 1st Bn. Suffolk Reg't, June 1944, WO 171/1381. The regimental War Diaries provide numerous first person accounts of the battle.

42 War Diary, ADMS 3 Br. Inf. Div., July 1944, appendix E, WO 177/377.

43 Stacey, *The Victory Campaign*, 156. See also T. Copp and R. Vogel, *Maple Leaf Route: Caen* (Alma: Maple Leaf Route Publications, 1983) and R. Roy, *The Canadians in Normandy* (Toronto: Macmillan, 1984) for accounts of the battle.

44 War Diary, Régiment de la Chaudière, 5 July 1944.

45 No precise figure is available, but medical units evacuated 370 Canadians on 4 July, 174 on 5 July and 110 on 6 July. These figures are 30 per cent greater than the number killed and wounded, and given the descriptive evidence must be assumed to include large numbers of battle exhaustion cases. We have estimated this conservatively at one half of the numbers evacuated without wounds. War Diary, ADMS, 3 Cdn. Inf. Div., NA, RG 24, vol. 15,661.

46 Ibid., 5 July 1944.

47 The ratio of neuropsychiatric casualties to battle wounded plus casualties in First United States Army rose from 11 in June to 23 during late July. Glass, *Overseas Theatres*, 292.

48 Crocker to Dempsey 5 July 1944 and Dempsey to Montgomery 6 July 1944, copies in Crerar Papers, NA, MG 30 E157, vol. 3. Montgomery was also unhappy with the performance of a number of British divisional commanders who in his view lacked "binge." He was particularly upset with the performance of 51st Highland and 7th Armoured Division and blamed their alleged shortcomings on their senior officers. D'Este, *Decision in Normandy*, 271. The research for this book suggests that all divisions in 21 Army Group had a very difficult time in Normandy and that there is little to choose between the performances of the various divisions. Each had to learn to cope with inadequacies of Allied equipment and tactical doctrine while fighting a tactically skilled enemy in possession of superior weapons.

49 General Crerar, the senior Canadian officer overseas, was not confident that he had a better replacement available. He was also uncertain that Montgomery's view was well founded. See Crerar to Simonds, 10 July 1944, in Crerar Papers.

50 Stacey, *The Victory Campaign*, 158.

51 See S. Zuckerman, *From Apes to Warlords* (London, 1978), 272.

52 Stacey, *The Victory Campaign*, 163.

53 We have used the same assumptions as for Carpiquet (see end note 45); 238 more men were evacuated through medical channels than can be accounted for as wounded in battle. War Diary, ADMS 3 Div, 8, 9, 10 July 1944.

54 The 59th Division was broken up to provide trained infantry reinforcements for other British divisions on 24 August. The official explanation for its selection as the unit to be removed from the order of battle was that it was the junior division in the army.

55 Complete casualty statistics by date and unit are available in NA, RG 24, vol. 18,611.

56 Appendix to War Diary, Canadian Scottish Regiment, July 1944. Reproduced in Copp and Vogel, *Maple Leaf Route: Falaise*, 34.

57 Ibid.

58 Information from interviews.

59 "Battle Exhaustion Casualties 6 June to 30 Nov. 1944," NA, RG 24, (File

133.065), vol. 18,611.

60 Ibid. Other statistics from Crerar Papers, vol. 4.

61 This description of the Chaudière may give offense and hurt the feelings of a number of veterans. It seems to me that the opposite conclusion should be drawn. The burden that circumstances placed upon the core of the regiment makes their contribution particularly noteworthy.

62 W.R. Bird, *The North Shore (New Brunswick) Regiment* (Fredericton: Brunswick Press, 1963).

63 Ibid.

64 "Battle Exhaustion Casualties, 6 June to 30 Nov. 1944."

65 The impressionistic view of the Queen's Own Rifles (QOR) is based on interviews over a period of five years. The statistics on battle exhaustion, desertion, absence without leave, and self-inflicted wounds confirm a picture of good leadership and high morale.

66 The attack on Le Mensil Patry, 10 June 1944, cost D Company of the QOR 96 casualties, 56 of them fatal. This ill-conceived venture, which involved the annihilation of a squadron of 1st Hussar tanks, was a terrible demonstration of the inability of Allied armour to take the lead in offensive operations against organized resistance. See Stacey, *The Victory Campaign*, 140, and Copp and Vogel, *Maple Leaf Route: Caen*, 84.

67 S.M. Lett who was a QOR company commander in Normandy and subsequently co of the Regiment told a historical officer that the QOR had "worked out a scheme whereby [battle exhaustion] personnel are not sos as casualties but are sent back to B Echelon for a few days rest. Here, relieved of all responsibility, they are cared for by the unit drivers and from this treatment most return quite fit." Memorandum of interview with Maj. S.M. Lett, 15 July 1944, DHIST. In fact all battalions attempted to use B Echelon in this way.

68 W.R. Bird, *No Retreating Footsteps* (Kentville: Kentville Publishing, n.d.).

69 Veterans of the Glens regard this period at Les Buissons or "Hell's Corners" as a particularly trying period, but statistically both physical casualties and battle exhaustion were comparatively low.

70 Stacey, *The Victory Campaign*, 162. For an account of the regiment's crucial battle on 8 July see A. Snowie, *Bloody Buron* (Erin, Ontario: Boston Mills Press, 1985).

71 "Battle Exhaustion Casualties, 6 June to 30 Nov. 1944."

72 When the Glens were ordered to prepare to join the battle on 25 July, the War Diarist wrote: "This is indeed a mental blow and is felt by all ranks. We need a rest and a refit ... The men and officers are looking worn out." War Diary, Stormont, Dundas, and Glengarry Highlanders, 25 July 1944.

73 The bare facts of this incident are mentioned in Stacey, *The Victory Campaign*, and in Copp and Vogel, *Maple Leaf Route: Falaise*. Interviews with

persons involved were unfortunately off the record so some rather colourful descriptions of events may not be printed. Brigadier Cunningham described the difference of opinion between himself and Keller in an on-record interview. Cunningham, interview with Copp and Dykeman, May 1983.

74 Quarterly Report, 1 July 44 – 1 Oct. 44, ADMS 3 Div, NA, RG 24, vol. 15,661.

75 Training for Operation Axehead dominated the 2nd Division's preparations in 1944. See War Diary, 2nd Canadian Infantry Division, March-June 1944.

76 Lt-Gen. Guy Simonds, "Operational Policy 2 Cdn. Corps," 17 Feb. 1944. Document is reproduced in Copp and Vogel, *Maple Leaf Route: Falaise*, 46-7.

77 Simonds had referred to "medium artillery concentrations directed onto the enemy tanks or self-propelled guns" as one of the methods needed for dealing with German counter-attacks. He did not, however, comment on the tendency of No. 18 radio set to break down under actual battle conditions. See, for example, "Report on Operation Windsor," NA, RG 24, vol. 10,791.

78 Dr John Burch, interview with Terry Copp, 18 Nov. 1982, and Burch to Van Nostrand, 5 Aug. 1944, NA, RG 24, vol. 12,630. By contrast Dr Burdett McNeel was welcomed by the division staff when assigned to the 4th Canadian Armoured Division. McNeel had begun the war as a medical officer in the 4th Division and remained with them until drafted into neuropsychiatry in early 1943. Burdett McNeel, interview with Terry Copp, 3 Dec. 1982.

79 Burdett McNeel, "History of No. 1 Canadian Exhaustion Unit 15 June, 1944–21 October 1944," n.d., (Fall 1944), McNeel Papers (in possession of the authors). These papers will be deposited in the Queen Street Mental Hospital Centre Archives (Griffin-Greenland Collection).

80 Ibid.

81 Burch to Van Nostrand, 5 Aug. 1944.

82 McNeel, "History."

83 McNeel, interview. Such attitudes were not confined to II Canadian Corps Headquarters. The medical order of battle for Normandy included the No. 1 Neuropsychiatric Wing, which was attached to a general hospital. Dr Glenn Burton, the co, and Dr Allan Walters arrived in the embarkation area to be told that their movement order had been cancelled and their unit disbanded. After an emergency phone call to Van Nostrand, they boarded ship anyway, arriving in France in early August. Once ashore they obtained permission to set up shop as part of No. 10 Canadian General Hospital. G.S. Burton, interview with Terry Copp, 26 Jan. 1983, and "Report No. 1 Cdn. Neuropsychiatric Wing, Period 5 Aug 44 to 30 Sept 44." Document from Dr Burton.

84 Montgomery to CIGS, 14 July 1944, quoted in Stacey, *The Victory Campaign*, 167.

85 Ibid., 176. Official casualty figures.

86 War Diary, 1 Cdn Exhaustion Unit, NA, RG 24, vol. 15,569.

87 Quoted in d'Este, *Decision in Normandy*, 383.

88 Stacey, *The Victory Campaign*, 174.

89 War Diary, 6 Canadian Infantry Brigade, 20 July 1944.

90 Stacey, *The Victory Campaign*, 176. For accounts of the battle see Copp and Vogel, *Maple Leaf Route: Falaise*.

91 War Diary I CEU.

92 War Diary, I CEU, 25 July 1944.

93 Brigadier W.S. Megill, interview with Terry Copp, May 1988. Megill, who commanded 5 Brigade, notes that a complete plan with routes and timings was handed down from division. It in turn had come from Corps. Megill believed the operation had been planned without reference to the terrain. His protests were overruled by Maj.-Gen. Foulkes, the divisional commander.

94 Casualty figures in Stacey, *The Victory Campaign*, 194. Battle exhaustion estimates from War Diary, I Cdn. Exhaustion Unit, July 44 and "Quarterly Report I CEU, 1 July–30 Sept 44," NA, RG 24, vol. 15,569.

95 See Robert Schneider, "Military Psychiatry in the German Army," in Richard A. Gabriel, ed., *Military Psychiatry: A Comparative Perspective* (New York: Greenwood Press, 1986). This article is the first attempt, in English, to write about stress reaction in the German Army on the basis of archival sources. Schneider has only been able to scratch the surface of the medical records available at the Militaerarchiv in Freiburg, but this is more than can be said for other writers on the subject.

   Dr Robert Vogel, Professor of History, McGill University, undertook a brief survey in this archive to determine what might be done with purely psychiatric records. "The files I looked at came under the acquisition list H20 and the files which dealt with psychiatry ran from 448 to 553 ... Each file ran to several hundred – sometimes thousand – pages." Clearly the history of battle exhaustion and of psychiatry in the German Army remains to be written. Letter, R. Vogel to T. Copp, October 1988.

96 This point is emphasized by most historians who write about the German Army. See especially M. Van Creveld, *Fighting Power: German and U.S. Army Performance 1939-1945* (Westport, Conn.: Greenwood Press, 1982). For a discussion of German military performance that integrates medical, disciplinary, and personnel records with combat see Omer Bartov, *The Eastern Front, 1941-1945, German Troops and the Barbarization of Warfare* (New York: St Martin's Press, 1986).

97 All of the statistics quoted here are from Manfred Messerschmidt, *Nazi Political Aims and German Military Law in World War II* (Royal Military College of Canada, 1981), 8-10.

98 Schneider, *Psychiatry in German Army*, 136.

99 Ibid., 136. Translation of term *Kameradschaftliche Zusprache*.

100 The phrases are from Messerschmidt, *Nazi Political Aims*, 18-19. He writes: "The exact figures for 1944-45 are unknown but one must expect these to be several thousands."

101 Dr B. McNeel, interview.

CHAPTER SEVEN

1 School of Military Neuropsychiatry, 312 Station Hospital (NP) US Army, *Combat Exhaustion*, NA, RG 24, vol. 10,066, 15.

2 A.J. Glass, ed., *Overseas Theatres*, vol. 2, *Neuropsychiatry in World War II* (Washington: Office of the Surgeon General, 1973) 285-6.

3 Ibid., 288.

4 Ibid., 282.

5 Ibid., 346-7.

6 Ibid., 304.

7 Ibid.

8 Ibid., 1012. United States Army Hospital admission for diseases rates per 1,000 mean strength were 405.0 in 1944 and 472.5 in 1945. British rates were less than half of this level. Ibid., 1,008 and W.F. Mellor, *Casualties and Medical Statistics* (London: HMSO, 1972), 226-7.

9 The non-battle injury rates per 1,000 strength for North-West Europe were: 1944 – British 29.9; US 82.6. 1945 – British 30.1; US 86.4. Glass, *Overseas Theatres*, 1,009; Mellor, *Casualties*, 226-7.

10 Canadian officers followed developments in the United States Army with some attention, and were aware of the high return to unit rates reported. Lieutenant-Colonel J.C. Richardson and exhaustion unit psychiatrists visited US facilities. The Canadians may have learned that not every American psychiatrist was confident that the return to unit policy was working exactly as claimed, but those interviewed had no specific recollections.

11 D.J. Watterson, "Report of Psychiatrist Attached 2nd Army, July 1944," War Diary, DDMS 2nd Army, July 1944, WO 177/321.

12 Ibid.

13 Parts of the Medical War Diaries of I British Corps, which included the 3rd Canadian as well as 3rd (Br.), 6th (Br.) Airborne and 51 (Highland) divisions, were destroyed by fire. WO 177/335 contains no material related to psychiatry for June, July, and August. A report written by T.T. Ferguson, the I Corps specialist in psychological medicine, was located in the files of DHIST, NDHQ, Ottawa (147.98009-D4). This report dated 22 Nov. 1944 reviews the experience of I Corps in Normandy.

WO 177/356 Medical War Diaries DDMS XXX British Corps contain good material for July. The June and August diaries are missing.

WO 177/343: The diaries for DDMS VIII Corps are complete with excellent detail. wo 177/350: The diaries for XII Corps are very poor for all periods. The only fairly complete British divisional medical War Diary for Normandy is that of 3 (Br.) Division, wo 177/377, though some material can be obtained from wo 177/405 51 (Highland), wo 177/409 53 (Welsh), and wo 177/399 49 (West Riding) divisions.

14 War Diary, DDMS VIII Corps, July 1944, annex 9.

15 "Psychiatry at 50 Field Dressing Station," 1 Aug. 1944, War Diary, No. 50 FDS, July 1944, appendix E, wo 177/925. The psychiatrist assigned to 50 FDS, one of Second Army's exhaustion centres, described the situation before the establishment of divisional psychiatry in these terms: "During rush periods, when as many as 50 a day supposedly A1 men were being evacuated to the UK, a feeling of disquietude arose – was one becoming party to a racket? This apprehension became more marked when one was critized by older officers ... 'we had nothing like this in the last war, they had to fight on frightened or not' – the loss of manpower was certainly staggering but I am convinced that few would have been of any use to their units in the near future, the facilities available at the time were such that we had no recourse save to send them home. The position is now improved. It was surprising how quickly the Field Dressing Station Medical Officers developed an aptitude for their work and their assistance was invaluable."

16 Watterson, "Report July." The War Diary, ADMS 53 (Welsh) Division, indicates that a divisional FDS began to function as an exhaustion centre at about the same time. A 53 per cent RTU rate was claimed. War Diary, ADMS 53 (Welsh) Div, July 1944, annex 1a, wo 177/487.

17 Second Army Medical Sitrep, 20 July 1944, War Diary, DDMS Second Army.

18 Medical War Diary, VIII Corps.

19 The ADMS also noted that: "Exhaustion continued to be a problem but the ratio of exhaustion to wounded was 2 to 7 compared to 2 to 5 in July – a distinct improvement but still a high ratio." 3 Division Monthly Medical Bulletin, August 1944, War Diary, ADMS.

20 "Minutes of a Conference of 21 Army Group Psychiatrists held at 32 (BR) General Hospital 12 and 13 January 1945, NA, RG 24, vol. 12,631.

21 F. Crew, The Army Medical Services Campaigns, vol. 4, North West Europe (London: HMSO, 1962), 558.

22 Hospital admissions for psychoneuroses, British troops, North-West Europe were 10.7 per 1,000 strength during the July-Sept. quarter, 7.71 Oct.-Dec., and 9.06 Jan.-March. Many variables, especially the intensity of combat, enter into the interpretation of this data. A simple comparison of psychiatric hospital admissions with admissions for wounds due to enemy action does not lend much support to the belief in a high return to duty rate.

	1945 July–Sept.	Oct.–Dec.	Jan.–March
NP Hospital Admissions	10.7	7.71	9.06
Injuries due to Enemy Action			
per thousand strength	103.68	26.88	44.32
Ratio NP Admissions			
NP Admissions + Battle			
Casualties	12	22	16

Source: Mellor, *Casualties*, 200-214.

23 Ibid., 194. There was, for example, a dramatic rise in the rates of hospital admissions for dermatitis among British troops. This outbreak led Lt-Col Watterson to invite the adviser in dermatology to address the psychiatrists of 21 Army Group in January of 1945. He noted that "in the early days the man with acute sepsis was afraid to leave his unit. Now he tended to draw attention to the last remaining spot, to see which a lens was needed." "Minutes of a Conference, 12 and 13 January 1945."

24 See the exchange of letters between Terry Copp and Brigadier P.A. Abraham, FRC Psych., Director of (British) Army Psychiatry in *British Army Review* 87 (Dec. 1987) for an indication of the problems of interpreting evidence on this controversial question. A careful search of the likely files in the PRO has failed to turn up any follow-up study, though there are references to the desirability of such research.

25 Ibid. Lt-Gen. Guy Simonds to Divisional Commanders, 29 August 1944.

26 Ibid. Crerar to Simonds, 2 Sept. 1944. Crerar was also upset by other manifestations of poor discipline in the Canadian Army. On 25 August, as the Battle of the Falaise Pocket was concluding, he admonished his Corps Commanders to enforce Routine Order 231 against "slackness regarding their appearance on the part of other ranks." The "recent combination of hot weather and heavy continuous fighting" was not an acceptable excuse. Ibid. Crerar to Corps Commanders, 29 Aug. 1944.

27 All psychiatrists interviewed for this study insisted that malingering was rare.

28 Appendix A, Quarterly Report – 1 Canadian Exhaustion Unit, 1 July – 30 Sept. 1944, NA, RG 24, vol. 15,569.

29 Crerar Papers, vol. 4.

30 Ibid. Absence without leave and desertion became a measurable problem only after Normandy. From 1 Sept. 1944 to Jan. 1945, 2nd Division had 243 AWL and 219 deserters. The 3rd Division figures were 348 AWOL and 72 deserters. The 4th Division accounted for 47 AWOL and 14 deserters in the same period.

31 War Diary, ADMS, 2nd Canadian Infantry Division, July 1944, NA, RG 24, vol. 15,569.

32 "Report on the Neuropsychiatric Division, BN & PS Hospital, 6 June 1944 –
18 July 1945," NA, RG 24, vol. 12,631.

33 T.T. Ferguson, "Psychiatric Report I Corps," 22 Nov. 1944, NA, RG 24,
vol. 12,630.

34 F.H. Van Nostrand to DMS, 13 Nov. 1944, NA, RG 24, vol. 12,631.

35 This estimate is based on Richardson's calculations in "Battle Exhaustion
Casualties as Reported to Stats. Sec. during period 6 June 1944 to 30 Nov.
1944," NA, RG 24, vol. 12,631. See also "Memorandum on Disposal of
Exhaustion Cases in Rear of the Army," 7 Dec. 1944, ibid.

36 Burdett McNeel, interview with Terry Copp, 3 Dec. 1982. When asked
about his scepticism towards Gregory's views recorded in the July War
Diary, 1 CEU, McNeel replied: "Bob was quite a salesman; he was kind of
a swashbuckling type – I think he was good for the division, but to refer
back – you can keep people from being evacuated but that is not always
the answer."

37 B.H. McNeel, "Preliminary Report on No. I Canadian Exhaustion Unit
RCAMC," 24 Aug. 1944, NA, RG 24, vol. 15,951.

38 Ibid. McNeel had initially tried to send the more promising cases to the
Second Army rest centre but it was full of British troops so they were sent
to the SEC.

39 C.H. Gundry, "Most Secret Report on Neuropsychiatric Work in 2 CBRG
for Months of May and Sept 44," NA, RG 24, vol. 12,583. The report of
I British Corps's psychiatrist for July-August 1944 claims a 12 per cent direct
RTU rate. It suggests that a further 18 per cent of the 1,458 exhaustion
casualties *may* have returned to unit after rehabilitation. Ferguson,
"Psychiatric Report."

40 McNeel, interview with Terry Copp, 3 Dec. 1982, and McNeel to Copp,
4 Jan. 1983. McNeel wrote in response to a query about his negative view
of the reinforcement units on the continent recorded in the interview.

41 15th (Scottish) Division had the most casualties of the British divisions. In
14 days of combat in August it suffered 1,742 casualties. "VIII Corps Battle
Casualties," War Diary, DDMS VIII Corps, August 1944. The NP casualty
rate in this outstanding division actually rose in August as much as the
Canadian rate did.

42 August figures from War Diary, DDMS 2nd Army, August 1944, "Monthly
Hygiene Report," 18 Sept. 1944.

43 J.C. Richardson, "Neuropsychiatry with the Canadian Army in Western
Europe – 6 June 1944 – 8 May 1945, typescript, 1945 (given to the authors
by Dr Richardson). There is a copy in NA, RG 24, vol. 12,631.

44 The 20 per cent figure was calculated by Richardson in "Battle Exhaustion
Casualties." Both Field Marshal Montgomery in his *From Normandy to the
Baltic* (London: Hutchison, 1947) and C.P. Stacey, *The Victory Campaign*
(Ottawa: Queen's Printer, 1960) mention the higher Canadian casualty rate
without explanation.

45 "Canadian Army Statistics – War 1939-43, Fatal Casualties," NA, RG 24, vol. 18,825.

46 Richardson, "Neuropsychiatry in Western Europe."

47 B.H. McNeel, "Re Cases of Exhaustion – 2 Cdn Inf Div," 1 Oct. 1944, NA, RG 24, vol. 12,583.

48 Ibid.

49 For the statistical basis of these statements and subsequent numerical statements about regiments see "Battle Exhaustion Period 1 June 44 to 9 August 44," appendix to War Diary 1 CEU Sept. 1944, and Crerar Papers, vol. 4.

50 The author of this chapter, Terry Copp, is presently researching a book on 5 Canadian Infantry Brigade and has conducted extensive interviews as well as a detailed analysis of casualties. Information on the leadership and morale of 5 Brigade units is based on the interviews.

51 For an account of the destruction of the SSRs and much else in 6 Brigade see T. Copp and R. Vogel, *Maple Leaf Route: Antwerp* (Alma: Maple Leaf Route Publications, 1984). Just 28 exhaustion casualties were recorded for the South Sasks to 9 August.

52 McNeel, interview.

53 War Diary, 1 Canadian Exhaustion Unit, August 1944.

54 The Lincs lost a good deal of equipment in their hasty withdrawal from the "sea of fire" about Tilly. Shortly afterwards they also lost their CO, who, despite a reputation as a fierce disciplinarian, proved unable to cope with the stress of battle. See G. Hayes, *The Lincs: A History of the Lincoln and Welland Regiment at War* (Alma: Maple Leaf Route Publications, 1987).

55 War Diary, 1 CEU.

56 Ibid. For an account of the destruction of the BCRs see T. Copp and R. Vogel, *Maple Leaf Route: Falaise.* The Algonquin Regiment, the third infantry battalion in 10th Brigade, suffered heavy casualties and a toll of PWs in this battle. There were few infantry exhaustion cases but then few men made it back.

57 British soldiers, chiefly from the 51st (Highland) Division accounted for 30 per cent of all admissions in August. J. Burch, "Quarterly Report – 1 Cdn Exhaustion Unit 1 July–30 Sept. 1944, NA, RG 24, vol. 15,569. The division's NP ratio in August was approximately 30, a level higher than during its "failures" in Normandy. Casualties from War Diary, ADMS 51 (H) Division, August 1944, WO 177/405.

58 The First Polish Armoured Division joined the Canadian Army in time for Operation Totalize, 8 August. Between that date and the end of the month the division lost more than a third of its total manpower, much of it in bitter fighting to close the Falaise Gap. The Polish ADMS reported that the division had "about 300 (exhaustion) cases in all and that the bulk of these had been retained in Division and returned to duty." McNeel, "Cases of Exhaustion 2 Div." This was not McNeel's impression but no reliable statistics are available.

59 "Battle Exhaustion and Battle Casualties by Arm of Service, 6 June 44 to 30 Nov 44," NA, RG 24, vol. 18,611.

60 F.H. Van Nostrand, "Memo to DMS," 29 August 1944, NA, RG 24, vol. 12,583. Van Nostrand added that Richardson was to combine the posts of adviser in neurology and adviser in psychiatry, which were split in the British Army.

61 This summary is based on J.C. Richardson, "Memorandum about Current Neuropsychiatric Problems in the Canadian Army in the European Theatre of Operations," 27 Oct. 1944, and on the Quarterly Reports of the units named. NA, RG 24, vol. 12,583.

62 These operations are the subject of a number of studies. See Copp and Vogel, *Maple Leaf Route: Scheldt*, and Stacey, *The Victory Campaign*, for the Canadian perspective.

63 "Deficiencies by Regiment," 7 Oct. 1944, NA, RG 24, vol. 10,517.

64 Casualty figures from War Diary, ADMS 2 Division, Oct. 1944, NA, RG 24, vol. 15,659.

65 Copp and Vogel, *Maple Leaf Route: Scheldt*, 38-9.

66 "Battle Casualties by Formation," Oct., Nov. 1944, NA, RG 24, vol. 10,517.

67 McNeel, "Quarterly Report NP Specialist 2 Cdn Corps 1 Oct. to 31 Dec. 44," NA, RG 24, vol. 15,951.

68 War Diary, ADMS 2 Division, Oct. 1944.

69 War Diary, No 1 Neuropsychiatric Wing, Oct. 1944, NA, RG 24, vol. 15,960. Richardson, in his post-war statistical summary, gives 839 as the total number of exhaustion casualties in the First Canadian Army for the period. Richardson, "Neuropsychiatry in Western Europe." This produces an NP ratio of 16 for the army.

70 War Diary, ADMS 2 Div., Oct. 1944.

71 "Battle Casualties by Formation."

72 McNeel, "Quarterly Report," 1 Oct. – 31 Dec. 1944.

73 Calculated from daily evacuations less wounded, War Diary, ADMS 3 Division, Oct. 1944, vol. 15,661.

74 R. Gregory, "Psychiatric Report, October 1944" War Diary, ADMS 3 Div.

75 War Diary, 1 CEU Oct., Nov. 1944.

76 T. Dancey, "Quarterly Report No. 1 CEU, 1 Oct. 44 – 31 Dec. 44," NA, RG 24, vol. 15,569.

77 Ibid.

78 Quoted in J.D. Griffin, "Memorandum, Psychiatric Standards, Opinions from Overseas," 9 Dec. 1944, NA, RG 24, vol. 12,637.

79 This summary of the mood of the infantry in October 1944 is based on interviews and correspondence with veterans conducted in connection with the author's *Maple Leaf Route* series. The accuracy of R. P. Typhoons in general, and specifically in the Scheldt battle is discussed in T. Copp, "Tactical Air Power in North-West Europe: An Analysis Based on Operations Research," unpublished paper, 1987.

80 The battle of Kapelsche Veer, 26 to 31 January 1945, involved two battalions of 10 Brigade, but 80 per cent of the 300 casualties were from the Lincoln and Welland Regiment, which bore the brunt of the attack. See Hayes, *The Lincs*, chapter 5.

81 McNeel, "Quarterly Report 1 Oct. – 31 Dec." There were 277 fatal casualties in November, 229 in December and 208 in January. "Canadian Army Statistics, Fatal Casualties."

82 Ibid.

83 Van Nostrand to DGMS, 2 Nov. 1944, NA, RG 24, vol. 12,631.

84 McNeel, interview.

85 Notes for Lecture "Psychology of Struggle," n.d., McNeel Papers.

86 B.H. McNeel, "Views on Management of Exhaustion in a Forward Area," appendix B, "Quarterly Report, NP Advisor 1 Oct. – 31 Dec. 1944."

87 "Medical Arrangements for Operation Veritable," 27 Jan. 1945. War Diary, DDMS XXX Corps, WO 177/357.

88 See Copp and Vogel, *Maple Leaf Route: Victory*.

89 War Diary, HQ Medical 53 (W) Div., March 1945 WO 177/357. The War Diary for 15 Scottish Division provides no statistics but on 22 February the diary notes "troops tired and disliked this fighting through woods under air burst artillery fire. Exhaustion rate going up." War Diary, 15 S Division, February 1945, WO 177/385. The official medical history provides casualty and battle exhaustion statistics for British divisions in Veritable – Crew, *History of the Second War*, 555. This table is taken from Watterson, "Report Quarter Ending 31 March 45," NA, RG 24, vol. 12,631. It lists 1,160 exhaustion cases for the period 8 Feb.–10 March. A second table in Watterson gives a figure of 2,914 psychiatric casualties for February 1945 alone. Unless we assume an incredibly high NP ratio among non-combat troops the figures suggest a much higher level of exhaustion than that reported in the official history.

90 McNeel, "Quarterly Report, 1 Jan. – 31 Mar. 45."

91 Watterson, "Report 31 March 45."

92 Ibid.

93 Crew, *History of the Second War*, 555.

94 Dancey, cited in McNeel, "Quarterly Report 31 March."

95 Ibid.

CONCLUSION

1 W.R. Feasby, *Clinical Subjects*, vol. 2, *Official History of the Canadian Medical Services 1939-45* (Ottawa: Queen's Printer, 1953-56) 91.

2 Ibid., 93.

3 B.H. McNeel, "War Psychiatry in Retrospect," *AJP* (January 1946): 500-6.

4 J.P.S. Cathcart to Colonel J.D. Griffin, 22 July 1944, NA, RG 24, vol. 19,466.

5 Charles Stacey has written that "the Canadian Army, though it got tremen-

dous dividends from its long training period in England still got rather less than it might have ... [it] suffered from possessing a proportion of regimental officers whose attitude towards training was casual and haphazard rather than scientific: like the traditional amateur actor, they were cheerfully confident that it would 'be all right on the night' without their having to exert themselves too much,'' Stacey, *Six Years of War*, 253. Commanders higher than the regimental level should be included in his stricture; they were responsible for preparing units for war. Unfortunately, there is no comprehensive study on Canadian Army training, its doctrine, assumptions, methods, or effectiveness. There are valuable insights in J.A. English's superb book, *A Perspective on Infantry* (New York: Praeger, 1981). Colonel English's doctoral thesis in preparation will be a notable companion. See also Captain R.A. Stanley, ''Why Did the Psychiatrist Turn Him Down?'' *JCMS* (May 1944): 329-37.

6 The lack of provision for administrative discharges caused much concern in the Canadian Pension Commission, many of whose officials had dealt with several thousand World War I veterans claiming neuropsychiatric disabilities. One memorandum described that perspective: ''Pension is not awarded for sacrifice made in the giving up of employment of civil life, or service or financial service, discomfort or weariness. Pension is awarded for disability resulting from injury or disease which was incurred on or aggravated during service. Social security for the veteran and disability pension are two distinct problems and there should be no comparison in this respect. Disability pension benefits are intended only for damage to the mind or body. It is determined on a medical basis.

''Scores of service personnel have been discharged on medical grounds when the MFB 227 records some trivial condition such as mental retardation, inadequate personality, emotional instability, dull intelligence. Many of such cases have been re-examined and after careful observation no evidence is discovered to support or justify the findings of the Medical Board. The impression is gained that the man is actually being retired as unlikely to become an efficient soldier, or as services no longer required, but discharge on medical grounds would appear to be the easiest way out. Apart from placing a stigma on the individual for future employment, the Medical Boards are leaving a potential pension on the doorstep of the Canadian Pension Commission.'' ''Chief Medical Advisor, Canadian Pension Commission, to the DMS,'' DV, n.d., NA, RG 24, vol. 2093.

7 The phrase is from Leo H. Bartemeier, et al., ''Combat Exhaustion,'' *Journal of Nervous and Mental Diseases*, 104 (1946). This article is the result of a comprehensive survey of US battlefield psychiatry undertaken by a blue-ribbon panel of American psychiatrists not directly involved in army psychiatry.

8 G.B. Chisholm to Adjutant-General, 21 August 1944, NA, RG 24, vol. 19,466.

9 Quoted in Glass, *Overseas Theatres*, xxi.

10 McNeel, "War Psychiatry in Retrospect."

11 J.C. Richardson, "Neuropsychiatry with the Canadian Army in Western Europe from 6 June 44 – 8 May 45" typescript with authors. Copy in NA, RG 24, vol. 12,631.

12 Robert Gregory, "Report of No. 3 Canadian Convaslescent Depot," May 1945, NA, RG 24, vol. 12,631.

13 Ibid.

14 A.E. Moll, "Psychosomatic Disease Due to Battle Stress," in Eric D. Wittkower and R.A. Cleghorn, eds, *Recent Developments in Psychosomatic Medicine* (Montreal: J.B. Lippincott, 1953), 436-7.

15 Griffin to Ewen Cameron, 31 August 1945, Griffin Papers.

16 Van Nostrand, "Neuropsychiatry in the Canadian Army (Overseas)." Paper given before the Inter-Allied Conference on War Medicine at the Royal Society of Medicine, 9 July 1945, NA, RG 24, vol. 12,631.

17 The explanatory triad of individual, situation, and organization frames the three volumes of E. Ginzberg et al., *The Ineffective Soldier* (New York: Columbia University Press, 1959). See also, Captain M.S. Straker, "Psychoneurosis and Psychopathic States," *JCMS* 3 (November 1945): 33-8.

18 The officer was in the Queen's Own Cameron Highlanders of Canada. He was one of hundreds who completed detailed questionnaires on their recent battle experience. NA, RG 24, vol. 10,450.

19 Infantry Captain, "Battle Experience Questionnaire," NA, RG 24, vol. 10,450.

20 Moll, "Psychosomatic Disease Due," 436-7.

21 Ibid.

22 Richardson, "Neuropsychiatry with the Canadian Army."

23 Van Nostrand to DMS, 8 January 1945, NA, RG 24, vol. 2089.

24 Richardson, "Neuropsychiatry with the Canadian Army."

25 Van Nostrand to DGMS, 2 November 1944, NA, RG 24, vol. 2089.

26 Feasby, *Clinical Subjects*, 77.

27 Van Nostrand, "Neuropsychiatry in the Canadian Army (Overseas)."

28 "Minutes of Inter-Service Conference of Psychiatrists," 12 June 1945, NA, RG 24, vol. 12,631. The discussions reflected the experience and concerns of psychiatrists in Canada, because the others were still overseas.

29 Griffin to DGMS, 16 November 1944, NA, RG 24, vol. 12,631.

30 Ibid.

31 Van Nostrand to DDGMS, 2 November 1944, NA, RG 24, vol. 2,089.

32 Dr Peter Van Nostrand, interview.

33 Richardson, interview.

34 Ibid.

35 R. Notman, "A Survey of 1271 Neuropsychiatric Casualties Passing Through No. 1 Canadian Exhaustion Unit in N.W. Europe Between October 1944 and May 1945: Follow-Up Studies of the Post-Discharge Adjustment of

346 Members of the Above Series," mimeographed report, Department of Veterans' Affairs, 1951. Copy in possession of authors.

36 Ibid., 136.

37 K. Ferguson, notes (in possession of authors), 1988.

38 Van Nostrand to DMS, 29 June 1945, NA, RG 24, vol. 12,631.

39 Colonel J.D. Griffin, "Reaction Stress – the Importance of a Preventive Programme," NA, RG 24, vol. 19,466.

40 Van Nostrand to DMS, 29 June 1945, NA, RG 24, vol. 12,631.

41 Brigadier C.S. Thompson to Dr G.H. Hutton, 23 September 1946, NA, RG 24, vol. 19,466.

42 Ibid.

43 Lieutenant-Colonel G.D. Dailey to Adjutant-General, 20 March 1948, NA, RG 24, vol. 19,466.

44 Ibid.

45 Ibid., DGMS minute.

46 H.F. Wood, *Strange Battleground* (Ottawa: Queen's Printer, 1966), 29-32, 67.

47 Ibid. See also Brigadier K.A. Hunter, "The RCAMC in the Korean War," *Canadian Services Medical Journal* (July-August 1954): 5-15; "Army Enlistment, August 1950," and relevant correspondence in NA, RG 24, vol. 18,221 (War Diary, Adjutant-General Branch); and the uninhibited account of an observer of recruiting in No. 6 Personnel Depot, Toronto, in DHIST 112.3H1.001 (D9). The appointment of psychiatrist in the fully integrated Commonwealth Division was filled by a Canadian.

48 The comment is from Stephen Wright, the comedian.

49 F.C.R. Chalke, "Psychological Aspects of Manpower Mobilization – the Lowest 10% – an Appreciation," NA, RG 24, vol. 19,466.

50 Hunter to VAG, 4 February 1953, NA, RG 24, vol. 19,466.

51 F.C.R. Chalke, "Psychiatric Screening of Recruits," DVA *Treatment Services Bulletin* (June 1954): 1-20. On other research proposed and conducted in this period see, "Medical Research and Development in the Canadian Army During World War II, 1942-1946," DHIST 147.013 (D6), and correspondence in NA, RG 24, vols 19,466 and 4,124.

52 All the above in Chalke, ibid.

53 Ken Tout, *Tanks Advance* (London: Grafton Books, 1989), 144-5.

Bibliography

ABBREVIATIONS

AJP	*American Journal of Psychiatry*
BMJ	*British Medical Journal*
CASF	Canadian Active Service Force
CMAJ	*Canadian Medical Association Journal*
CPHJ	*Canadian Public Health Journal*
DHIST	Directorate of History, National Defence Headquarters, Ottawa
DND	Department of National Defence (Canada)
DVA	Department of Veterans' Affairs (Canada)
HMSO	Her Majesty's Stationery Office
JCMS	*Journal of the Canadian Medical Services*
JRAMC	*Journal of the Royal Army Medical Corps*
MJA	*Medical Journal of Australia*
NCMH (C)	National Committee for Mental Hygiene (Canada)
NPAM	Non Permanent Active Militia
USMHI	United States Military History Institute

I PRIMARY SOURCES

Archival

The National Archives of Canada
  Record Group 24 National Defence
  Manuscript Group 30 E157 Crerar Papers
  Manuscript Group 27 III B11 Ralston Papers

Directorate of History, Department of National Defence (Ottawa)
  Miscellaneous Papers, National Defence

The Public Record Office (United Kingdom)
   War Office 171 Unit War Diaries
   War Office 177 Medical Unit War Diaries

The Osler Library, McGill University
   The Colin Russel Papers

Griffin-Greenland Archives, Queen Street Mental Health Centre (Toronto)
   Jack Griffin Papers

United States Military History Institute
   Manuscript Collection

Papers in the possession of the authors
   Travis Dancey Papers
   Burdett McNeel Papers

Interviews

With Terry Copp

Dr Harry Botterell	Kingston, October 1986
Dr John Burch	Winnipeg, October 1982
Dr G.S. Burton	Kitchener, January 1983
Brig. D.G.B. Cunningham	Kingston, October 1981
Dr Travis Dancey	Montreal, July 1983
Dr Kingsley Ferguson	Guelph, May 1986
Dr Jack Griffin	Toronto, October 1982
Dr Bill Keith	Toronto, October 1985
Dr Burdett McNeel	Toronto, November 1982

With Bill McAndrew

Major-General B.M. Hoffmeister	Vancouver, 1979
Dr Bert Moll	Ottawa, 1987-88
Dr Clifford Richardson	Toronto, December 1982
Dr Peter Van Nostrand	Toronto, October 1985
Dr Allen Walters	Toronto, October 1982
Dr Bill White	Toronto, October 1985

II BOOKS AND ARTICLES BY
PARTICIPANTS IN THE MILITARY
PSYCHIATRIC SERVICES DURING
WORLD WAR II

Canadian Authors

Baillie, W. "A Summary of 200 Neurological and Psychiatric Admissions from the Canadian Army Service Forces." *AJP* 48 (1941).

Boyer, G.F. "The Psychoneuroses of War." *CMAJ* 43 (1940).

Brown, A.J. "Mental Tests." *CPHJ* (1938).

Carver, H.S.M. *Personnel Selection in the Canadian Army*. Mimeographed typescript. Directorate of Personnel Selection. Ottawa, 1945.

Cathcart, J.B.S. "Recent Advances in Neuropsychiatry." Paper read before Ottawa Chirurgical Society, March 21, 1941. NA, RG 24. Vol. 12,631.

- "The Neuropsychiatric Branch of the Department of Soldiers' Civil Re-Establishment." *The Ontario Journal of Neuro-Psychiatry* (1928).

Chisholm, G.B. *A Platoon Leader's Responsibility for the Morale of his Men*. Ottawa: DND, 1941.

- "Problems of Morale." *JCMS* 2 (1945).

- "Psychiatric Casualties in the Middle East." *JCMS* 3 (1944).

- "Psychological Adjustment of Soldiers to Army and to Civilian Life." *AJP* 101 (1944).

Dancey, T.E. "The Awarding of Pensions on Psychiatric Grounds." *Treatment Services Bulletin* 5 (1948).

- "Psychiatry." *Treatment Services Bulletin* 4 (1947).

- "Treatment in the Absence of Pensioning For Psychoneurotic Veterans." *AJP* 101 (1950).

Doyle, A.M. "Practical Aspects of Community Mental Health." *CJMH* (1938).

- "Psychiatry with the Canadian Army in Action in the CMF." *JCMS* 2 (1946).

- "Report of the Canadian Medical Rest Station in the Sicilian Campaign." *JCMS* 1 (1944).

Dunn, W.H. *Gastro-Duodenal Ulcers: An Important Wartime Medical Problem*. Typescript, 1942. Griffin-Greenland Archives.

Elliot, H. "Head Wounds – Canadian Army World War II." *Treatment Services Bulletin* 6 (1949).

England, Robert. *Discharged: A Commentary on Civil Re-establishment of Veterans in Canada*. Toronto: Macmillan, 1943.

Farrar, C.B. "Sigmund Freud." *University of Toronto Medical Journal* (January 1940).

Gliddon, W.O. "Discharge Problems in the Neuropsychiatric Group: An Analysis of 500 Recent Discharges. *JCMS* 2 (1945).

- "Psychiatry and Post-Discharge Problems." *JCMS* 1 (1943).

Griffin, J.D. "The Contribution of Child Psychiatry to Mental Hygiene." *CPHJ* (1938).

- "Mental Hygiene in Canada." *CPHJ* (1941).

- "Neuropsychiatry in the British Army in the Last War 1914-1918." Bulletin No. 1. in the series *Mental Hygiene and the War*. NCMH(C). Toronto, 1939.

Griffin, J.D. et al. "Psychiatry in the Canadian Army." *AJP* 100 (July 1943).

Griffin, J.D. et al. "Psychoneurotics Discharged from the Canadian Army." *CMAJ* 52 (1945).

Gundry, C.H. "Classification and Reallocation of 'Exhaustion' Casualties in a Theatre of War." *AJP* 103 (1946).

Hawke, W.A. "Common Problems in Canadian Army Psychiatry: A Survey of 250 Consultations at an Advanced Training Centre." *JCMS* 2 (1945).

Hincks, C.M. "The Future of Canadian Psychiatry." *CMAJ* 54 (1947).

Hyland, H.H. "Psychoneuroses in the Army Overseas." *CMAJ* 51 (1944).

Hyland, H.H. and J.C. Richardson. "Psychoneurosis in the Canadian Army Overseas." *CMAJ* 47 (1942).

Line, W. "Psychology." *Treatment Services Bulletin* 4 (1947).

Line, W. and J.D.M. Griffin. "Personnel Selection in the Army." *CMAJ* 48 (1943).

McFarlane, J.A. "Dieppe in Retrospect." *The Lancet* (7 April 1943).

McKerracher, D.G. "Psychiatric Problems in the Army." *CMAJ* 48 (1943).

McNeel, B.H. "War Psychiatry in Retrospect." *AJP* 103 (1946).

McNeel, B.H. and T. Dancey. "The Personality of the Successful Soldier." *AJP* 102 (1945).

Meakins, J.C. "The 'Pulhems' System of Medical Grading." *CMAJ* 48 (1943).

- "The Returning Serviceman and His Problems." *CMAJ* 50 (1944).

Moll, A.E. "Psychosomatic Disease Due to Battle Stress," in *Recent Developments in Psychosomatic Medicine*, edited by E.D. Wittkower and R.A. Gleghorn. Montreal: J.B. Lippincott 1953.

Park, F.S. "Causes of Rejection from the Army and Incidence of Defects in Recruits." *CMAJ* 51 (1944).

Richardson, J.C. "Clinical Experiences with a R.C.A.M.C. Neuropsychiatric Division in England 1940-1944." *Proceedings of the Royal Society of Medicine* (May 1944).

Russel, C.K. "The Nature of War Neuroses." *CMAJ* 41 (1939).

- "A Study of Certain Psychogenetic Conditions in Soldiers." *CMAJ* 7 (1918).

- "War Neuroses – Some Views on Diagnosis and Treatment." *Archives of Neurology and Psychiatry* (1919).

Russel, E.M. "The Origin, Organization and Scope of the Canadian National Committee for Mental Hygiene." *CMAJ* 39 (1937).

Sharpe, N. "M.F.B. 227 – Memoirs From Boards." *JCMS* 3 (1946).

Sheps, J.G. "A Psychiatric Study of Successful Soldiers." *Journal of the American Association* 126 (1944).

Sheps, J.G. and F.E. Coburn. "Psychiatric Study of One Hundred Battle Veterans." *War Medicine* 5 (1945).

Stanley, R.A. "Why Did the Psychiatrist Turn Him Down?" *JCMS* 1 (1944).

Straker, M.S. "Psychoneurosis and Psychopathic States." *JCMS* 3 (1945).

Van Nostrand, F.H. "Three Years of Neuropsychiatry in the Canadian Army Overseas." *CMAJ* 49 (1943).

Watson, M.C. "Medical Aspects of the Normandy Invasion." *CMAJ* 52 (1945).

Wellman, M.D. and J.F. Simpson. "Psychiatric Casualties in the Canadian Navy." *AJP* 102 (1945).

us *Authors*

Aita, J.A. "Neurological and Psychiatric Examination During Military Mobilization." *War Medicine* 2 (1942).

Appel, J.W. "Incidence of Neuropsychiatric Disorders in the United States Army in World War II." *AJP* 103 (1946).

Appel, J.W. et al. "Comparative Incidence of Neuropsychiatric Casualties in World War I and World War II." *AJP* 103 (1946).

Bartemeier, L.H. et al. "Combat Exhaustion." *Journal of Nervous and Mental Disease* 104 (1946).

Braceland, F.J. "Psychiatric Lessons From World II." *AJP* 103 (1947).

Coleman, J.V. "The Group Factor in Military Psychiatry." (Paper by Neuropsychiatrist 38th us Infantry Division). June 1945. Manuscript Collection usmhi.

– "Prognostic Criteria in Soldiers with Psychiatric Problems." Paper. n.d. Manuscript Collection usmhi.

Cooke, E.D. *All But Me and Thee*. Washington: Infantry Journal Press, 1946.

Flicker, D.S. "Psychiatric Induction Examination." *War Medicine* 2 (1942).

Glass, A.J. et al. "Psychiatric Prediction and Military Effectiveness." Typescript. usmhi.

Grinker, R.R. and J.P. Spiegel. "Brief Psychotherapy in War Neuroses." *Psychosomatic Medicine* (1944).

– *War Neuroses in North Africa: The Tunisian Campaign (Jan.-May 1943)*. New York: Josiah Macey Jr. Foundation, 1943.

Jonas, C.H. "Psychiatry Has Growing Pains." *AJP* 103 (1946).

Link, H.G. "The Errors of Psychiatry." *American Mercury* (July 1944).

Manson, M.P. and H.M. Grayson. "Why 2276 American Soldiers in the Mediterranean Theatre of Operations were Absent Without Leave, Deserted or Misbehaved Before the Enemy." *AJP* 103 (1946).

Menninger, W.C. "Psychiatric Experience in the War 1941-46." *AJP* 103 (1947).

– *Psychiatry in a Troubled World*. New York: Macmillan, 1948.

Needles, W.N. "A Statistical Study of One Hundred Neuropsychiatric Casualties from the Normandy Campaign (with Control Material)." *AJP* 102 (1945).

Porter, W.C. "Military Psychiatry." *War Medicine* 2 (1942).

Salmon, T.W. and N. Fenton. "Neuropsychiatry in the American Expeditionary Force," in *Neuropsychiatry*, vol. 10, *The Medical Department of the United States Army in the World War*, edited by M.W. Ireland. Washington, 1929.

Schwab, R.S. "Observations of Anxiety and Fear in Non-Hospitalized Functioning Combat Personnel." *Transactions of the American Neurological Association* (1946).

Spiegel, H.X. "Preventive Psychiatry with Combat Troops." *AJP* 101 (1944).

Tureen, L.L. and L. Linn. "A Study of Morale, Psychosomatic Symptoms and

Neurotic Tendencies in Groups of Overseas Soldiers." *Transactions of the American Neurological Association*, 1946.

British and Commonwealth Authors

Aiken, M.H. "Psychoneuroses in the Second New Zealand Expeditionary Force." *New Zealand Medical Journal* 40 (1941).
– "A Review of Psychiatric Casualties Among New Zealand Troops in Italy." *New Zealand Medical Journal* 44 (1945).
"Alienist." "Some Recollections of Army Psychiatry." *JRAMC* 84 (1945).
Allan, C. "Acute War Neuroses." Letters to the Editor. *The Lancet* (13 July 1940).
Anderson, C. et al. "Psychiatric Casualties from the Normandy Beach-Head: First Thoughts on 100 Cases." *The Lancet* (12 Aug. 1944).
British Historical Section, Central Mediterranean. *The Problem of Desertion*, Administrative monograph no. 5, March 1946. Directorate of History, Ottawa.
Cooper, E.L. and A.J.M. Sinclair. "War Neuroses in Tobruk." *MJA* 2 (1942).
Culpin, Millais. "Acute War Neuroses." Letters to the Editor. *The Lancet* (13 July 1940).
Curran, Desmond and W.P. Mollinson. "War-Time Psychiatry and Economy in Manpower." *The Lancet* (14 Dec. 1940).
Cutler, E.C. "A Surgeon Looks at Two Wars." *The Lancet* (30 Sept. 1944).
Davis, P.J.R. "Divisional Psychiatry Report to the War Office." *JRAMC* (1946).
Debenham, Gilbert et al. "Treatment of War Neuroses." *The Lancet* (25 Jan. 1941).
Dibden, W.A. "Psychiatric Casualties as a Repatriation Problem." *MJA* 5 (1945).
Dillon, F. "Neuroses Among Combatant Troops in the Great War." *BMJ* (1939).
Fidler, R.F. "A Psychiatrist's Observations in the B.L.A." *JRAMC* (1947).
Finny, C.M. "An A.D.M.S.'s Experiences with the B.E.F. – May 1940." *JRAMC* (1941).
Goulston, S.J.M. "A Regimental Aid Post in Tobruk." *MJA* 2 (1942).
Guttman, E. and E. Thomas. *A Report on the Re-adjustment in Civil Life of Soldiers Discharged from the Army on Account of Neurosis*. London: HMSO 1946.
Haldane, F.P. and John Rowley. "Psychiatry at the Corps Exhaustion Centre." *The Lancet* (26 Oct. 1946).
Hunter, D. "The Work of a Corps Psychiatrist in the Italian Campaign." *JRAMC* (1946).
James, G.W.B. "Psychiatric Lessons from Active Service." *The Lancet* (22 Dec. 1945).
The Lancet (Editorial). "Neurotics in the Forces." *The Lancet* (7 Sept. 1940).
L'Etang, H.J.C. "A Criticism of Military Psychiatry in the Second World War." *JRAMC* (1951).
Love, H.B. "Neurotic Casualties in the Field." *MJA* 2 (1942).
Mackeith, S.A. "Lasting Lessons of Overseas Military Psychiatry." *Journal of Mental Sciences* 92 (1946).
– "Psychological Aspects of the Problem of Anti-Malarial Precautions." *JRAMC* (1945).
Miller, E. "Psychiatric Aspects of Rehabilitation." *JRAMC* (1945).

– "Psychiatric Casualties Among Officers and Men from Normandy." *The Lancet* (24 Mar. 1945).

Miller, E., ed. *The Neuroses in War*. London: Macmillan, 1940.

Mira, E. "Psychiatric Experience in the Spanish Civil War." *BMJ* (1939).

Palmer, Howard. "Military Psychiatric Casualties: Experience with 12,000 cases." *The Lancet* (13 Oct. 1945).

– "The Problem of Neurosis in Ex-Soldiers." *New Zealand Medical Journal* 48 (1948).

Rees, J.R. *Reflections*. Washington, 1948.

– "Three Years of Military Psychiatry in the United Kingdom." *BMJ* 1 (1943).

Rodger, Alex. "Personnel Selection By Whom." *Proceedings of the Royal Society of Medicine* (Jan. 1946).

Sargant, W. "Physical Treatments of Acute Psychiatric States in War." *War Medicine* 3 (1943).

Sargant, W. and N. Craske. "Modified Insulin Therapy in War Neuroses." *The Lancet* (23 Aug. 1941).

Sargant, W. and H.J. Shorvon. "Acute War Neurosis." *Archives of Neurology and Psychiatry* (Oct. 1945).

Sargant, W. and Eliot Slater. "Acute War Neuroses." *The Lancet* (6 July 1940).

Sinclair, A.J.M. "Psychiatric Aspects of the Present War." *MJA* 4 (1944).

– "The Psychological Reactions of Soldiers." *MJA* 5 (1945).

Symonds, C.P. "Anxiety Neurosis in Combatants." *The Lancet* (25 Dec. 1943).

– "Neurology and Mental Disorders." *The Lancet* (15 March 1941).

Wyllie, A.M. "Electrical Convulsion Therapy." *The Lancet* (19 July 1941).

Yellowless, H. "Anxiety States." *JRAMC* (1940).

Youngman, N.V. "The Psychiatric Examination of Recruits." *MJA* 2 (March 1942).

III   SECONDARY SOURCES

Ahrenfeldt, R.H. *Psychiatry in the British Army in the Second World War*. London: Routledge and Kegan Paul, 1958.

Allard, J.V. *Memoirs*. Vancouver: UBC Press, 1988.

Babington, A. *For the Sake of Example*. London: Leo Cooper, 1983.

Bartov, O. *The Eastern Front, 1941-1945, German Troops and the Barbarization of Warfare*. New York: St Martin's Press, 1986.

Baynes, J. *Morale: A Study of Men and Courage*. London: Cassel, 1967.

Beattie, K. *Dileas: History of the 48th Highlanders of Canada, 1929-1956*. Toronto: 48th Highlanders, 1957.

Belenky, G. ed. *Contemporary Studies in Combat Psychiatry*. New York: Greenwood Press, 1987.

Bird, W.R. *No Retreating Footsteps*. Kentville: Kentville Publishing, n.d.

– *The North Shore Regiment*. Fredericton: Brunswick Press, 1963.

Birney, Earle. *Turvey*. Toronto, 1976.

Blaxland, G. *Alexander's Generals*. London: William Kimber, 1979.

Bogacz, T. "War Neurosis and Cultural Change in England, 1914-22: The Work of the War Office Committee of Enquiry into 'Shell-Shock.' " *Journal of Contemporary History* 24 (1989).

Botterell, E.H. "Kenneth George McKenzie, MD FRSC, 1923-1963." *Surgical Neurology* 17 (1982).

Bourne, P.G., ed. *The Psychology and Physiology of Stress*. New York: Academic Press, 1969.

Brown, M.W. and F.E. Brown. *Neuropsychiatry and the War: A Bibliography with Abstracts*. New York: National Committee for Mental Hygiene, 1918.

Brown, S. *The Loyal Edmonton Regiment*. MA thesis. Wilfrid Laurier University, 1984.

Brown, T. "Shell Shock in the Canadian Expeditionary Forces, 1914-1919: Canadian Psychiatry in the Great War," in *Health, Disease and Medicine: Essays in Canadian Medical History*, edited by Charles Roland. Toronto: Clarke Irwin, 1983.

Brownlee, R.L. and W.J. Mullen. *Changing an Army: An Oral History of General William E. DePuy, USA Retired*. Washington: US Center of Military History, 1988.

Burns, E.L.M. *General Mud*. Toronto: Clarke Irwin, 1970.

– *Manpower in the Canadian Army*. Toronto: Clarke Irwin, 1956.

Canadian Army Headquarters Reports. No. 63. "Manpower Problems of the Canadian Army During the Second War"; No. 37, "The Policy Governing the Finding and Selection of the Officers for the CASF"; No. 91, "Some Aspects of Disciplinary Policy in the Canadian Service, 1914-1946." Directorate of History.

Canadian Department of National Defence. *General instructions for the Medical Examination of Recruits for the C.A.S.F. and N.P.A.M.* Ottawa: King's Printer, 1940.

Canadian Military Headquarters Reports. No. 134, "Historical Sketch: Rates of Wastage of Personnel, Canadian Army Overseas, 1939-1945"; No. 133, "The Organization of the Canadian Reinforcement Units (UK): Historical Outline, 1940-1945"; No. 156, "Selection and Training of Officers for the Canadian Army Overseas, 1940-1945"; No. 164, "The Problem of Selection and Reallocation of Personnel in the Canadian Army Overseas, 1939-1946." Directorate of History.

Cederberg, F. *The Long Road Home*. Toronto: General Publishing, 1984.

Chalke, F.C.R. "Psychiatric Screening of Recruits." DVA, *Treatment Services Bulletin* 9 (1954).

Collins, Anne. *In the Sleep Room*. Toronto 1988.

Comfort, C. *Artist at War*. Toronto: Ryerson, 1956.

Copp, T. "Battle Exhaustion and the Canadian Soldier in Normandy." *British Army Review* 85 (1987).

Copp, T. and R. Vogel. *Maple Leaf Route*. 5 vols. *Caen. Falaise. Antwerp. Scheldt. Victory*. Alma, Ontario: Maple Leaf Route Publications, 1983-1988.

Craig, Norman. *The Broken Plume*. London: Imperial War Museum, 1982.

Crew, F., ed. *History of the Second War: United Kingdom Medical Services – Army Medical Services, Campaigns*, vols. 1, 2, 4. London: HMSO, 1957-1962.

D'Este, C. *Bitter Victory*. London: Collins, 1988.

– *Decision in Normandy*. London: Collins, 1983.

Dinter, E. *Hero or Coward*. London: Frank Cass, 1985.

Dixon, N. *On the Psychology of Military Incompetence*. London: Jonathan Cape, 1976.

Ellis, J. *Cassino: The Hollow Victory*. New York: McGraw Hill, 1984.

– *The Sharp End of War*. London: David and Charles, 1980.

English, J.A. *A Perspective on Infantry*. New York: Praeger, 1981.

Feasby, W.R. *Official History of the Canadian Medical Services, 1939-1945*, vol. 1, *Organization and Campaigns* and vol. 2, *Clinical Subjects*. Ottawa: Queen's Printer, 1953-56.

Frost, C.S. *Once a Patricia*. St. Catharines: Vanwell Publications, 1988.

Gabriel, R., ed. *Military Psychiatry: A Comparative Perspective*. New York: Greenwood Press 1986.

Galloway, S. *Bravely into Battle*. Toronto: Stoddart, 1988.

– *Some Died at Ortona*. London: The Royal Canadian Regiment, n.d.

– *With the Irish Against Rommel*. Vancouver: Battleline Books, 1984.

Ginzberg, E. et al. *The Ineffective Soldier: Lessons for Management and the Nation*, vol. 1, *Breakdown and Recovery*, vol. 2, *The Lost Divisions, Patterns of Performance*. New York: Columbia University Press, 1959.

Glass, A.E., ed. *Neuropsychiatry in World War II*, vol. 2, *Overseas Theatres*. Washington: Office of the Surgeon General, 1973.

Gould, S.J. *The Mismeasure of Man*. New York: Norton, 1981.

Graham, D. and S. Bidwell. *Tug of War: The Battle for Italy*. New York: St. Martin's Press, 1986.

Granatstein, J.L. *Broken Promises*. Toronto: Oxford Press, 1977.

Grinker, R. and J. Spiegel. *Men Under Stress*. New York: McGraw-Hill, 1945.

Hall, B.H., ed. *A Psychiatrist for a Troubled World: Selected Papers of William C. Menninger, MD*. New York: Viking, 1967.

Hayes, G. *The Lincs: A History of the Lincoln and Welland Regiment at War*. Alma: Maple Leaf Route Publications, 1986.

Hillsman, J.B. *Eleven Men and a Scalpel*. Winnipeg: Columbia Press, 1948.

Hitsman, J.M. "The Problems of Personnel Selection in the Canadian Army Overseas 1939-1946." CMHQ (1946).

Holmes, R. *Acts of War: The Behavior of Men in Battle*. New York: The Free Press, 1985.

Hunt, D. *A Don at War*. London: William Kimber, 1966.

Hunter, K.A. "The R.C.A.M.C. in the Korean War." JCMS (1954).

Irvine, S.H. and S.E. Newstead, eds. *Intelligence and Cognition: Contemporary Frames of Reference*. Dordrecht 1987.

Jackson, W. and T.P. Gleave. *The Mediterranean and the Middle East*, vol. 6, part 2, *June-October 1944*. London: HMSO, 1987.

Janowitz, M. and E. Shils. "Cohesion and Disintegration in the Wehrmacht in World War 2." *Public Opinion Quarterly* 12 (1948).

Jefferson, Lewis. *Something Hidden: A Biography of Wilder Penfield*. Toronto, 1981.

Keegan, J. *The Face of Battle*. New York: Vintage Books, 1977.

Kellett, A. *Combat Motivation*. Boston: Kluwer-Nijhoff Publications, 1982.

Kitching, G. *Mud and Green Fields*. Vancouver: Battleline Books, 1983.

Lewis, N. and B. Engle. *Wartime Psychiatry: A Compendium of the International Literature*. New York: Oxford University Press, 1954.

Linderman, G.F. *Embattled Courage*. New York: Free Press, 1987.

Lindsay, M. *So Few Got Through*. London: Collins, 1946.

Marshall, S.L.A. *Men Against Fire*. New York: William Morrow, 1947.

McAndrew, W.J. "Eighth Army at the Gothic Line: Commanders and Plans, the Dogfight." *RUSI Journal* 131 (1986).

– "Fire or Movement? Canadian Tactical Doctrine, Sicily – 1943." *Military Affairs* 51 (1987).

– "Recording the War." *Canadian Defence Quarterly* 18 (1988).

– "Stress Casualties: Canadians in Italy – 1943-1945." *Canadian Defence Quarterly* 17 (1987).

McNaughton, F.L. "Colin Russel, a Pioneer of Canadian Neurology." *CMAJ* 77 (1957).

Mellor, W.F. *Casualties and Medical Statistics*. London: HMSO, 1972.

Menninger, Karl. "Sigmund Freud." *Bulletin of Menninger Clinic* (November 1939).

Millet, A. and W. Murray. *Military Effectiveness*, vol. 3, *The Second World War*. Boston: Allen Unwin, 1988.

Montemaggi, A. *La Linea Gotica*. Roma: Edizion Civitas, 1985.

Montgomery, Field Marshal Lord. *From Normandy to the Baltic*. London: Hutchinson, 1947.

Moran, Lord. *Anatomy of Courage*. 2nd ed. London: Constable, 1966.

Morton, D. "The Supreme Penalty: Canadian Deaths by Firing Squad in the First World War." *Queen's Quarterly* (1972).

Mowat, F. *And No Birds Sang*. Toronto: McClelland and Stewart, 1979.

– *The Regiment*. Toronto: McClelland and Stewart, 1973.

Myers, C.R. "Edward Alexander Bott." *The Canadian Psychologist* 15 (May 1974).

Myerson, Abraham. "The Attitude of Neurologists, Psychiatrists and Psychologists Toward Psychoanalysis." *AJP* (1940).

Newby, E. *Love and War in the Apennines*. Newton Abbey: Readers' Union, 1987.

Nicholson, G.W.L. *The Canadians in Italy*. Ottawa: Queen's Printer, 1956.

Notman, R. "A Survey of 1271 Neuropsychiatric Casualties Passing Through No 1 Canadian Exhaustion Unit in N.W. Europe Between October 1944 and May 1945: Follow-up Studies of the Post-Discharge Adjustment of 346 Members of the Above Series." Mimeographed report. DVA 1951.

Opinion of George Cooper, Q.C., Regarding Canadian Government Funding of the Allan Memorial Institute in the 1950s and 1960s. Ottawa, 1986.

Origo, I. *War in Val D'Orcia*. London: Jonathan Cape, 1947.

Pasture, N. "The Army Intelligence Test and Walter Lippman." *Journal of the Behavioural Sciences* (1978).

Pearce, D. *Journal of a War*. Toronto: Macmillan, 1965.

Pos, R. *History of Psychiatry at Toronto General Hospital*. Griffin-Greenland Archives, Toronto.

Redlich, F.C. "Metrazol Shock Treatment." *AJP* (1939).

Rees, J.R. *The Shaping of Psychiatry by War*. New York: W.W. Norton, 1945.

Resch. G. "Combat Stress Reaction Casualty Management: Canadian Personnel Conservation Experience in a Theatre of War." Paper presented for the Sixth Users' Workshop on Combat Stress, San Antonio, Texas. 30 November-4 December 1987.

Richardson, F.M. *Fighting Spirit: Psychological Factors in War*. London: Leo Cooper, 1978.

Roy, R. *1944: The Canadians in Normandy*. Toronto: Macmillan, 1984.

Ryder, R. *Oliver Leese*. London: Hamish Hamilton, 1987.

Sabshin, M. "Twenty-five Years After Men Under Stress," in *Modern Psychiatry and Clinical Research*, edited by D. Offer. New York, 1972.

Sargant, W. *The Unquiet Mind*. London, 1967.

Sarkesian, S., ed. *Combat Effectiveness: Cohesion, Stress and the Volunteer Military*. Beverly Hills: Sage Publications, 1988.

Sevareid, E. *Not So Wild a Dream*. New York: Atheneum, 1976.

Smith, W. *What Time the Tempest*. Toronto: Ryerson, 1953.

Smoler, F. "The Secret of the Soldiers Who Didn't Shoot." *American Heritage* (March 1989).

Snowie, A. *Bloody Buron*. Erin, Ontario: Boston Mills Press, 1985.

Solomon, Z. and Rami Benbenishtz. "The Role of Proximity, Immediacy and Expectancy in Frontline Treatment of Combat Stress Reaction Among Israelis in the Lebanon War." *AJP* (1986).

Somers, F. "A History of Psychiatry at the Toronto General Hospital." Typescript. Griffin-Greenland Archives.

Spencer, J.C. *Crime and the Services*. London: Routledge and Kegan Paul 1954.

Spiller, R. "Ison's Run: Human Dimensions of Warfare in the 20th Century." *Military Review* (1988).

– "S.L.A. Marshall and the Ratio of Fire." *RUSI Journal* 133 (1988).

– "The Tenth Imperative." *Military Review* (1989).

Stacey, C.P. "Canadian Leaders of the Second World War." *Canadian Historical Review* (March 1985).

– *Six Years of War*. Ottawa: Queen's Printer, 1955.

– *The Victory Campaign*. Ottawa: Queen's Printer, 1960.

Stevens, G.R. *A City Goes to War*. Brampton: Charters Publication, 1964.

– *The Royal Canadian Regiment*. London: London Printing, 1967.

Stout, T.D.M. *War Surgery and Medicine*. Wellington: War History Branch, Department of Internal Affairs, 1954.

Thompson, R. *The Pelican History of Psychology*. London, 1968.

Tout, K. *Tanks Advance*. London: Grafton Books, 1989.

Truscott, L. *Command Missions*. New York: Dutton, 1954.

United Kingdom. *Neuroses in Wartime*. London: HMSO, 1940.

– *Statistical Report on the Health of the Army*. London: HMSO, 1948.

Van Creveld, M. *Fighting Power: German and U.S. Army Performance 1939-1945*.

Westport, Conn: Greenwood Press, 1982.

Vernon, P.E. and J.B. Parry. *Personnel Selection in the British Forces*. London: University of London Press, 1949.

Vokes, C. *Vokes: My Story*. Ottawa: Gallery Books, 1985.

War Office (UK). *Operations of British, Indian and Dominion Forces in Italy, 3 September 1943 to May 1945, Part 5, Administrative Monographs, No. 13, Medical Papers and No. 5 The Problem of Desertion*. British Historical Section Central Mediterranean, 1946.

– *Report of the War Office Committee of Enquiry into Shell Shock*. London: HMSO, 1922.

Wavell, Field Marshal Lord. *The Good Soldier*. London: Macmillan, 1948.

Whitaker, W.D. and S. Whitaker. *Tug of War*. Toronto: Stoddart, 1984.

Winter, D. *Death's Men*. London: Penguin, 1979.

Wood, H.F. *Strange Battleground*. Ottawa: Queen's Printer, 1966.

Wright, M.J. and C.R. Myers, eds. *History of Academic Psychology in Canada*. Toronto, 1982.

Index